PRAISE FOR
THE ART OF THE PRESIDENCY

"He makes me believe in an America I didn't think possible."
—Lachlan Batchelder, Pittsburgh Press

"Knowing that someone of Jermanski's caliber was working in the White House somehow makes the last nine months understandable."
—Phillip Armbruster, Providence Patriot

"The only insight in this book is that President Drumpf has managed to identify our worst traits and use them against us."
—Michael McMichaelson, Salt Lake City Sentinel

"One can only hope that this is political satire and not reality."
—Walter O'Malley, Chicago Trumpeter

"Too close to home. This scares me."
—Rachel Jackson, San Diego Post

DRUMPF
THE ART OF THE
PRESIDENCY

Ronald G. Drumpf
and
Martin Jermanski

PAYNE PUBLISHING

Published by Payne Publishing

THE ART OF THE PRESIDENCY.
Copyright © 2018 Ronald G Drumpf and Martin Jermanski.

ISBN 9780692042519 (paperback)
ASIN 0692042512 (paperback)

Design and layout by 52 Novels (http://www.52novels.com/)
Cover design by Payne Publishing
Cover painting by Jonathan Cusick (http://www.jonathancusick.com/)

First Edition

mjermanski@gmail.com

For Gabrielle

CONTENTS

CAST OF CHARACTERS
(IN ORDER OF APPEARANCE OR MENTION)

MARTIN JERMANSKI
Low-level White House Staffer

RONALD G. DRUMPF
President

MIKE SPENCE
Vice President

AMANDA CHUNG
Low-level White House Staffer

ROB POTTER
White House Staff Secretary

IVANIA DRUMPF
Daughter of the President

BETSY DEVOE
Secretary of Education

SHAWN HANNITY
Fox News Personality

MIKE POMPEII
Head of the CIA / Secretary of State

REX TILLESON
Secretary of State

JOHN KELLNER
White House Chief of Staff

MADELEINE WATTERHOOT
President's Personal Secretary

JAMES "BULL DOG" MATTHEWS
Secretary of Defense

SCOTT BOKOR
Low-level Administration Staffer

STEVE MUNCHKIN
Secretary of the Treasury

ALEX AZARRO
Secretary of Health and Human Services

ALEX ACOATTA
Secretary of Labor

HOPE HILLS
Former White House Communications Director

STEVE BANYAN
Former Chief Strategist

MELANYA DRUMPF
The First Lady

STEVEN MILLS
Senior Speech Writer and Advisor

KELLY CONVILLE
Counselor to the President

DENNIS RODDMANN
Former NBA Basketball Player

JOHN BELTEN
The National Security Advisor

SARAH SAUNDERS
White House Press Secretary

ROBERT MEILLER
Special Investigator

MARK SKORT
Director of Legislative Affairs

DAN MCGOHN
White House Counsel

ANDREW BREIBURG
Director, Domestic Policy Council

LESLIE CORNACRE
Up-and-Coming Conservative Television Personality

JEFF SESSOMS
Attorney General

KRISTEN NELSON
Secretary of Homeland Security

SONNY PURDY
Secretary of Agriculture

WILBUR ROSE
Secretary of Commerce

PROLOGUE

Martin Jermanski and his father were sitting in the back yard. It was a Sunday afternoon in early December, 2017. His father was at the grill, standing where he could look into the house to watch the Jaguars game through the sliding glass door. Martin was sitting upwind of the grill, trying to enjoy the sun and high-sixties temperature in peace.

"So, Marty. I forgot to tell you."

Martin didn't respond, which was typical of him.

"Marty. News. I think you'll actually find it interesting."

Martin lifted the sunglasses that covered his eyes—a sign to his dad that he was paying attention.

"I spoke to The Ronald the last time he was in town."

Martin dropped the glasses and shifted in the rickety lawn chair. Life had always been a little strange, it seemed to Martin. His father worked at Mer-a-Lago, somewhere in middle management, high enough to have met Ronald Drumpf many times. Martin had met him a few times as well; he seemed like an okay dude.

Life was strange when Drumpf was a reality television star. With him as President, life was even more bizarre. Not that it changed much for his dad at work, but it certainly changed how his dad acted. More so than before, he was about "always putting our best foot forward" and "protecting the Drumpf name."

'Had Drumpf ever protected the Jermanski name?' Martin wondered.

His dad insisted on keeping the house clean and the yard perfectly manicured. As if The Ronald was going to visit the Casa del Jermanski. It wasn't going to happen.

"How is The Ronald, dad?"

"We actually didn't talk about him. We talked about you."

Martin couldn't blame his parents. They were certainly proud. He didn't think graduating from UNF was that impressive, but to hear his mom tell it, he had graduated from an Ivy League.

"Really?"

"Yeah. I told him about you graduating and your degree in English. And how you haven't really done much since."

"What did he say?"

"That's it. He said you should take a job at the White House."

That was a surprise. Martin sat up in the chair. "Huh?"

"Yeah! He said they're always looking for hard workers in the White House. People loyal to the family. People he could trust."

"Seriously?" Martin didn't know what to think. Him? In the White House? It was almost laughable. No, it *was* laughable. He knew nothing about politics, cared nothing about politics. Actually, he avoided the topic like the plague.

"Yeah. He said he'd be happy to have you. Happy to have another Jermanski working for him."

"Dad. You didn't have your nametag on at the time, did you?"

"What? No."

"He doesn't know our name, dad. He read it off your nametag."

"You know that we have to wear those now, Martin. An extra layer of security. Secret Service rules and all."

"Whatever. He wasn't serious. He was just playing 'Good Ronald.'"

"Ha. Knew you'd say that. But if he didn't mean it, he wouldn't have given me this." His dad pulled a sheet of paper from his front pocket, carefully unfolded it, and stretched out his hand toward Martin.

Martin, willing to play along, took the paper and looked it over.

Quality paper. Mer-a-Lago, Ronald Drumpf letterhead. The gigantic Drumpf signature at the bottom.

Martin read it aloud, "To Whom It May Concern. Blah blah blah. Has my highest confidence. Worthy of working in the White House. Blah blah blah." Martin found his dad eyeing him expectantly. "What am I supposed to do with this?"

"Flip it over. The number? That's the White House switchboard. Call it, schedule yourself an interview. You're going to Washington, DC!"

"Really?" Voice flat, Martin wasn't convinced.

"It's better than any of the other jobs you've had."

"Dad. You know I'll find something—"

"You took too long. I found you something."

The argument lasted far shorter than Martin intended; he caved. They agreed he would make the trip after the New Year. 2018 was to start with an adventure! If going to Washington, DC could be called an adventure.

After the Jaguars game, the three sat at the small dining room table. "I got you this," Martin's dad said, sliding a softcover book across the table.

Martin looked at it. *The Art of the Deal* by Ronald Drumpf. "Dad, you've had this book for as long as I can remember."

"Look inside."

Martin opened the cover. A hand-written inscription read:

> Bill,
> Thanks for all your years of hard work at the Club. It's a great organization – the best in the country. Good luck to your son.
>
> The Ronald
> December 2017

Martin realized his dad was watching him. 'What should I say?' "Cool." That seemed to satisfy his father.

"You could write the sequel," his mom suggested.

"What do you mean?"

"Well, he wrote that book a long time ago, sometime in the eighties. He's President now; maybe it's time for a sequel."

"But why me?"

"Martin. You were an English major at UNF," his mom said. "You've always enjoyed writing. You're good at it."

"Mom. A novel is, what, fifty-thousand words? The longest thing I've ever written was just over thirty, and it almost killed me."

"I still have that box of notebooks from when you were in elementary school, full of stories that you wrote yourself. You're a good writer!"

"I'm decent." But his mother was right. Martin did enjoy writing; he always had. He didn't know if he was any good. He got decent grades at UNF, really enjoyed his creative writing electives. It was something to think about.

"Great! It's settled." His mother always seemed to have the ability to read his mind.

Martin looked down at *The Art of the Deal* still in his hands. 'Ronald G. Drumpf with Anthony Schwartzman.' He figured he would take the book with him to Washington, DC.

DC BEGINNINGS

Getting off the plane at Washington Dulles surprised Martin. He thought that he had dressed warmly—jeans, a short-sleeved polo, and a windbreaker. His parents had said otherwise, but he didn't believe them. Maybe he should have or maybe he should have checked The Weather Channel app.

The air was cold. The sky was gray. A slight drizzle fell. Luckily, his Uber driver arrived within seconds of his request. He climbed in. Black leather seats, cracked and faded, but at least it was clean.

"State Plaza Hotel, please."

"Address?" The driver was Caucasian but spoke with an accent Martin didn't recognize. European. Why was he asking for the address? As the driver, wasn't he supposed to know?

"Corner of E Street and Virginia Avenue Northwest, I think. Lemme check."

The driver pulled away before Martin could pull the phone from his jacket pocket. It didn't seem that *he* was checking anything.

"Yeah. E and Virginia," Martin said. "Apparently, there's an entrance on F Street as well."

"Where're you from?"

"Florida. Palm Beach."

"Warm there?"

"Warmer than this."

"What're you doing in town?"

"Job interview tomorrow."

"Hmm. Good luck. Where're you going to work?"

"The White House."

For the first time, the driver looked at him through the rear view. Martin couldn't read his eyes. But it seemed that the driver kept his eyes on him for far longer than would be safe driving away from the airport.

．　　　　．　　　　．

"Your stay will be for two nights, Mr. Jermanski?"

"At least two, maybe longer. Not quite sure yet."

"Well, that's fine. If you need to extend, you can just call down to the desk."

Martin looked around. The lobby was clean, but gray. Everything was gray.

"Here's your key. Enjoy your stay."

"Thanks." He started to walk away, then stopped.

The girl behind the counter looked up and smiled. She was dark-skinned with vibrant white teeth. Indian? Like, from India. Very cute.

"Is there somewhere close to eat?" he asked.

"There's a Dunkin' Donuts a short walk from here, just east on E Street. There's also a place close by on 21st called Tonic. They have decent sandwiches."

"Which way to Tonic?"

"Leave the lobby and turn right, then turn left when you come to the first intersection. It's just a few minutes up the street on your right."

"Thanks."

The entire hotel was gray. Standing waiting for the elevator, Martin glanced up the hallway. Gray carpet, slightly different color gray walls, darker gray trim on the walls, gray doors to rooms. Depressing. Then the elevator dinged.

He climbed on and pressed the button. The inside of the elevator was also gray, only a darker shade. Were all DC hotels like this? Was all of DC like this? The sky had been.

Opening the door to his room, he was relieved to see that the walls of the room were white. 'Thank you,' he thought. But the sky outside the window was still gray. He dropped his suitcase on the bed and opened it up. *The Art of the Deal* was on top.

.   .   .

The next morning, Martin sat across from a middle-aged woman. Forty-eight, he guessed. She wore a nametag on her blazer: 'Jennifer.' She didn't look like a Jennifer, but he wondered if he actually looked like a Martin. He was nervous. This was his first interview for a "real" job. He wore an ill-fitting navy blue business suit and a red tie, which he had to tie eight times before he was happy with it.

Martin had been called into the office after sitting in a waiting room for thirty minutes.

Jennifer asked him to sit and then spent fifteen minutes looking through a small manila envelope. Finally, she looked up and asked, "James?"

"James? Me? No, Martin."

"Martin?"

"Yes, ma'am."

She raised an eyebrow at him and then reached for a pile of manila envelopes on the desk. She flipped through three before pulling the fourth from the pile. "Martin Jermanski?"

"Yes."

Somehow, despite the fact that she called him by name into her office and then proceeded to peruse the wrong envelope, she seemed annoyed with him.

"Not much of a resume," she said.

"No, ma'am." It was true. The resume listed his college information, including his two summer internships, and the two jobs he held in the time since graduation.

"English major from University of North Florida?"

"Yes, ma'am." It was right there; why did she need to ask about it?

She looked at him, arranged the thin stack of papers that made up his 'file,' and then slid them into the folder and set it aside. "Facebook account?"

"Yes, ma'am."

She turned in her seat to face a massive Apple monitor, pulled a thin white keyboard from a drawer, and began to type.

"Do you mind if I friend you?"

"What?"

"Do you mind if I friend you on Facebook?"

"I've only known you for twenty minutes." He could tell by the look on her face that his joke had fallen flat.

"Uh, sure."

She typed for a moment. He felt the phone in his pocket vibrate.

Martin reached into his pocket, withdrew the phone, and opened the app. There she was – Jennifer Saalfeld. He approved the friend request.

"What about LinkedIn?"

"I have a profile there."

"Will you accept a connection request from me?"

"Sure." He did the same again.

"Is there anything you want to tell me before I begin?"

"What do you mean?"

"Is there anything in either of these profiles that will give me reason to not hire you?"

"I don't think so." Martin wasn't sure what kinds of things would disqualify him. "Like things that are illegal?"

"Illegal?" she chuckled. "Not necessarily. Have you ever posted anything critical of then-candidate Drumpf, President Drumpf, Vice President Spence, or the Republican Party?"

Martin racked his brain. Maybe? He wasn't sure. He didn't really trust either of the parties. "Maybe the Republican Party?"

"But no Drumpf?"

"No."

"Don't worry. He's not much of a fan of the Republican Party either." Jennifer was scrolling and clicking through one or both of his profiles.

"My father works at Mer-a-Lago. He'd lose it if I posted anything negative about Mr. Drumpf."

She just kept on scrolling and clicking. Occasionally, an eyebrow would raise, or both. Once or twice, she pursed her lips.

Martin began to grow uncomfortable. His left butt cheek was starting to go numb. He tried not to fidget.

"Okay. That seemed fine, but one question: Were those pictures a Spring Break trip from a year or two ago?"

"Shit," he muttered under his breath. There wasn't any pictures of pot or nudity, was there?

"Just kidding. It looked like a fun trip." She laughed at her own joke and then pulled a form from his file and scribbled some notes on it. "Snapchat? Instagram? Pinterest? Tinder?"

"Uh, no. And no, and no. Maybe?"

"Wipe it. Today. Any blogs, vlogs, YouTube channels? An old MySpace account?"

"MySpace? Ha! No."

She scribbled some more on the form. "The others?"

"No."

"I recommend you wipe them. And I hope you're telling me the truth. I'd hate to find something later."

"You don't believe me?"

"You're 23. How many 23-year-olds do you know who don't have at least three or four social media accounts of some kind?"

'Good point,' he thought.

"In fact, you should double wipe them."

"Double wipe? What's that?"

"I don't know. You're the Millennial." She laughed out loud. "When I was your age, I didn't have to worry about people learning about my stupid adventures. The point was to keep the stupid private." She chuckled more to herself. "Also, do you have a Twitter account?"

"No."

"Establish one. Immediately."

"I'm 'wiping' all of my other accounts. Why do you want me on Twitter?"

"To follow the boss." She looked at him as if it were the most obvious thing in the world. "Once you open your account, follow @realRonaldDrum1."

"But I don't—"

"Doesn't matter. Need to keep his numbers up."

"You said I'm a Millennial. Millennials don't use Twitter anymore. That's so 2014."

"Don't care. Do it." She glanced down at the form, apparently to find her spot. "Anything in your history that would call into question your loyalty to Mr. Drumpf?"

"No." A mark on the form.

"What about the Drumpf family?"

"Like what?" He didn't know any of those people, although he had seen one or two of the sons at the club one time.

"Please answer the question, Mr. Jermanski."

"No." Another mark on the form.

"Mr. Drumpf places great importance on loyalty. I cannot stress to you the importance that Mr. Drumpf and his family place on personal loyalty." It sounded to Martin like she was reading from a canned speech. She stopped speaking and looked at him.

Was she waiting on a response? He just sat there looking at her.

She waited an additional second and then continued, "If accepted for a position at the White House, will you do everything in your power to ensure the success of Mr. Drumpf and his Administration?"

'Power? What power will I have?'

She just sat there waiting for a response.

"Yes." Another mark on the form.

"If accepted for a position at the White House, will you do everything in your power to maintain the trust and confidence of Mr. Drumpf?" Her pen hovered over the form.

'What did that even mean? What the hell.' "Yes."

"If accepted for a position at the White House, will you work tirelessly to achieve the policy aims outlined by Mr. Drumpf as voiced in official correspondence, interviews, press conferences, commercial appearances, and tweets?"

'Wow.' "Yes."

Two more marks on the form.

Jennifer placed the form flat on the desk, leaned over it, and scanned it intently.

Martin didn't understand what she was examining. The form wasn't very long, certainly wasn't very complicated, and she had literally just completed it.

Finally, she looked up at him. "Mr. Jermanski. On behalf of the Drumpf Administration, I'd like to offer you a position in the White House. It will be probational in nature for a period of 90 days. If you last those 90 days and maintain good standing, a contract for a period of one year from that date will be extended to you. Do you have any questions?"

FIRST DAY

Martin showed up at 1650 Pennsylvania Avenue at the appointed time. He found out that it was the Eisenhower Executive Office Building. Someone should have told him it wasn't the White House; it certainly would have made it easier to find the place. But finding it was only the first challenge. The next was figuring out how to enter it. There were security checkpoints, guards, and metal detectors.

Standing on the sidewalk, Martin shivered. It was cold, unpleasantly so. The sky was overcast; a cold wind blew. He pulled his phone from his pocket and re-read the email, trying to discern where, specifically, he was supposed to go.

"You Jermanski?" said a loud voice, extremely close to him.

He looked up in shock to find a woman staring at him. The first things that registered were her red hair and red lips. She was somewhere between her early twenties and late thirties. He couldn't tell, and that freaked him out. Usually, he was an expert at determining women's ages.

"Uh—" he stammered.

"Martin Jermanski? New staffer? Starting today?" She talked quickly, loudly, and her eyes pierced his with their intensity. She looked at a piece of paper she held in one hand and pulled her collar tighter around her neck with the other.

"Yes."

"Good. Follow me." She turned and marched away from him, not pausing to see if he followed. "They told me I should wait for you inside, for you to find your way into the building. I might have. Especially because it's cold, and I hate the cold. But I have a busy day—too busy to waste time fucking with the new lost puppy."

Martin rushed to follow. Hearing her wasn't a problem; her voice echoed off of the exterior of the Eisenhower Building. Keeping up with her was a different story; he jogged to catch up. "You are?"

She ignored the question. She walked past a line of people waiting to be granted entrance, stepped to a second door, showed the guard standing there a badge, and then turned to him. "You coming?"

'Cute redhead,' he thought, glancing down at her hands. 'Is there a ring?'

"Starting tomorrow, you'll have a badge. For now, we'll get you inside to fill out some paperwork." The guard nodded at her and held the door open. She disappeared inside before Martin could catch up to her.

The guard started to close the door. Martin moved faster. The guard looked at him and started to close the door in front of him.

"Come on!" She called from inside.

The guard reluctantly re-opened the door.

Martin was happy to get out of the cold. Two men in suits sat at a desk in the small room; neither looked up at him. He looked around, confused; the redhead was gone.

"Excuse me," Martin said.

One of the men tilted his head toward the doors that exited the room. He didn't even look up at Martin.

Martin walked to the door and pulled on it. It didn't budge. As he turned back to ask the men for help, he felt and heard a loud click in the door.

"Try again," the other man said, also without looking up.

This time the door opened, into a long hallway. The polished floor reflected the fluorescent lights from the ceiling. The place was crowded with people, all wearing badges. The redhead was twenty feet down the hallway, waiting for him with an exasperated look on her face.

He rushed to catch up to her. As he approached, she turned on her heel and began moving again. "There'll be a bunch of intake paperwork for you to fill out. Shouldn't take more than a few hours. After lunch, I'll take you over to the West Wing. As a new employee of the Federal Government, there are a series of briefings and some indoctrination you are required to complete before actually starting your job. You might just skip those. You probably won't be here longer than a few months, anyway."

"Wait. What?"

"Don't take it personally," she said, as *everything* about her face and mannerism told him to take it personally. "There's a lot of turnover in the Staff. The boss fires people all the time. Not sure if he realizes it trickles down to us at the worker-bee level as much as it does. But it does."

"The boss?"

"The President? Ronald Drumpf?" she asked, shaking her head. "You've heard of him, right?"

"Well, sure."

She stopped at a doorway, knocked twice, and went in. A middle-aged woman sat at a desk and looked up at her and then turned to him.

"Helen will take care of you," the redhead said. And then, turning to Helen, she said, "New hire. Hasn't completed any of the package. Probably should complete the badge paperwork first. I'll be by at one to take him in. Thank you!" She smiled at Helen, turned, and left without saying another word.

Martin turned back from the closing door to see Helen shaking her head with a slight frown. She said something under her breath that Martin couldn't make out, except for the word 'typical.'

Immediately, the frown vanished from Helen's face. She looked up at him with a smile. "Good morning!" She swiveled around in her chair, opened an old gray filing cabinet, and pulled from it a thick manila envelope. "You can sit right over there," she said, indicating a small table through the doorway behind her desk. "Start with the top form. Fill them all out in black ink. Please write neatly. You have no idea how many people have hideous penmanship."

He took the envelope and sat down. And spent the next three hours filling out a series of forms. Several were redundant, and most, due to being photocopies of photocopies of photocopies, were barely legible.

.   .   .

Helen was much friendlier than the redhead had been. Martin plowed through the paperwork, had his picture taken, was given a badge, and then sent to lunch. He was standing outside Helen's office at one o'clock when the redhead reappeared.

"All done!" he said cheerfully as she approached.

She didn't seem impressed. She turned and nodded for him to follow. "They haven't decided where you're going to work so, for now, you'll be placed temporarily."

Again, she walked fast. Martin kept up, but only barely. She came to a door, knocked on it, and stepped in without waiting for a response.

Two desks were crammed into a small office. A guy sat at each desk. There were no other chairs. They looked up at her and then at him.

"Hey, boys. New office-mate for you. Don't worry; he won't be here long." She laughed. "I mean, he won't be in your office for more than a few days. They're still trying to figure out where to put him."

"What about the White House?" Martin asked.

"What about it?"

"You told Helen you'd take me there this afternoon."

"Yeah. No. Plans changed. Once the higher-ups figure out what to do with you, we'll figure out where to put you. You'll get to see it at some point. Any questions?" Her tone made it clear that she didn't want to answer any questions.

"No?"

"Good." She stepped out and closed the door behind her.

Martin turned to his new office-mates. "Hey."

"Hey," said the first. Short, ruddy, and thick-necked. "I'm Lucas. Call me Luke."

"She's the worst," said the second, who then stood up and offered his hand. He was tall with a scruffy explosion of blond hair. "Michael; call me Mike."

Martin shook his hand. "Hey, Mike. Luke. Martin."

Mike's grip was less than firm. Luke's handshake was better, despite his hand's diminutive size.

"Don't let Brianne bother you," Mike said. "She's like that to everyone."

"Almost everyone," Luke offered. "The first thing we need to do is find you a chair. Shouldn't be too hard. We just have to steal it from one of the offices further than four or five doors in either direction."

"I'm on it," Mike said, with obvious glee in his voice. He opened the door and surprised a man standing just outside holding a large cardboard box in his hands.

The man stepped into the office, completely blocking Mike's escape. "I know I'm a little late today."

Mike and Luke both groaned in reply. "Seriously?"

The man dropped the box on a desk. "At least Amanda didn't bring the box." Based upon the boom it made striking the desk top, the box must have weighed a ton. He looked Martin up and down and saw the fresh badge hanging around his neck. "Besides. It looks like you have some help!"

"I'll get started," Luke said, "You find Marty that chair."

"It's Martin!" Martin said.

The delivery man left. Mike followed him out. Luke motioned for Martin to sit at Mike's desk and removed the lid from the cardboard box. Inside was a stack of folders. Luke pulled several out and carefully set them on the desk. Despite his care, several small pieces of paper fluttered from the top folder. "Shit," he said under his breath.

"What's this?" Martin asked.

"This, Marty, is the Document Reconstruction Team," Luke said.

Martin almost said 'Martin' again but held his tongue.

"Some call it hell. It's our primary duty." Luke opened the folder. Inside was a large pile of torn-up paper pieces. Each piece was no larger than a square inch. Many were smaller.

"Okay, but what is it?"

"So there is a law, or a regulation—or policy? I don't know," said Luke. "But there's a rule that says every piece of paper the President touches must be saved, filed, and stored. For posterity's sake, or some bullshit."

"Okay," Martin said.

"Well, the boss isn't a fan of that policy. Or maybe he's just used to doing things his way. Whatever. But he has a tendency to rip up every piece of paper that crosses his desk." Luke bent down, opened a desk drawer, and pulled from it five rolls of scotch tape. He tossed them on the desk; one slid and fell into Martin's lap.

"You're telling me we have to tape them together again?"

Luke sat down across from Martin. "I said Document Reconstruction Team, didn't I?"

"What?" Martin didn't believe it.

"Oh, yeah. Believe it." Luke pulled the top folder closer to him and grabbed the few stray pieces of paper that had earlier leaked out. "The D.R.T., the 'dirt,' staffer doom, spelled 'DRT.' Call it what you will."

Martin shook his head.

Without saying another word, Luke began to carefully arrange the little pieces of paper on the desk in front of him.

Martin watched in disbelief.

Luke set out about thirty pieces and then began to compare edges and the type on them, trying to find matches. It reminded Martin of his parents' puzzle hobby. They LOVED to do puzzles. Just watching them drove him crazy.

While Martin watched, Luke found a match and carefully taped the two little pieces of paper together. He found another and then another, each time carefully taping them together. Then he stopped and looked at Martin. "Well?"

"Oh," Martin said. He reached over Luke's pile of scraps for the next folder in the pile.

"Be careful!"

Luke's hand flew out and grabbed Martin's wrist. In the process, several of the pieces of paper were blown from his carefully arranged rows and columns.

"Shit," Luke muttered at the same time that Martin said, "What?"

Luke looked down at the pieces that had almost blown away and then shook his head. "Rookie mistake. Listen. You have to be careful. Pieces fall out, or get further jumbled, if you don't handle the folders gently. This is hours and hours and hours every week. You quickly learn to treat these bullshit little piles of paper with the respect they deserve. Anything that makes it easier on us to put them all back together."

Martin looked at him; he understood the individual words but wasn't sure he understood the meanings of the sentences coming out of Luke's mouth.

"All. Back. Together. Dude, not kidding. Every piece of paper that crosses the President's desk has to be kept. He seems to take joy in making that extremely difficult on us."

"That's fucked up," Martin said.

"Oh, yeah, it is," Luke agreed. "But that's how it is."

"Has anyone told him about this?" Martin asked. "I mean, does he know that someone has to fix all this?"

"Of course! Numerous times. Everyone, up to the Chief of Staff, has told him."

"Chief of Staff?"

"Our boss," Luke said. "Well, our boss's boss."

"I thought the President was our boss."

"Well, yeah. He is. But we're staffers; we work for the Chief of Staff. A retired Four Star General. A Marine."

Martin didn't know much about the military, so he said nothing.

"Kind of a hard-ass, but he's a good guy. A lot of the staff who was here from the beginning don't like him that much, but he's fair."

Martin listened. Luke taped.

"You better get to taping," Luke said. "This is the rest of our day."

"You said the boss's boss?" Martin asked.

"Yeah," Luke said. "We, the DRT, work for the Staff Secretary, Rob Potter, but he—all of us—work for the Chief of Staff. Make sense?"

The door opened. Mike slid in, pushing a nice, rolling, leather office chair in front of him.

"Where'd you get that?!" Luke was obviously excited.

Martin could understand the excitement. They were sitting on two old, decidedly uncomfortable metal chairs topped with non-existent padding. Compared to their two chairs, Mike's new chair was a Lamborghini.

"Don't worry about it. All that matters is I have it!"

"That's fantastic!" Luke only became more excited.

Martin stood and dragged his chair aside to make room for Mike's. The metal legs scraping across the floor made a miserable sound.

Mike pushed the chair into the room and collided with the desk. He pulled it back into the hallway, re-aimed, and pushed it into the room again.

"You gotta get that in here," Luke warned.

"You think I don't know that?" Mike asked. His blond explosion rocked from side to side as he attempted to maneuver the massive chair into their cramped office. Finally, it was in, but it blocked the door.

"Slide the desk!"

Martin pulled at the desk; it screeched across the tile floor. "That's gonna leave a mark."

Mike shoved the chair against the desk and then pulled the door past it. Finally, he sank into the chair. He let out a contented, and exaggerated, sigh.

Martin couldn't help but smile.

"How long do you think it lasts?" Luke asked Martin.

Before Martin could answer, Mike said, "As long as we keep the door, and our mouths, shut … a day or two."

"Yup," agreed Luke. "The real owner will come looking for it before too long."

Martin quickly grew to loathe the chore. And he wasn't very good at it. By five o-clock that afternoon, he had reassembled nine sheets of paper. The other two had taped fifteen and eighteen, respectively.

"Are you sure that someone said something about this to the President?" Martin finally asked.

"Yes," Luke answered. "Drumpf doesn't care."

"Does he know that he has people spending hours a day on this?"

"Yes!" both answered simultaneously, and then Mike continued, "This is literally your first afternoon. Whatever you feel right now, wait until you've been here for several months."

"Why don't we just stop taping them back together?"

"I think it's a case of the staff trying to protect the President from himself," Luke responded glumly.

"That's retarded," Martin fumed.

"You can't say that," Luke said.

"Retarded or not, it is what it is," said Mike. "Besides, Drumpf says 'retarded' all the time."

Martin finished his first day as a White House staffer after ten o'clock that evening, without having set foot in the White House. He didn't even see the White House that day.

Stepping into the cold air, Martin thought to himself, 'What have I gotten myself into?' His first day was not at all what he thought it would be. He made his way back to his hotel and fell asleep almost immediately.

ONE WEEK DOWN

The fancy office chair was reclaimed the very next day, and from then on, they all sat in ancient, beaten-up chairs.

The next several days were nothing but taping documents. Martin didn't meet any other staffers beyond his office mates; he never made it into the White House.

He came to work each morning, walked to his office, and waited for the first pile of folders (on a good day) or pile of loose paper (on a bad day) to start the reconstruction process.

Each day was the same: Leaning over a desk, carefully examining tiny pieces of paper in an attempt to match them and then tape them together. The human body was not designed for it, and the aches and pains it caused were sharp. And the pains seemed to start earlier and earlier with each passing day.

On his sixth day, Martin's pain became unbearable two hours in. He sat up and attempted to stretch the agony away. "You guys think the President does this to torture us?"

"Torture us?" Luke shook his head. "Worse than that. He doesn't even think about us when he does it. It doesn't even cross his mind that an actual person has to clean up after his mess."

"He's right," Mike said. "I mean, in an abstract way, some small part of him knows that someone, somewhere has to do this work.

But on a daily basis, he doesn't think about it. I think he thinks he's sticking it to 'the man.'"

"That makes no sense," Martin said. "He is 'the man.' By definition, there is no other man. He's the fucking President."

"Okay, so 'the man' isn't right," Mike said.

"Deep State!" Luke said. "He's sticking it to the Deep State!"

"Whatever," Mike said. "He's sticking it to the rules and regulations that cover how the government is supposed to work. That's his thing—rolling back government stupidity."

"By destroying the lives of his staffers?" asked Martin.

"Bit extreme, don't you think?" Luke retorted.

"Yeah, maybe," Martin conceded then tried a different tack. "By creating his own stupidity?"

"Every organization has its own," Luke reasoned.

"Whatever," Martin said.

To prevent the insanity that was surely approaching, Martin turned the tedium into a game. How many pages could he complete in a day? How many pages could he complete in an afternoon? How many pages could he complete in an hour? Gamifying the pain started his competitive juices flowing. But on that day, the game had lost its luster.

"Isn't there an app for this?" Martin asked. "Some kind of software that could do this for us?"

"We were told that those options had been investigated and didn't work," Mike said.

"Bullshit. No one bothered to look," Martin said.

"He's going through the stages," Luke said to Mike, a slight grin on his face.

"Absolutely," Mike responded.

"Somewhere between denial, anger, and bargaining," Luke said.

"He'll get through it," Mike said.

"I've told you guys that I hate it when people talk about me as if I wasn't there, right?" Martin asked.

"Certainly the anger," Mike commented, again to Luke.

"Nice." The sarcasm rolled off Martin's tongue.

"Where've you been staying?" Luke asked.

"State Plaza Hotel," Martin said.

"Why there?" Mike asked.

"Why aren't you staying at the Drumpf International?" Luke asked.

"I can't afford that place. Do you know what they charge a night?"

"You said your dad works at Mer-a-Lago," Mike said. "Family discount? Special rate?"

"Have you been looking for a place to move into?" Luke asked.

"I've only been in town for a week," Martin answered. "Where do you guys live?"

"I live down near the Navy Yard," Mike said.

"In the Wharf," Luke said.

"Don't know where either of those places are," Martin said.

"You don't get out much, do you?" Luke asked.

"You two are about the only people I know in this city," Martin said. "Where would I go? What would I do?"

"What have you been doing when we get out each day?" Mike asked.

"Grabbing a bite," Martin answered. "Heading back to my hotel room. Waiting on one of my coworkers to call me."

"No, shit!" Mike said. "Well, you're a fucking loser. Waiting on a coworker to call you? That's poor."

Luke laughed.

"Sorry, man," Mike said. "I just figured you were set."

"Thought wrong, I guess," Martin said.

"We're fixing that tonight!" Luke said.

"What're we going to do?" Martin asked.

"Club, bar, restaurant," Luke laid out the options. "Which do you prefer?"

"I just want to talk to something pretty," Martin said. "Someone prettier than the two of you."

"You mean something prettier than your right hand," Mike said. "Or are you a lefty?"

"Ha! That's old," Martin answered. "Have anything better?"

Mike's mood seemed to shift. "You're gonna need something better in this town."

"Wait, what?" Martin asked. "What do you mean?"

"Word of warning," Mike said.

"Okay."

"Most of the eligible ladies in DC don't really like us," Mike said.

"Us?" Martin asked.

"Drumpf staffers," Luke said.

"What do you mean?"

"Exactly what he said," said Mike. "If you tell a chick that you work for the administration, more than likely she won't be interested."

"You're full of shit," Martin said.

"No, seriously," Luke responded. "Most of the women around here don't like Drumpf and won't like you."

"What about college girls?" Martin asked.

"College?" Mike asked. "What're you talking about?"

"Dude. College girls?" Luke asked. "How old are you?"

"Twenty-three," Martin said. "I only graduated last year. How old are you two?"

"I'm twenty seven," Mike said.

"Twenty eight," Luke answered.

"Really?" Martin couldn't believe it. He laughed, "And you guys are still taping paper together?"

"We haven't worked here that long," Mike said.

"We both started only last fall," Luke added.

"I might be doing this for several months?"

Mike shrugged. "It's possible."

"You have your father's connection," Luke said. "That might work in your favor."

"I wouldn't know how to use that connection if I wanted to," Martin said.

"Uh, maybe call your dad," Mike said. "He might have an idea or two."

"Nope," Martin said. "Not calling the old man."

"Seriously?" Luke asked. "If my dad had connections, you can bet I'd be calling."

"You're twenty-eight years old," Martin said.

"Maybe," Luke replied. "But family connections are forever."

"It works for the Drumpfs," Mike said. "Do you really think The Ronald would hire either of his sons if they weren't his sons?"

"I don't think that much about them," Martin said. "I wouldn't know."

"And then there's Ivania," Luke added.

"What about her?" asked Martin.

"Ever read her book?" Luke asked.

"Didn't know she wrote a book," Martin said.

"Well," Mike said. "She wrote two, but I think he's talking about the first one. It was called 'The Drumpf Card.'"

"Yeah?"

"It's written as a self-help book for women," Mike said. "Talks about how to overcome adversity and succeed. In it, she even claims that her wealth and privilege have been handicaps to her success."

"I think that since she's talking about adversity, she felt the need to come up with some examples that she has dealt with," Luke said.

"Sure!" Mike said. "Because she hasn't dealt with any adversity. She had to come up with something."

"So what does any of this have to do with me?" Martin asked.

"If you read 'The Drumpf Card,' you'll realize a lot of what she recommends doesn't work for people who don't have connections, who don't have a wealthy, powerful father, who don't have a name," Mike explained. "The book is about protecting the value of her name."

"And?"

"Well, you don't have a name, but you have a father who has a connection," Luke said. "You should try to use it."

"What if my connection works?" Martin asked. "What if I leave you two behind?"

"We won't hate you," Luke deadpanned.

"Speak for yourself," Mike said to Luke, then to Martin, "I'll despise you. Forever!"

"Who would I even talk to?" Martin asked. "The redhead?"

"Brianne?" Luke asked.

"She's the worst," Mike said.

"You said that before," Martin said.

"He'll probably say it again," Luke said. "And again. Go ahead, say her name again."

"Brianne," said Martin.

On cue, Mike said, "She's the worst."

"Hey, Mike," Martin asked. "Anything I need to know about?"

"He'll never tell you," Luke answered.

"Listen," Mike began. "The Presidential Personnel Office. That's who you need to get in with."

"True," Luke agreed. "The PPO."

"Get in with?" Martin asked.

"Who interviewed you?" Mike asked.

"Jennifer," Martin said.

"Okay, Jennifer. Then Brianne dragged you around on your first day," Mike said. "You spent some time with Helen, and then you came to us. Right?"

"Sounds right," Martin said.

"Jennifer. Brianne. Helen," Mike said, "All are part of the PPO."

"Doesn't tell me anything," Martin said.

"They're the HR department for the staffers." Luke said.

"Okay," Martin said. "Can one of them help me?"

"Probably not," Mike said.

"But they'll probably know who can," Luke added.

"So I should talk to one of them?" Martin asked.

"Brianne, first," Luke said.

"She's the worst," Mike said.

"But if you can't get to her," Luke said.

"You won't be able to get to her," Mike interrupted.

"If you can't, go to Helen," Luke finished.

"Most of the people in the PPO are idiots," Mike said. "Helen might be the oldest person in the office. She's certainly older than the people who run it."

"She should be able to help you," Luke said. "She's even friendly."

"Think I should head over there now?" Martin asked.

"No," Mike answered. "Your page count is too low." He pointed to the five reconstructed pages on the desk in front of Martin. "You need to keep chuggin'."

"Try to hit Helen up first thing tomorrow morning," Luke advised. "Before the party starts."

"Party?" Martin asked.

"Don't ask. You'll see."

NIGHT ON THE TOWN

Martin was excited. His first night out with other people since arriving in DC! He had gone out twice alone in the previous week but found that, after a day of reconstructing documents, all he wanted to do was vegetate in his room. He was hopeful that adding other people to his nightlife would be an improvement over the nights out alone.

He took an Uber to the bar that Luke suggested. Bright lights, lots of people, noisy; it looked and sounded right. No sign of the others at the bar, but he saw a sign pointing to the second-floor bar. Luke was standing at the far end, talking to the bartender.

Martin made his way through the crowd. More than once, the pleasant smell of perfume or a nice shampoo slowed his progress. The ladies were attractive. Luke saw him as he closed the last few steps.

"I thought Mike was going to join us," Martin said to him over the din of the bar.

"Mike? Hell, no!"

Martin was surprised; he'd assumed the two were tight.

"It's cool," Luke said. "We hung out a bit when we first started, but quickly learned that we had nothing left to talk about after spending the day together. We'll occasionally run into each other, but that's about it."

The place was packed; the clientele was mostly twenty-somethings. The music loud, and the bare brick walls only made it louder. One flat screen was showing a Capitals game; one was tuned to ESPN.

Martin perused the crowd. He prided himself on being able to guess any woman's age—it was his little trademark party trick. Every female in sight was at least twenty-two years old. Most, in fact, were older than him. Perhaps this was the wrong place.

"What're you drinking?" Luke asked.

"I'll have what you're having," Martin said. "What's the word on this place?"

"Mostly young professionals, like us," Luke said. "Most aren't staffers, although you'll sometimes see a few. I know a few of the bartenders."

"Are we meeting anyone else?" Martin asked.

"No," Luke said.

'You invite me out,' Martin thought, 'but aren't going to introduce me to anyone else? What's the point?'

Luke handed him a beer.

"D'you see anyone you recognize?" Martin asked.

"Only the two bartenders," Luke said.

Someone scored a goal in the hockey game. Several people cheered. "Were you guys being serious about the women in DC and Drumpf staffers?" Martin asked.

"Think we'd lie? But don't take my word for it," Luke said. "Try it out."

Martin didn't fear rejection; he actually took perverse pleasure in it. Over the next 45 minutes, he approached six different ladies. He opened with a witty joke, told them he was new in town, and then told them that he had just starting working at the White House.

Girl #1: "I'm sorry. You're not my type."

Girl #2: "Ew. Get away."

Girl #3: "Fuck you."

Girl #4: "Are you also a misogynistic, homophobic, narcissistic, asshole?"

Girl #5: "Fuck you."

Girl #6: "Fuck. Seriously? Fuck. Goodbye!"

"Well, that was singularly impressive," Martin said to Luke afterward.

Luke had been watching all of it from a safe distance. His smile grew wider with each interaction, although Martin couldn't tell if he was smiling at the show or with each additional beer.

"Please," Luke said. "You got off easy."

"How so?" Martin asked.

Luke raised his index finger. "You didn't get threatened."

Middle finger. "You didn't get slapped."

Ring finger. "Didn't get a drink thrown in your face."

Pinky finger. "You didn't, not really at least, get cussed out."

Thumb. "And you didn't have the girl ask the bartender to stop serving you."

"No shit!" Martin said.

"I'm not making this up," Luke said.

"You've seen all those things happen?"

"Those and more," Luke said. "Regularly."

"So how do you recover from that?" Martin asked, more to make conversation than to hear Luke's wisdom.

"You recover by moving on to the next one. By forgetting it ever happened."

"The crazy thing is, I was feeling good with each of them until I mentioned the White House," Martin said.

"You made it look easy," Luke said.

"Never had a problem with talking to the ladies," Martin said. "Never had a problem making them laugh. Never even had a problem getting phone numbers. The problems always seemed to start after that."

"Cry me a river," Luke said.

"What can I say?" Martin said. "I've a way with the ladies."

"You have a way with the ladies?" asked an extremely attractive lady who had just sidled up to Martin's side.

"That's what I've been told," Martin responded smoothly.

"By who?" she asked. "Your mom?"

"Ouch!" Martin said.

"Damn," Luke said.

Martin sensed that Luke was going to be checking out of the conversation, which was fine by him. He turned to face the young lady. He took in her entire face and refused the urge to look elsewhere.

"Twenty-five and a half," he said definitively.

"What?" And then his comment registered, and she laughed. "Yeah, almost to the day, actually."

"I know," he said. It was the type of smart-ass comment that could score him some points or completely backfire. It all depended on the flow of the moment and whatever chemistry may or may not already exist between them.

"I'm Gabrielle," she stuck out her hand.

'You don't hear that name often,' he thought. "Martin," he said and took her hand.

Warm hand, firm handshake, slightly plump fingers. He could get used to that hand.

"Come here often?" she asked.

"Did you really just ask me that?" he asked.

"Touché," she answered.

Their witty repartee continued for a few moments, and then Martin noticed Luke over Gabrielle's shoulder, looking decidedly glum, drinking a beer and half-heartedly watching ESPN. Martin leaned in slightly closer to Gabrielle. "Can you excuse me for just one quick moment?"

"Sure, but you better hurry back," she said.

"Don't worry. I'm not going far." He took two steps past her and moved into Luke's field of view.

"Well?" Luke asked.

"So far, so good," Martin said. "You?"

"I'm ready to go," Luke said. "This is number four." He took another swig. "Told her where we work?"

"And ruin the opportunity?"

"You'll have to at some point," Luke insisted.

"Maybe," Martin said. "But not tonight." He glanced over his shoulder. Gabrielle was only a few feet away, talking to another young lady.

"I'll see you tomorrow?" he asked Luke.

"I wouldn't miss the opportunity to practice my arts-and-crafts skills. Learned 'em in kindergarten, and they're still useful."

Martin smiled at the joke and then turned back to his new friend. The reintroduction line had to be good, or the earlier good-will could evaporate in an instant. "So, I think you were telling me about your undercover career as a finger-painting cellist for that classic punk band, Deaf Monkey Hammer?"

"Actually, I was," she laughed. "Where was I?"

They talked for the next two hours, always remaining in each other's orbit. The conversation came easily.

'Is this too easy?' Martin thought to himself.

He purposefully avoided any mention of what he did and, to be fair, always steered the conversation away from what she did. He was impressed that they were able to talk for that long without hitting the subject of work. Unfortunately, he wasn't able to ascertain where she fell on the political spectrum. He needed a clue one way or another but wasn't getting any.

And then his opportunity ended.

Gabrielle, who was still laughing at his latest brilliant joke, looked down at her watch and frowned. "Marty, I'm sorry. I've had a really nice time, but I need to go."

'That was abrupt.'

She took his phone number, while refusing him hers, and then disappeared. The whole transition from conversation to standing alone was less than a minute. Climbing into his Uber five minutes later, Martin still couldn't understand what had happened.

      ·   ·   ·

His mind raced during the ride back to his hotel. It kept racing from the sidewalk to his room and then through his tooth brushing. He replayed the last ten minutes of their conversation several times in his mind. Nothing seemed amiss.

He told himself that sometimes things just don't work out. He knew it was true but found the entire experience unsatisfying. Lying in bed, he couldn't stop thinking about it. He tossed and turned. Nothing could get Gabrielle out of his head.

He decided to try something that he hadn't done since prior to graduating from college.

He climbed out of bed, went to the dresser, and pulled out the small leather-bound book his mother had given him as a going-away gift. It was a journal, completely blank on the inside, waiting for him to open it for the first time.

He grabbed a pen and started writing, describing Gabrielle and then backtracking to describe Luke and then the bar itself. He filled nine small pages. When he'd written everything about the evening that he thought was worth writing down, he decided to start from the beginning. He wrote of the last nine days, starting with his stepping off the plane.

Two hours later, he had caught up to that day. It felt good to write. He was tired but clear.

His mother had asked him to journal about his experience at the White House. When she mentioned it to him, he didn't care for the idea. He assumed that he wouldn't write anything in the journal.

Climbing into bed, yawning uncontrollably, he decided that he would write all about his time in DC. With that decision made, he rolled over and quickly fell into an exhausted slumber.

PRESIDENTIAL PERSONNEL OFFICE

"Shit, man," Mike said. "You must have had a fantastic evening!"

Martin slept through his alarm and made it into work almost two hours late. He knew it didn't really matter – no one seemed to track the comings and goings of the Document Reconstruction Team. All that mattered was that they reconstructed documents.

"Tell us about your new friend," Mike continued. He had obviously assumed the best.

"Her name is Gabrielle," Martin said. "She's easy on the eyes; she's a brilliant conversationalist. And she high-tailed it out of there at about ten forty-five, without giving me her number."

"What?!" Luke exclaimed.

"Holy shit!" Mike added.

Both of them sat up from their hunched positions over piles of ripped-up documents and dropped their rolls of scotch tape almost simultaneously. 'Theirs, and mine, is a miserable existence,' Martin thought.

"What happened?" Luke asked.

"I really don't know," Martin shook his head. "It was going great, and then she was gone."

"You told her about the White House," Luke suggested.

"No! It never even came up."

"You shared with her your strict conservative views," Mike said.

Martin shook his head.

"You asked her why she voted for Hillary," Luke said.

"No. Nothing. She was just … gone," Martin said.

"It would have been a better story if it ended with her bitch-slapping you and then storming off," Mike said, as he bent back over his current project and resumed taping.

"Sorry to disappoint."

"You going to head over to the PPO?" Luke asked.

"Yeah. Anything I need to know?"

"A bunch of those guys can be assholes," Mike offered.

"Yeah, if you get there at the wrong time, there'll be a whole gang of them, just sitting around, vaping up the joint," Luke said.

"Don't they have jobs to do?"

Luke spread his arms over the mass of papers on their desk and the pile of folders waiting to be reconstructed. "You would think so, but apparently not."

·   ·   ·

Martin arrived at the PPO to find over a dozen staffers, hanging out, all doing nothing. They were standing, sitting, or leaning on walls or furniture, not one seemingly doing any real work. He couldn't tell who was in charge, if anyone was. There were at least five different conversations occurring.

"Yeah, just the other day was Religious Freedom Day," one staffer was saying to a group of three. "I helped write the proclamation."

Another laughed at the comment. "Yeah, if you consider passing the draft from one principal to another as 'writing.' You didn't write shit."

"I spent three hours editing that proclamation!"

"Did they take any of your changes?" another asked.

"Beside the point," the first said sheepishly. The other three burst into laughter.

Only a few feet from Martin, two other staffers were complaining to each other.

A thick staffer with a wrestler's ear was just finishing a sentence, "…the events for National School Choice Week."

"But what does that even mean?" a tall, thin staffer with a hawk nose asked the wrestler. "Like, what's the point?"

"It's an important issue," Wrestler Ear responded.

"Was it important before you began working it?"

"Not to me," Wrestler Ear admitted. "But Bell Biv is taking it seriously."

The tall one laughed, "Bell Biv? That's what you're calling her these days?"

"Bell Biv DeVoe! Hell, yeah! That's her nickname this week. It changes weekly, sometimes daily."

"Has she ever heard that one?" Hawk Nose asked.

"Doubt it," Wrestler Ear said. "I don't think she'd know who they are, anyway."

"I'm surprised you know who they are," Hawk Nose said.

"Shit, man," Wrestler Ear said. "I'm up on my early-nineties hip hop."

"Were they *really* hip hop?" Hawk Nose asked.

Martin wished he had time to crack jokes about… whoever it was they were cracking jokes about. But not as much as he wished someone would acknowledge his existence.

A third conversation was about the upcoming State of the Union.

"…should be interesting. Are you guys gonna go?"

"No. Don't think I'm even going to watch it."

"Why not?"

"It's all just words, man. The Prez is going to say what he's going to say. The Republicans will stand and clap; the libtards will sit in silence. The Prez will go off script, probably say something completely off the cuff, and then we'll have to play damage control for three days."

"That's the truth. But that's not as bad as working a policy for three weeks and then having him change his mind for no reason other than someone said something on CNN."

"We've all been there."

"Do you ever wonder what life was like under other Presidents?"

"That way leads to depression; I don't want to think about that."

The conversations went on. Martin continued to stand in the doorway for several minutes before someone noticed him.

An Indian guy taking part in yet another conversation took a deep drag on an e-cigarette, gave Martin a cursory glance, and said, "Be right with you." He was wearing khakis that were obviously too large for him, a sweater, and a turtleneck. He continued his conversation for another three minutes.

During that time, not a single other person in the office even acknowledged him.

"Yes?" Baggy Khakis asked.

"Yeah. Good morning," Martin said. "I was hoping someone could help me."

"Depends what kind of help you're looking for," Baggy Khakis answered.

Martin wasn't in the mood for his nonchalant bullshit. "I'm a new hire, been here a little over a week. Brianne told me that I'd be moving before now to a more permanent position."

At the mention of Brianne, every conversation in the room abruptly ceased.

"Aw, Brianne," said a voice behind Martin. "What I wouldn't do to Brianne."

Martin turned to the guy who commented on Brianne. He was tall, with dark circles under his eyes. Dude was creepy.

"I'll tell you what she wouldn't do to you," said another.

"What?" asked Tall and Creepy.

"Everything!"

The room exploded into laughter.

When Baggy Khakis stopped laughing, he moved to sit down at a desk. "What are you doing now?"

"Document reconstruction," Martin said.

Several of the staffers behind Martin snickered. He turned, only to see several of them shaking their heads.

"Been there," Wrestler Ear said sympathetically. "Longest six weeks of my life."

"Name?" Baggy Khakis asked. He was typing at a computer and then stopped, waiting for Martin to answer.

"Jermanski. Martin Jermanski." Martin turned back to Wrestler Ear. "I'm with two guys who've been at it for months."

"You mean Mike and Luke?" Hawk Nose asked.

Before Martin could answer, several staffers laughed. "Not those two."

"There's a reason they're still taping documents." Tall and Creepy said. "Do they still have their motto on a little poster on the wall?"

"Let's see, Jermanski, Martin," said Baggy Khakis. He examined the monitor and clicked and looked some more.

Martin was trying to listen to Baggy Khakis and Tall and Creepy. "I don't think so. What was their motto?" he asked.

"So we have a system for assigning people based on their resumes," Baggy Khakis said. "I have your resume right here. Let's see ... Well, I can see why you were put there."

"You tear it; we'll repair it!" Tall and Creepy said, before falling into a fit of laughter.

"What do you mean?" Martin asked Baggy Khakis.

"Dude. There's, like, nothing here," Baggy Khakis said. "Your resume basically says 'graduated college, dead end job, dead-end job, dead-end job.' It's accurate, right?"

"Yeah, it's accurate."

"Good," Baggy Khakis said. "We've had problems lately with some ... less than experienced personnel making the news for ... inaccuracies on their resume."

"Seriously?" Martin asked.

"Oh, yeah," Baggy Khakis responded. "We had to let go of a high profile staffer, because he lied on his resume. Worse than that, it was picked up in the news."

"No," said Martin. "Not that. You look at *my* resume and ask if it's false?"

"Hey, man," said Baggy Khakis. "Can't be too careful."

"No doubt," another staffer who had been silent up to that point said. "A higher-up screws up, lies, or does something illegal and nothing happens. If one of us does, they let us go lickety split. Apu there is just covering his ass."

"Apu?" Baggy Khakis asked. "That's some racist, fucked-up bullshit."

"Look, Apu," Previously Silent said. "If the shoe fits, wear it. If your skin's brown, own it."

"That's fucked up," Baggy Khakis repeated without looking up from the computer. "Wait a minute…"

Martin waited for several seconds and then could wait no longer. "What is it?"

"There's a special note here. It says…Oh." Baggy Khakis looked up at him. "I don't know what to tell you."

"What does that mean?" Martin asked.

"You got a special recommendation?" Baggy Khakis asked.

Martin assumed he was talking about the note from The Ronald, but he didn't know that it was 'in the system.' "Yeah."

"That's why you're still with documents. I think they're trying to find a place for you. Your resume doesn't really support much, but the recommendation's worth a lot."

"How long'll I be in documents?"

"No clue," Baggy Khakis answered. "Any idea where you want to go?"

Martin shook his head.

Baggy Khakis typed for several seconds. "If you don't hear from someone, check back here in about a week."

"Another week taping documents together?"

"Sorry, man," Baggy Khakis shrugged. "Someone has to."

SCOTCH-TAPE PURGATORY

Martin almost didn't have the will to return to his office. The feel of scotch tape on his fingers was becoming unbearable. He didn't know how Mike or Luke were still at it, months after being hired. He couldn't do it, but it seemed like he wouldn't have to. He just needed some patience.

The conversation in the PPO made him wonder. What was the story with Mike and Luke? Why were they still taping documents together after so long? He decided it best not to ask.

He got back to the office to find the two of them still at their desks, bent over, and taping furiously. And then he noticed an additional box on the floor. He opened one flap. It was full to the top with red folders, something he hadn't seen before.

"What're these?"

"Red ones?" Luke asked. "Classified documents,"

"Like secret and shit?" Martin asked.

"Yeah," Mike answered.

"Am I allowed to work on those?"

"We told them that you were with us," Mike said. "They were in a hurry, said not to worry about it."

"You sure?"

"Don't worry," Luke said. "We've seen tons of shit that is marked 'Confidential' or 'Secret' that doesn't seem like it should be either. No worries."

"Really?"

"Calm down. Promise," Luke said. "But we need to get through all of the normal shit before we can start on that."

"Seriously, man. Don't be a sweatpump," Mike added. "Apparently, we're falling behind, and they want us to catch up. We're here tonight until we finish this."

·   ·   ·

The three worked until the day's pile and the new box of classified papers were gone. 'Here tonight until we finish' meant after nine that night.

Martin stuck with the 'normal' papers. Mike and Luke concentrated their efforts on the classified materials.

"What do you need to do to get access to that?" Martin asked late into the afternoon.

"Officially?" Luke asked.

"Yeah," Martin said.

"Not sure," Mike said.

"What do you mean?" Martin asked.

"You're like my two-year-old nephew!" Luke said. "That kid asks a thousand questions. Daily."

"I haven't even been here two weeks; I'm still trying to figure the place out." He turned to Mike. "But seriously, what do you mean you're not sure?"

"Oh. Well. I'm not sure what I did to get access. Not sure I did anything. What'd you do?" Mike asked Luke.

"Filled out a bunch of paperwork. Was interviewed by someone," Luke answered. "Pain in the ass."

"I don't remember doing that," Mike said.

Luke laughed, "Maybe you didn't."

"You sure you should be looking at that?" Martin asked.

"I've been looking at it for months," Mike said. "Not going to stop now. Besides, I don't think they'd let me stop. Too many documents to rebuild."

Martin knew that he shouldn't, but he couldn't help himself. "What kinds of things have you learned?"

"What? You mean secret shit? I couldn't tell you," Mike said. "Like Luke said earlier, I don't know what's secret and what isn't."

"Each individual paragraph in those documents is marked," Luke said. "So you can tell which paragraphs contain classified information and which ones do not. But that doesn't help. At all."

Mike nodded in agreement.

"I've read some things in an unclassified paragraph that I would've bet were some kind of secret," continued Luke. "And I've read multiple pages of paragraphs marked confidential or secret and would've bet that nothing I read was classified, or even important."

"Makes no sense," Mike added.

"I don't get it," Luke agreed.

"All that shit's above our heads, anyway," Mike said. "We're just the document guys."

At the end of the night, the three were organizing folders of reconstructed documents. Martin was handing a red folder from Mike to Luke when a sheet of paper fell from it. It appeared to be a page from a comic book, with six panels of crudely drawn pictures.

"What's that?" Martin asked.

"That's the daily intel brief," Luke said.

"Say what?"

"Every day, the President receives a daily intelligence brief. Apparently, for previous President's, it came in a binder—a fairly thick document," Luke said.

"President Drumpf doesn't like to read," Mike said. "So he wasn't reading them. The intel types began to shorten the brief. He still didn't read it. They shortened it some more. Still no reading."

"Eventually, they shortened it down to comics pages," Luke said. "The Director of the CIA briefs the President using comics pages. Apparently, he likes the pictures."

"You're shitting me," Martin said.

"Look," Mike said, handing a sheet to Martin. "Comics page. Secret marks at the top and bottom. Cartoon Bashar al-Assad."

"Check this one," Luke said. "Cartoon Kim Jong Un."

"Cartoon Vladimir Putin," Mike said, waving another at Martin.

"Cartoons," Martin said.

"Yup!"

．　　　　．　　　　．

Martin was first in the next morning. The daily box hadn't arrived yet, so he sat down and tried to get comfortable. Impossible: Shitty chairs, cramped office. Martin sat and wallowed in his misery.

Thankfully, a knock at the door a few minutes later signaled the arrival of the box. Except this one contained something new.

"What's this?" Martin asked as he removed the lid.

"Apparently, some of the papers were wetted."

"Wetted?" Martin asked.

"Water spilled on them or something."

"Shit," Martin said.

"Don't complain; there have been times when papers were burned."

Martin let that pass. "So what am I supposed to do with these?" he asked, picking up a ziploc bag that contained soaked pieces of paper and a decent amount of what he hoped was water.

"Your first time with widdy?"

"'Widdy'?" Martin asked.

"W.D.I."

"W.D.I.?" Martin asked. "You're going to have to give me something."

"Water Damaged Items."

"Oh," Martin said.

The guy stared at him. "Yeah, so. First time?"

"Yeah," Martin said.

"They have a hair dryer around here somewhere. Paper towels? I don't know. You'd have to ask Mike or Luke."

"Guess I'll start on the dry stuff first," Martin said.

"I wouldn't. Longer it soaks, harder it is to repair."

"Great," Martin muttered.

By the time Luke showed up twenty minutes later, Martin had found two hair dryers in the filing cabinet and several rolls of paper towels. He had unrolled several sheets of paper towel onto the desk and was carefully laying out the soaked and ripped pieces of paper onto the towels. Air dry seemed to be the way to go.

He had tried to use the hair dryer, but it only blew the pieces around. It didn't do a good job drying them either.

Luke looked over and laughed. "You're in the big leagues now!"

Martin just shook his head. "I think I may have destroyed some pieces early on."

"Yeah," Luke said. "You have to be extra careful separating the smaller ones when they're soaked like this. They rip easily."

"Tell me about it," Martin lamented, looking at the desktop. "Has it really come to this?"

"Yes, Marty. It has," Luke said. "Mike should be in any minute now. With three of us working, it'll go pretty fast."

"That's just the drying," Martin said. "We still need to assemble and tape them."

"True," Luke agreed. "And they're typically harder to tape, because they tend to curl up as they dry."

"Oh yeah," Mike said as he walked through the door. "Document reconstruction at its best! So what's the liquid?"

"Don't know," Luke answered. "I just beat you by a few minutes. Marty?"

"Water, I think," Martin said. "What else could it be?"

"Coffee," Mike said.

"Orange juice," Luke said.

"We had scotch one time," Mike said.

"Yeah," Luke agreed. "Various alcohols. A beer or two?"

Martin looked at them. "You guys aren't joking," he said.

"No," they responded simultaneously.

"There's been worse," Mike offered.

"Impossible," Martin said. "It can't get worse."

"Imagine reconstructing a burned document," Mike said.

"Burned?"

"Burned," Luke said.

"Shouldn't there be some kind of forensic experts doing this?" Martin asked.

"Too expensive," Mike said. "So the government gets us."

"Best that money can buy," Luke said.

Without another word, they got down to it. Hours into the day, after they had fully discussed all the intricacies of WDI reconstruction and only made the smallest dent in the daily box, Luke turned to Martin. "Hear from Gabrielle yet?"

"No," Martin said.

"Sure she didn't figure out where you worked?" Mike asked.

"Tried my best to hide it," Martin said. "I've no idea where she works."

"She was on to you," Luke said. "She probably read you in the first ten minutes."

"You know that's bullshit," Martin said. "If she did, she would have left then—not string me along for the rest of the evening to ghost me at the end."

"She probably just wanted to milk you for a few free drinks," Mike insisted.

"It's only been a few days," Luke said. "The window's still open."

"Dude. I can't do any more wet docs," Martin said. "I need to move to some dry."

"There's only two Ziploc bags left!" Mike said.

"We haven't even started on the folders. There's a whole stack of those," Martin said. "You know this is going to be a late one; I'm not hurting anything by shifting to the dry folders."

"Fine. Have at it," Mike said.

It was a late one. Through lunch and through dinner, the three worked until nine that evening.

·   ·   ·

Martin stepped out of the Eisenhower Building into the chilly night air. He ached from taping all day and wasn't in a good mood. He glanced at his phone and noticed he had missed a text from his mother. "Call me" was all it said.

He realized that he hadn't spoken to his parents since arriving in DC and decided to call; it would be the easiest way to pass the time on his walk.

His mother picked up the phone before the first ring ended. "It's going okay?"

"Yeah, mom. Job's going okay so far."

"You must be really busy," she said. "We haven't heard from you since your first day in DC."

"Sorry. I have been busy. Working really late nights."

"I bet you're doing important work."

"Working hard," he said.

"And have you met Drumpf yet?" she asked.

"Mom, you know I met him before. I was with you the first time, wasn't I?"

"You know what I mean. In DC."

"No, mom. I haven't met the President since being here, but I'm sure it's only a matter of time."

"What're you doing?"

"Right now, I'm doing a lot of document work for the administration."

"Document work, eh? That's exciting. Important documents, I hope?"

"Everything that's seen by the President."

"Wow!" Her excitement blasted his ear. "That's great, Martin. I'll tell your dad. He's going to be proud."

"Thanks, mom," he said and shivered against the cold. "But it's not that big a deal."

"Are they using your writing skills at all? Do they know about your degree?"

"You *could* say they're taking advantage of my writing."

"How exciting. We are so proud of you, Martin. You know that, right? Even your dad is excited."

"I know, mom. I know. It means a lot to me." Martin paused, and then he remembered the other thing he wanted to tell her. "I started journaling in that journal you gave me."

"That's great, Martin. I bet you're having plenty of adventures to write about."

He laughed, mostly at the irony of her comment. "Something like that, mom."

"We love you, handsome. And miss you. A lot."

"I miss you, too, mom." Martin did, and it was good to hear his mother's voice. "Hey, mom. I gotta go."

"Oh, do you?" she asked coyly. "Going out with the guys? Going out on a date?"

"Something like that. I love you."

"Take care, Martin. Love you. Bye!"

"Bye, mom." He wasn't going out, and he didn't have a date. He didn't want to do anything but lay down. His back, shoulders, and neck ached too much to do anything else.

MOVIN' ON UP

Martin, Mike, and Luke were an hour into another miserable day in the DRT. The initial morning bitching had ended, and they sat in silence sorting and taping. They had already received a box for the day, so it was a shock to all of them when there was another knock at the door.

"They wouldn't bring another box so soon, would they?" Martin asked.

"Wouldn't put it past them," Luke said. "Maybe red?"

"They wouldn't do that to us," Mike insisted, and then loudly, "Come in! It's open."

The door opened, and a short Asian female stuck her head in. "What's up, losers?"

Martin immediately perked up. She was cute.

Luke just shook his head and went back to taping.

Mike sighed. "What's up, 'Manda?"

She ignored the two taping professionals and looked at Martin. "You're Jermanski."

He sat up a little straighter. Perhaps the day was looking up. "Yes, ma'am," he said, in a fake southern drawl, an attempt to be friendly. It backfired.

"Ma'am? Do I look like a 'ma'am' to you?" Her cute smirk was replaced with fierce anger.

Martin couldn't tell if she was being serious or joking.

"I don't," she insisted. "But if that's how you want it, we can play it that way."

"Hey, I—" Martin attempted.

She cut him off. "Guess that means you're going to be my bitch. Whaddya think?"

Martin didn't know what to think, or say.

"What do you losers think?" she said to the other two. "Huh?"

Luke looked up. "He was just trying to be friendly."

"Just trying to be…" Amanda mocked Luke in a sniveling voice. "Please. He was being condescending. 'Ma'am'? Please."

Martin thought it better to remain silent.

Mike tried to steer the conversation. "What can we do for you today?"

Amanda looked at him and then back to Martin. Without taking her eyes off Martin, she said to Mike, "PPO contacted me. Told me that Jermanski was moving in with me. I complained, said there's no room in my office—barely enough room for me—and they told me to suck it up. So I'm here to grab him."

"No shit!" Mike said.

"Your wish came true," Luke said to Martin. And then cocked his head toward Amanda. "Well, maybe not."

"What do you mean by that, loser?" Amanda demanded of Luke.

"I'm surprised you listen to them," Luke responded. "PPO says jump and apparently you jump."

Martin was impressed. He'd never seen backbone in Luke.

Luke continued, "And what is it, exactly, that you do in that little hole of an office?"

"Don't start with me, tape boy. I can tell you what I'm not doing in my office – taping bullshit documents together."

"You were here once, too," Mike said to Amanda. "You remember those days."

Amanda's only response was a firm middle finger in Mike's direction.

"You can call us losers. But a hundred years from now, our descendants will be able to review those documents that were whole only because of us," Luke said. "But your descendants won't know a thing about you. Other than that you might have fetched coffee for some DC bigwig."

"Fuck you, loser."

"Whoa. Calm down, Amanda," Luke said. "We know it's important to fetch coffee, or maybe a remote, or put nametags out on a table. You're doing a great job."

Amanda growled and then pointed at Martin. "You. Out. Now."

Martin was happy to let the little drama play out without him. He stood up and looked at Mike and Luke. "Well, men. I can't say it's been fun."

"Oh, you'll miss us!" Mike said.

"Come on, Jermanski," Amanda said, and then to the other two, "Now you guys can be alone together again. Enjoy, losers."

Martin grabbed his coat, bag, and cup of coffee. "Let's go!" He tried to sound enthusiastic, although he wasn't sure if he was doing it to impress Amanda or motivate himself.

Amanda turned and left. Martin walked to the door.

Mike mouthed a quiet, "Good luck."

Luke said, "Have fun."

As the door swung shut behind him, Martin heard Luke call out a joking, "Don't forget us!"

Amanda was already on her way.

Martin hurried to catch up. He was excited to be leaving the DRT behind but wasn't sure about Amanda. He was hoping that his first impression was wrong—that she wasn't a raging bitch. He decided to chalk up the morning to a personality conflict between Amanda, Mike, and Luke.

"Your office is in the White House?" he asked.

"Yup." Curt.

"Will I be working with you?" he asked.

"Yup."

"What do we do?" he asked.

She stopped and spun to face him. "Listen. We do whatever the higher-ups ask us to do. We *do* fetch coffee, if we need to. We *do* fetch remote controls, if we need to. We do all the stupid shit that needs to get done in the White House, like in any big organization." She stepped closer to him. "Now shut the hell up."

"Okay." Martin wasn't sure what to say.

They left the Eisenhower Building and walked the short distance to the White House. Martin was excited. It was his first time in the building.

"Prepare yourself," Amanda said in sarcastic deadpan.

Martin couldn't help but smile.

And then they arrived. The tiny office was in the bowels of the White House. The room, little larger than a closet, was occupied by two desks facing each other. There wasn't room to fully push out a chair to stand. There were no windows; the carpet was torn; and one of the two fluorescent bulbs in the ceiling clicked and flickered.

Martin's smile started to fade.

"Whaddya think, bitch?" she asked.

Martin let the 'bitch' pass. He wasn't going to let it bother him—not on his first morning away from the DRT. In his best teenage girl voice, "It's awesome!"

"You'll soon realize it's not," she replied and then sat at one of the desks. "So I considered not telling you anything, letting you struggle for a few days and then quit, but I realized that my life gets easier if you're around. As much as I already dislike you, you being here could be a good thing."

"Gee, thanks," he said. "That was … nice?" He sat down at the desk opposite her and ran his hands over the desktop. Old, chipped, and dirty.

"Cleaning supplies are in the closet down the hall," she said. "I don't care if you clean your desk or not, but you'll clean mine twice a week, on Mondays and Wednesdays. You'll vacuum the carpet every other day. And try to get the lightbulb replaced. That flicker is driving me crazy."

'First day in the White House,' he kept telling himself. 'She must be under a lot of stress.' He decided to ignore Amanda's crazy. As far as doing chores for her, he'd cross that bridge when it came.

"Do you have your IT accounts set up?" she asked.

"No."

"Of course not, you don't need those in the DRT," she muttered. "You'll have to get that taken care of, but don't think you'll get to use the computer. It's mine."

It was the first time that he noticed that only her desk had a computer. Another bridge to cross later.

She threw a small booklet at him. "The staffer's handbook. Read it. Bunch of do's and don'ts."

He caught it and glanced through it. "This official?" he asked. It didn't look official.

"Who knows? But it has some good info in it," she said. "It has some bullshit, too, but anyway …"

He opened the booklet and thumbed through it. If it was official, it was extremely poorly done.

"DO be at your desk at 0700 SHARP."

"Do NOT make eye contact with the Chief of Staff before 0700."

"Do NOT talk to the First Daughter, Ivania Drumpf."

"Do NOT extend your hand to shake the President's hand. If he wants to shake your hand, he'll extend his."

Was it some document written by a smart-ass staffer? Was it a joke?

While Martin was pondering the booklet, Amanda slid a single sheet of paper across the desk toward him. He needed to lean forward to reach it.

"That's not important right now, but eventually you'll meet the President."

"What is it?" he asked. It was just a list of words with a date at the bottom.

"Oh," she said. "That's the current list of banned words."

"Banned words?"

"Yeah. Words that you should never say in front of the President. Banned."

The two that most jumped out at him were 'Impeach' and 'Impeachment'.

"What happens if you do?"

"It could be anything. One staffer got a stern look. The President blew up at another. I know of at least one who was fired."

"Just for saying a word?" He didn't believe it.

"Believe it." She paused to let it sink in. "Bathrooms are down the hall, around the corner. There's a coffee maker for us nearby."

"Have you met him?"

"Yeah. It's possible to run into him anywhere. Although he typically doesn't come down here. He tends to avoid the... dirtier... areas. He seems to just wander the halls sometimes. Probably when he's bored with whatever he should be doing."

Martin didn't feel it necessary to tell Amanda he had met the President a few times. It had been years ago. His dad had introduced them; Drumpf didn't seem interested in interacting with the then-12-year-old Martin.

"What's the typical day like?" he asked.

"Get in around seven. Check the schedule. He ignores it by the way. Completely ignores it. I don't even know why we create one. But if there's something that requires us, our day revolves around that. If there isn't, we sit here and wait for the call."

"The call?"

"The phone call asking us to do whatever needs to be done."

"Oh," he said. "So we sit here and wait."

"That sums it up!"

"That's it?"

"Actually, no," she said. "They'll send out emails with last minute or late-breaking work to do. That's why you need to get your accounts set up. If they task you with something over email, and you didn't know because you didn't read the email, you're outta luck.

More importantly, if there is an email that tasks me with something that you miss, I'll be pissed. You don't want that."

He couldn't tell if she was joking or not.

"I'm not joking, bitch. If I get tasked with something, you'll help out with it, or straight up do it yourself. Got it?"

He didn't answer the question. He was trying his best not to be bothered by the 'bitch' thing. It was getting harder.

"And you better get used to being called 'bitch,' bitch." She wiggled the mouse to wake up her computer. It woke up, and she immediately lost interest in him.

Martin sat back. 'May as well read this staffer's handbook,' he thought. His mind began to wander before he finished the first page.

Amanda was lost in her computer.

He wondered what Mike and Luke were doing and then realized that he knew what they were doing. 'Was this office better? Was this job better?' He wasn't sure, but he did know that he was in the White House now and no longer a member of the DRT. At that moment, it seemed enough.

SHAWN

Martin was carrying a pile of folders from one senior White House official's office to another. It was boring and all-too-common. Didn't these people use email to transfer documents? Why was he carrying folders of paper?

He knocked on the appropriate door, and a voice within called out. He pushed it open slightly.

"Come on in, kid. I'll take those."

He stepped into the office. Six people were present, three sitting, two standing, and one leaning against the wall. Two of them appeared to be his age. Why was he "kid"?

The man behind the desk reached out to take the folders.

"What's going on, here?" The President!

Everyone jumped to their feet. Where had he come from?

"They treating you, okay?"

Martin turned around to see that the President was talking to him.

"Uh, sir—" He quickly dropped the folders on the desk.

"Don't you worry about him, sir." The man whose office it was spoke up when Martin hesitated. "We're taking good care of him."

The President laughed, as did everyone else in the office. Martin didn't see what was funny.

"What can we do for you, sir?" One of the other young staffers asked. Female, brunette, vaguely attractive.

"Nothing. Just taking a short break from the pressures of running the government. Thought I'd pop in to see how everyone's doing."

Martin had been told that the President often "popped-in" and usually offered the same explanation why. Some of the staffers believed it; others didn't. Martin didn't know what to think.

"Guess who I just got off the phone with?"

The room was silent. Martin was sure that not one of them cared about the answer, but all were wearing the 'I-can't-wait-to-hear' expression on their faces.

"Just got off the phone with Shawn! The most honest, authentic, real journalist on television today. I know that we usually talk later in the evenings, but he felt he had some important information for me. Of course, I took the call immediately."

"What was the information, Mr. President?" Vaguely Attractive asked.

"Wouldn't you like to know!"

All of them laughed. 'Obsequious,' Martin thought. He had just learned the word and thought it fit.

"You know, sir," one of the other staffers said. "At some point, you're going to have to tell us. We can't do your business unless we know."

"Good point, Mark. Good point. Let's just say he thinks the Republican Party is failing. They're failing the American people, they're failing themselves, and they're failing me. He had some ideas on how we can fix them."

"The midterms are coming up this fall, sir."

"It's not looking good for them. I'll be fine, of course. But unless they fix themselves, they could be in trouble."

"Sir, are you sure that you should talk to Shawn as often as you do?" Another staffer asked the question, mid-thirties or so, slightly unshaven.

"Absolutely!" The President glared the word more than actually saying it. "He and I are very similar. I mean, he's not as successful as I am, or as rich, but he is a New Yorker like me. He understands the media like I do, knows that they tell lies. We get each other."

"Sir," said Mark. "The media will have a field day if they find out that you speak to him regularly."

"Let 'em! You know the media can't touch me. And my people, my followers, don't trust the media anyway. And so what if I speak to Shawn? What does it matter?"

"Sir," said Mark. "It won't look good if it's known that your staunchest supporter on television, who lambasts all of your opponents, is actually a good friend of yours."

"What? Why? That's what friends are for." The President looked around and shrugged at all of them. "To do favors for one another, to pull strings, to make phone calls."

'Seems reasonable to me,' Martin thought.

"Certain segments of the American population would call that crooked," Slightly Unshaven said.

"Crooked?" the President scoffed. "Hillary was crooked! Is crooked. The press should be investigating her. I'm not crooked. I'm a businessman trying to fix this city!"

"You know that we all agree with you, Mr. President. We wouldn't be here if we didn't," Mark said. "The problem with Shawn is that he's a voice in the media, a powerful voice, and the media draws its power from its unbiased views."

"Unbiased? Mark, we talking about the same media? They're all biased. And most are biased against me. What's the matter if one's biased in my favor? It only levels the playing field."

"I just think it's something to be careful about, sir," Slightly Unshaven warned.

"Don't worry. I'm careful. I'm always careful." Drumpf looked around, waiting for any other questions. Finally, his eyes settled on Martin. "How's *he* doing?"

"He's relatively new in the White House, sir. But it looks like he'll be a good addition."

Martin hated when people talked about him as if he wasn't there. He hated it even more when they looked him up and down, sizing him up, just as the President was doing at that very moment.

"Is he loyal?" The question was directed at the room, and then Drumpf turned toward him. "Are you loyal?"

"Sir?" Martin wasn't sure how to answer. 'Loyal to who?'

"He is, sir," Mark answered for him. "He passed the vetting process. Clean."

Drumpf glanced at Mark and nodded and then looked Martin up and down one last time.

"I hope so. I'm sure that he is. I'm sure that you are." The President smiled at everyone and then turned and ducked out.

"Your first time meeting him?"

Martin turned; it was Vaguely Attractive that asked him the question.

"Yeah," he said. "First time."

No one replied. They returned to their positions from prior to the President's surprise arrival. And then they looked at him.

Martin looked from face to face. 'Are they waiting on me to say something or to leave?' "So. Shawn who?"

They burst out laughing. The laughter lasted for several seconds.

"Hannity. Shawn Hannity," Mark said. "Fox News? Hannity?"

Martin thought he knew who Shawn Hannity was, but wasn't sure. He just shrugged.

"You should watch him," Slightly Unshaven said. "He's on Fox."

"Listen, kid," Mark said. "If you want to understand the President, watch Hannity. Hannity speaks for the President."

"Wait," Martin interrupted. "Literally?"

Mark shook his head and looked at the others. "Where do they get these people?" And then back at Martin. "Not literally. At least I don't think so, but he may as well. He also speaks for most of Drumpf's supporters."

"Maybe he just speaks for himself," it was another staffer, a red-head with a large Adam's apple, who had been silent up until that point. The others just looked at him.

Mark continued, his eyes narrowed in Adam's Apple's direction, "Regardless of who he speaks for, he and the President are almost always on the same page." Mark looked back at Martin. "It doesn't really matter whose page it is—"

"Don't tell the President that!" Adam's Apple said.

"—but they are on the same one."

"Got it."

"Anything else?" Adam's Apple asked Martin dismissively.

"No. I guess not."

They sat in silence again, looking at him. Martin finally took the hint. He backed out of the office and pulled the door shut. Muffled laughter bled under the door.

THE OVAL OFFICE

The next morning, Martin came in to find Amanda already at her desk, already logged on to her computer. It was a few minutes past seven.

"Where you been, bitch?"

Surely, there was some HR policy against her always calling him 'Bitch.' At some point, he might need to research that. Maybe the guys in the Presidential Personnel Office could answer the question. Maybe Apu. 'That was offensive and probably racist,' he thought to himself. 'But it *was* funny.'

"Day starts at seven," she said. "Didn't I tell you that?"

"Good morning, Amanda. How're you today?"

"You stopped at Starbucks and didn't get me one?" she asked, looking at the towering coffee in his hand.

Martin actually wasn't a huge coffee drinker, but there was something about starting work in a new office that prompted him to grab one on his way. He should've realized she'd take offense.

"Sorry," he said. "But I didn't know what you liked. I figured you'd have told me what your favorite was."

"It's your job to know," she insisted. "I shouldn't have to tell you."

"Do you ever stop?" he asked, pulling out his chair and plopping onto its ruined padding.

She didn't answer. She seemed lost in the computer.

"Anything interesting on the schedule?"

She ignored the question.

"Are we going to swing by the Oval Office today?" He had joined Amanda three days prior and had yet to see the Oval.

His first full day was entirely spent establishing computer accounts. The experience made him wonder if the entire Federal Government suffers from shitty IT. No wonder people complained about the government; you couldn't get anything done with the systems they're forced to use.

Day Two started with a quick tour of the offices in the White House and the Eisenhower Building. Apparently, as a member of the DRT, he had no need to know where people worked or where the various offices were. Now, he was required to know where everyone worked—if only to run items from office to office. Before the tour was even finished, he was tasked with various busy-work items: Run this to that office; pick up this from the other office; make photocopies of this stack of documents and deliver them to yet another office.

The day prior was more of the same. It involved a lot of getting lost, taking apparently too long to accomplish things for Amanda's liking, and then being called 'Bitch'. He came to the conclusion that being called *that* didn't bother him as much as he assumed she intended it to. He decided to ignore it.

The one plus to Day Three was that he met several other staffers and ran into several he had seen in the PPO. He also spent part of the day looking for Brianne, but he never did find her. At one point, he even stopped in on Mike and Luke in the DRT.

"How's Amanda treating you?" Luke asked.

"Well?" Martin answered. He wasn't sure how to answer the question.

"Typical," Mike said. "She's been like that as long as I've been here."

"How often do you guys actually interact with her?" Martin asked.

"She would occasionally bring the box over from the Oval Office," Luke answered. "Other than that, not at all."

"She never did while I was here," Martin said.

"Guess you got lucky," Luke said.

"What's up with her—?" Martin began.

"Calling you 'bitch'? That's just her, man," Mike said.

"You could lodge a complaint," Luke said.

"What would happen then?" Martin asked.

"Good question," Luke said, and then said nothing else.

Martin waited, expecting more of an answer, and then he realized that he wasn't going to get one. Then he realized that the two of them were growing impatient.

They sat at their desk, partially re-assembled documents spread across the surface in front of them, looking up at him expectantly.

He glanced down; the box beside the desk was looking a bit full for that time of day. It must have been slow going. He almost offered to sit down and help them for a while. Almost.

"Guess I'll get out of your hair," Martin said. "Talk to you guys later." Walking away from their office, he thanked the good Lord that he no longer worked there.

Sitting in his office on Day Four trying to ask Amanda some questions was frustrating, but it wasn't DRT frustrating. And then Martin thought it was sad that the highlight of his Day Three was talking to people who were miserable in their jobs. He was hoping that Day Four would end up better. He rephrased and asked his question again. "Any chance you'll run me past the Oval Office today?"

This time, Amanda looked up from her computer. "Yeah," she answered. "I think so."

She had told him on his first day with her that while any staffer could walk to, and sometimes even in, the Oval Office, the higher-ups typically didn't like random bodies just appearing. He couldn't tell if she was lying or not, but it made sense to him, so he didn't push the issue. He was growing impatient, though.

"Really?" He was surprised.

"You have a quick interview with the Chief of Staff. I'd have to take you that way whether I wanted to or not."

"I know I can always count on you," he said.

Her slight frown told him that she didn't appreciate his sarcasm.

"What do I need to know about the Chief of Staff?" Martin asked.

"Other than he's a former Marine," she said. "He's a hard-ass. He doesn't put up with bullshit. Well, except from one person, but that person happens to be the boss. I don't think there's much you need to know."

"What about this interview?" he asked.

"What about it? He does it with everyone on the staff. Ten minutes, fifteen minutes tops," she said. "You'll be in and out."

"What time is it?" he asked.

She looked at her computer. Her face twisted into a contorted expression of fear. She jumped to her feet. "Oh, shit! Five minutes ago!"

He jumped up, panicked and ready to move.

And then she collapsed into her chair in a hysterical fit of laughter.

"What is it?!" he screeched.

She laughed only harder.

And then he got the joke. It was firmly on him.

"What is it?" she mocked in a high-pitched whine. And laughed even harder.

He could only stand there and take it. He took a deep breath and then dropped slowly into his seat.

She laughed for another minute. After catching her breath, she glanced at him. "That. Was. Hilarious," she said. "That actually made it worth it to be stuck with you in this shitty little office. The look on your face." She giggled. "The only thing that would have made that better is if I had taken a picture. The look on your face!"

Martin could only sit there and take it.

"So what time is this interview?" he asked.

"Eight-thirty. I recommend that you be there at least five minutes early," she said. With a serious face, "That's a no-shit. No later than 8:25."

"Got it," he said. "And the Oval Office?"

She looked at him and shook her head, then glanced again at her computer. "Schedule's clear. No urgent taskers. Office is probably empty. Let's go now."

"Probably empty?" he asked as he stood to leave.

"Oh, yeah," she said. "It's—what? Not even 7:30 yet? There's no way the Prez is in the Oval right now."

"Whaddya mean?" Martin asked.

"He's probably still in the Residence, maybe not even dressed yet—that's a sight you don't want to see, believe me—watching TV," she stood and led him from the office. "Probably 'Fox and Friends'. Or, if he wants to get pissed off at something, CNN or MSNBC."

"When does he get in?" he asked.

"Depends. Fox and Friends runs until nine," she said. "Then he'll get ready or maybe watch more television. Shoot out a tweet or two. Hard to say; somewhere between ten and eleven. The first thing on his schedule is the daily intel brief. If you can call it daily."

"Who briefs him?" he asked.

"Pompeii," she said and glanced at him. The glance told her all she needed to know. "Head of the CIA? Former Congressman. Some say future Secretary of State …"

"Secretary of State! Great!" he sang. "Is he already Senate-approved?"

This time, her glance told him all he needed to know. 'Not a Hamilton fan,' he thought.

"No! He's not Senate-approved." She looked at him as if he were the stupidest person in the building. "Tilleson is still in the job. And both he and the President say he'll be there for the long term."

Martin only shrugged. His parents owned some Exxon stock and liked the SecState, but other than that, he didn't know much about the man.

"You probably helped reconstruct some documents from the intel brief," she added. "Red folders?"

He nodded.

"Yeah. The minor stuff gets sent to the DRT, but Pompeii keeps a hold of the more sensitive shit," she said. "We certainly couldn't have that stuff sent to the DRT."

Her last sentence dripped with sarcasm. Martin didn't know much about security and secrecy. When he was in the DRT, he had read plenty of Secret documents. What was more sensitive than Secret? Top Secret? He thought that was made up for movies and video games.

"And here we are," she announced.

He looked around. Here where? He'd walked past this spot in the hallway a few times, running errands back and forth. Nothing special here.

"Seriously?" she asked and pointed. "That door."

"Wait, what?" he asked. "That door?"

"Yes. That door!"

"No shit," he said.

"He's not in," she said.

"How d'you know?"

"If he was, there'd be a Secret Service agent or a Marine close by. None of them—none of him."

"Got it. Can we go in?"

"Go ahead!"

He took a step toward the door then stopped. She was a little too enthusiastic with the answer. He turned around to her.

"You're learning, bitch," she said. "You're learning."

"So where is the Chief of Staff's office?"

"Seriously?" she scoffed. "Do I have to show you everything?"

Martin only looked at her, trying to maintain a flat stare.

"But let's go in anyway," she said as she stepped past him and to the door to the Oval Office.

"But I thought—" he started.

Amanda opened the door and stepped into the Oval. He walked to the doorway but didn't step through.

"It's fine," she shrugged. "You may as well take a look. We're here."

He hesitated and then stepped in. "It's not as … *gold* as I thought it'd be. Well, except for those curtains. They kinda hurt the eyes."

"It's not his apartment in New York City," she said.

He walked toward the desk across a sea of thick carpet, perhaps the thickest carpet he had ever walked upon. Was it "rich-people" carpet? He walked past sofas, a coffee table, armchairs, and end tables to stand right in front of the President's desk. He considered taking a seat behind it and then reconsidered. He looked around. A grandfather clock, paintings, statues. It wasn't as gilded as he thought'd be. "What're all these flags?"

She rolled her eyes and said, "They're the service flags—the flags of the Armed Services."

"I guess that's patriotic," he said.

Amanda shrugged.

"How often do you come in here?" he asked.

"For work? Fairly often. If there's some low-level task that needs to be done, they call me. I'll probably start sending you now. But that reminds me."

"What?"

"The Chief of Staff is important. Obviously. But you also need to know about Maddie."

"Maddie?" Martin asked. 'Is she attractive?'

"Madeleine Watterhoot. The President's Personal Secretary. She's the gatekeeper."

"What?" Martin asked. "Like Zuul?"

"Who?" Amanda asked and then growled. "Shut up and listen. Watterhoot is the President's closest aide. She controls who sees him and when; she'll always be in the Oval Office or close by."

"Do we work for her?"

"No. Not really," Amanda said. "We do different things than she does. But if she asks you, tells you to do something, just do it."

"So we do work for her."

"Fuck. No. You'll see."

'That was helpful,' Martin thought. 'Is she attractive?'

Martin was still looking at the service flags. "What are all these ribbons?" he asked. He had moved next to the U.S. Army flag, the top of which was enveloped in dozens of ribbons, so much so that he couldn't really even see its top half.

"Not sure. Don't care," she said. "I'm not here to answer your stupid questions."

"Ms. Chung?"

They both looked up to see an older gentleman standing in the open doorway through which they had entered. Martin didn't know who it was.

Amanda's demeanor immediately changed. "Good morning, sir," she said in a voice more professional than Martin had previously heard her use.

"What're you doing in here?" the man asked.

"I was taking a few minutes to show Jermanski the Oval, sir. Part of his orientation. He hadn't seen it yet, and I knew the office would be empty."

The man nodded, his face neutral. He looked at Martin. "That's Jermanski? My 8:30?"

"Yes, sir," she said.

Martin tried to ignore the fact that they were talking about him in his presence. He realized that the gentleman was John Kellner, the Chief of Staff. He was taller than Martin, thin, and mostly bald. He looked like a doctor; Martin could easily picture a stethoscope hanging around his neck. Kellner did not look like a Marine—or at least the stereotypical image that Martin carried in his mind.

"You have time now, Jermanski?" Kellner asked. "It's a little early but my schedule's open."

"Yes, sir." It felt weird to call anyone 'sir'. Martin figured he should probably get used to it.

"Follow me," Kellner said, leaving the door open as he left the Oval.

THE CHIEF OF STAFF

Martin followed the Chief of Staff into his office.

"Sit down, Jermanski. This shouldn't take long."

Martin sat in a comfortable chair in front of the Chief of Staff's desk. What he wouldn't give for a comfortable chair of his own.

Kellner walked around his desk and pulled his chair out. "Ever know anyone in the military?"

Martin shook his head. "No, sir."

"Doesn't matter," Kellner said as he sat. "I sit down with most of the new hires for a few minutes. It's something I learned a long time ago – you have to know your people to know how they'll perform, to know *if* they can perform. It's served me well for a long time. Shit, probably longer than you've been alive."

Kellner thought for a moment.

"You're in a bit of an interesting situation." The Chief of Staff looked at him, put on his reading glasses, and then opened a folder on his desk. He spent a moment looking through a small stack of papers.

"Most of the junior staffers in the administration work in specific topical areas, have areas of expertise, or work for higher-ranking staffers who do: National Security Affairs, Domestic Policy,

International Negotiations, Economic Policy, and so forth. They found their way into those positions based upon their degrees, or their interests, their prior work. Many of the higher-ranking ones worked for the President's campaign. Personally, I don't think that's how important positions should be filled, but that's politics."

"When I came in as Chief of Staff, I cleared a lot of chaff. The place was chaos, and I did what I believed best for the President and the country. Most of the people who remain are, in fact, the wheat. Take Ms. Chung, for instance. She's a Priebus hold-over, but I like her. She works hard; she's smart; she doesn't take shit from people. She can be a bit abrasive."

Kellner shrugged. Martin nodded, trying not to give away his initial opinion of Amanda.

"But try to learn from her," Kellner said. He removed his reading glasses from his face and dropped them on the desk in front of him. "As I said, you're an interesting case. You have an English degree, not a bad degree by the way. Some of my very best Marines were English majors. But it's not one that lends itself to any specific office or role. That might have been different if you had done any important writing, something that we could hang a hat on. But you didn't."

Kellner paused. Martin waited; he wasn't sure where this was headed.

"I'll be honest with you," Kellner continued. "If it weren't for the letter the President gave to your father, we wouldn't have hired you. Wouldn't have looked twice at you. Frankly, I'm still skeptical of the decision...But that left the PPO, and me, with a problem: What to do with you. I couldn't leave you in the DRT, but there wasn't any natural fit for you."

Kellner's comments weren't pleasant to listen to, but they made sense to Martin.

"You'll continue to work with Ms. Chung. You'll continue to do what she's been doing for months now—whatever it is that needs to be done in and around the White House. You're kinda outside of the more formal White House structure, but it allows me to keep an eye on you. As time goes by, and if you desire it, you might be able to move into a more formal role."

Martin nodded. It didn't sound much different than what Amanda had said when he started.

"Since you'll probably start to interact more and more with the President, you need to watch your behavior. You need to be well-dressed, and you need to be respectful at all times."

"None of those things'll be a problem, sir," Martin said.

"While you are, in fact, one of the lowest, you are still a civilian staffer. Many of the military personnel in the building will defer to you. Make sure you treat them with respect. If I hear you are anything less than courteous and professional toward them, we'll have a conversation."

"The same goes for the Secret Service. They tend not to take shit from anyone, but they will also, out of their sense of professionalism, defer. Do not take advantage."

'Are there people who actually require being told this stuff?' Martin thought to himself as he nodded.

"Finally, as someone who works in and around the White House, you'll be privy to information, whether or not it is formally classified, that's highly sensitive." Kellner's voice changed, and he stared hard at Martin. "I expect you to keep your mouth shut and keep that information to yourself. At all times, and for all time."

Martin nodded again; he took the hint.

Kellner sat back. His look changed. Martin couldn't decide if he was smiling or not.

"D'you have any questions for me?" Kellner asked.

Martin was sure that he should have had questions, but he couldn't think of any. He started to shake his head and then one popped into his head. "Sir, does this mean that I'm done with the DRT?"

The Chief of Staff smirked. "Officially, yes. But when things get busy, all of the junior staffers put in some time doing reconstruction. Anything else?"

"No, sir."

Kellner raised an eyebrow and then stood up and offered his hand.

Martin stood to meet him and shook the Chief of Staff's hand. 'The man has a strong grip,' Martin thought.

"You know where to find me, if necessary," Kellner said. "Have a good day."

"Thank you, sir," Martin said and left the office.

.   .   .

"How'd that go, bitch?"

"Fine," Martin said. "How'd you expect it to go?"

"About like that," Amanda said. "I told you. I like the guy. He doesn't take any shit."

"So what else is on the schedule?" he asked, picking up and taking a sip from his cold Starbucks.

"You have a phone. Haven't you set up your email to go to your phone? Can't you get to the page on your phone?"

He showed her his phone. Old.

"Oh," she cracked up. "The bitch has a bitch phone!" Then she stopped laughing and shook her head. "You'll need to report to the Comms Agency and get an official phone." Her tone indicated that she didn't want to share that information.

"You mean I get a new phone?"

"Yup," she said. "On the government's dime."

'Wow,' he thought. 'Things are looking up.'

"You might want to do that today. I can probably, for a price, tell you where their office is."

"I'd expect nothing less."

"Since I'm feeling some pity for you and that shitty-ass phone, I'll tell you that there isn't anything on our schedule for today. It might be a boring one."

"But," she continued. "There is a Cabinet Meeting tomorrow. We lend a hand with the preps, make sure the room is set – which it always is; they don't need us for that at all. They might use us to usher people in and out. Or not. We even, if we wanted, could hang out and observe. As long as the topics are unclassified."

"I've never been to a Cabinet Meeting."

"No shit, jackwad. Stupid thing to say, but you'll get your chance tomorrow."

"Hurray?"

She shrugged then went back to her computer.

.   .   .

Amanda had been right. It was a boring day, which turned into an early day—his earliest since starting work. Martin left the White House and stepped into a cold but sunny afternoon.

He had to admit that getting a new phone, which he was told would be ready in the next day or two, was an exciting prospect.

'Maybe the mere fact that I have a new phone will cause Gabrielle to call me!' Martin thought. 'On the old one.' He was often glad that people couldn't read his mind.

It had been a couple of weeks since his night on the town with Luke. Gabrielle never did call him. 'Did I misread the situation?' He kept thinking back to that night. Despite his best efforts, he was having trouble forgetting her.

His phone vibrated in his pocket.

'Could it be? Cha-ching!'

He answered without even checking who it was. "Hello?"

"Hey, Martin!" It was his mom.

He tried to hide his disappointment. "Hey, mom. How are you guys?"

"I feel so loved knowing that you're happy to hear from me."

"Sorry, mom," he said and tried to sound upbeat. "I'm happy to hear from you. How's dad?"

"We're both good, Martin. Everything is fine. I didn't think you'd answer your phone this early. I was going to leave a message."

"What was the message going to be?"

"To call your loving mother."

"Well now I don't have to!" It was time to head home; he started walking.

"I just wanted to see how you're doing and ask if anything's new."

"Actually, mom," he said. "There's a bunch that's new. I've changed jobs."

"Are you still working for Drumpf?"

"Yeah, still working for the administration. But I got a promotion. And I now have an office in the White House."

"Wow! That's great, Martin!"

"And I briefly met the President a few days ago."

"Great. Did he remember you?"

"I doubt it, mom. And there really wasn't time. It was a very short meeting."

"And I'll be getting a new phone in the next few days. An official White House phone."

"You're becoming a real mover and shaker, aren't you?"

"Yeah, mom. Something like that."

They spoke for a few more minutes. And when they hung up, Martin was in a really good mood.

WHO'S WHO IN THE ZOO

"So the Cabinet Room is right next to the Oval Office," Amanda said to Martin as they made their way in that direction. "There won't be anything for us to do, but we go anyway."

'Seems pretty straightforward,' Martin thought. 'In a bizarre, massive-bureaucracy sort of way.'

"Have you met any of the Secret Service Agents yet?"

"I've seen a few, but I haven't met any."

"That makes sense," she said. "They typically don't hang out near our office. But as you spend more time in and around the Oval Office, or the Cabinet Room, or even the Residence, you'll see them more and more."

Martin was impressed. Amanda seemed willing to teach him things, as opposed to continuously ragging on him. But he wasn't so easily fooled. 'Maybe she's waiting for me to drop my guard,' he thought. "When we stopped by the Oval Office the other day, I didn't see any Secret Service."

"True," she said. "They only stand watch when the President is present. So if you don't see an Agent, you can bet that he isn't around. Same for the Marines outside, like literally outside, of the Oval. If the President is present, a Marine will be stationed on the walkway or balcony outside of the Oval."

Martin nodded. That all made sense.

"But you have to watch out for the President," Amanda continued. "That man has a tendency to just show up places, out of the blue, and surprise people. I don't know how he does it."

"Even the Secret Service?" he asked.

"I think they'd tell you he never surprises them. It's their number one job, right, to know where he's at? But I bet he surprises even them sometimes."

"What're they like?"

"They're good guys," Amanda said. "I enjoy busting their balls. Giving them shit whenever I can. They take it well."

'That's the Amanda I know,' Martin thought.

"The staffers have given most of the Agents nicknames," Amanda continued. "No one can remember their real names, so they get call signs."

"So there's 'Ben.' I don't remember why he was given that name. He's also called 'the Chin,' and you'll know why when you see him. There's 'Phil' who looks like Clark Gregg, the actor who plays Phil Coulson in the Avengers movies. There's 'Chad' who looks like every stereotypical white, rich, young guy that I can't fucking stand. There's 'Lex' because of his shiny, bald head. Let's see. Who else?"

"Do the Agents know the staffers have names for them?" Martin asked.

"Not sure," Amanda said. "But I'm pretty sure they do. I mean, seriously, how could they not? Then there's 'Jake.'"

"Jake? That's his nickname?"

"Yeah," she said.

"What's the joke there?" he asked.

"Don't know. His real name is Joe, though."

'That's stupid,' Martin thought.

They stopped in front of a doorway. Amanda turned to Martin. "Know where you're at?"

"Yeah," he said. "The Oval Office is right down that way."

"Yup. And this is the Cabinet Room." She stepped in; Martin followed.

'Impressive,' Martin thought. Big oval table, plush seats arranged around it, paintings, statues, and thick curtains covering a wall of windows.

"Each Cabinet Official has his or her own seat," Amanda said. "Like, literally, their very own seat that no one else sits in. See, each has a little engraved marker."

Martin didn't know how to take this helpful and informative Amanda. It was bizarre, so he just kept his mouth shut and let her continue.

"The President sits there." She pointed to a seat in the center of the table on its far side. "The Vice President sits right beside him. The other Cabinet officials sit around the table. There's a standard order when they're all present. You'll learn it after a few meetings."

Amanda looked at her watch. "They're going to start arriving any minute. Each will show up with an assistant, sometimes two. Depending on the discussion, the assistants will stay in the room, or hang out somewhere close by. Our job is to be present, ready to help with anything, but completely disappear. We stay off to the side, out of the way. Got it?"

"Sure," Martin said. 'Seems pretty straightforward.'

"If a photographer is going to take a picture, and it looks like we might end up in it, we discretely, but quickly, get the hell out of the way. Got it?"

"Yup," he said.

She looked at him closely.

"Yes, Amanda," he insisted. "I get it!"

"While you were listening to this bullshit, I was making sure the room is ready. Places are all set. Pens, notebooks, pre-staged. This is going to be a full Cabinet, so I did a quick count of the chairs. Everything is, as always, in order."

"So now what?" he asked.

"We stand off to the side and don't do anything."

A moment later, Scott Bokor, a staffer in Domestic Policy, entered the Cabinet Room. Martin had met him a few days earlier when he was moving into his new apartment. He and Scott lived in the same apartment building.

Scott walked up to them. "'Manda. Marty."

She nodded curtly at him. "Punk."

"Hey, at least you're only a punk," Martin said to Scott. "I'm a bitch."

Scott cracked up. "We're all bitches at one point or another."

"Funny," she frowned at both of them. "Not."

"Your first Cabinet meeting?" Scott asked Martin.

"Yessiree," Martin said. "Should I be excited?"

"Oh yeah. You've finally made it."

"You losers are pitiful." Amanda stormed off, to the far side of the room where she attempted to look busy.

"I would ask you what her deal is," said Scott, "but I already know the answer."

Martin laughed. It seemed that Amanda was known far and wide amongst the staffers.

"How's the new place?" Scott asked.

"It's good," Martin said. "Certainly better than the hotel." Martin observed more people walk into the room. "Been to many of these?"

"More than I'd care to," Scott answered. "Have you met any of the Cabinet, yet?"

"Not a one."

Scott shook his head. "They come from a different world."

"Which world is that?"

"The world of money," Scott said.

"Does that make them bad people?"

"No. Just different. Most are okay. One or two are obviously assholes. One or two seem to be down to earth."

"Who do you like the most?"

"Matthews. Without a doubt."

"Secretary of Defense, right?" Martin hoped he was right. He didn't want to look like a complete fool.

"SecDef," Scott said. "Yeah. He's a good dude. Just watch out for the knife hand."

"Knife hand?" Martin asked.

"Oh, yeah. The knife hand. You'll know it when you see it."

Martin waited for further explanation. None seemed to be coming, so he flashed the 'what-the-hell' look.

"Oh. Apparently, it's a Marine thing."

"What the hell does that mean?" Martin asked.

"Here," Scott said, typing something onto his phone and then turning it to show Martin. "Look at this."

Martin looked at a picture of the Secretary of Defense in uniform, his hand pointed strongly ahead of him. "Got it. That's a knife hand."

"That's not a knife ... hand," Scott said in a terrible Australian accent. "This is a knife ... hand."

"That was horrible," Martin said laughing. "One of the worst ever."

"You losers are having too much fun." Amanda had rejoined them. "Put that shit away. They're here."

The first were, in fact, arriving.

"So who's that?" Martin asked, indicating a middle-aged dude with black hair and black glasses.

"Steve Munchkin," Amanda said. "Treasury."

Scott leaned in close to Martin. "You should see his wife."

Amanda glared at him.

"Her?" Martin asked of another woman who'd just entered the room. "She looks like my third grade teacher."

"Good call, man," Scott said.

"It's Betsy DeVoe," Amanda said. "Secretary of Education. I hate that bitch."

Martin and Scott both looked at her in surprise. It seemed a bit extreme—even for Amanda.

"She recently came out and said that states can't regulate student loan companies," Amanda said. "Do you know how much I still owe in student loans? And the company is trying to screw me over. Fuck her."

"So that's Bell Biv, and Amanda hates her," Martin said under his breath, and then aloud, "There he is." He was referring to the Secretary of Defense, who had just entered the room. "He's shorter than I expected."

"I think you should tell him that," Scott said.

"What?" Martin asked. "And subject myself to that knife hand? No way."

"Losers," Amanda grumbled under her breath.

"How about that guy?"

"Alex Acoatta," Amanda said. "Secretary of Labor."

"He's … unfortunate looking," Martin said.

"That's fucked up," Scott said. "And extremely shallow. Who'd've guessed that about you, Marty? You're a shallow S.O.B."

"Get off my case, man. I just pay attention to how people look. Who's he?"

"Alex Azarro. Health and Human Services," Amanda said. "You'll like this, bitch. He's been the Secretary for less time than you've been a staffer."

"Nice," Martin said. "But, who are all these people?"

"What d'you mean?" Scott asked.

"That guy, that guy," Martin said, indicating Acoatta and Azarro. "I've never seen them, never even heard of them."

"You're working in the White House, now," Scott said. "You better get on it."

"Shh! Everyone quiet," Amanda said.

The Chief of Staff walked up to the three of them. "Jermanski, Chung." He just looked at Scott and didn't say anything, and then to Amanda, "We set?"

"Yes, sir," Amanda said. "Preps all complete. We were going to stay and observe; this will be Martin's first Cabinet Meeting."

Kellner nodded. "Just stay out of the way."

"Yes, sir," all three responded in unison.

The room was almost full. A white-haired man walked in.

"That's the Vice President, right?" Martin asked.

"You've been here almost six weeks," Amanda protested. "Are you seriously not sure?"

"I figured he was, but no one ever told me for sure."

"You do know how to use Google, right? Surely, you've seen some of the tourist literature that's strewn about the building. His picture is everywhere." She shook her head. "You're terrible."

Martin turned to Scott and mouthed, "I knew it was the Vice President. I just wanted to hear her reaction."

"What was that, bitch?" Amanda asked.

"Nothing, Amanda. I guess that means that the President will be here any minute."

As Martin finished the sentence, the President walked in. Everyone else was still standing; at the President's arrival, they all moved to stand behind their chairs.

"Good morning, everyone. Good morning. It's so nice to see everyone today. It's a great day in Washington, DC, isn't it?" He slowly moved around the table, toward his seat. He greeted each of the Cabinet members as he passed but didn't shake anyone's hand.

Drumpf finally got to his seat and sat down. Everyone else then sat down as well.

Martin scanned the table. He still didn't know who half the Cabinet members were. Had no clue.

"Everyone," the President began. "It's an exciting time for America. The country is doing well, amazingly well, unbelievably well. The economy is humming. Our friends are growing to love us more. Our enemies are learning to fear us again. I have, we have, kept the promise to make America great again!"

The room burst into a round of applause. At the center of it sat Drumpf, a huge smile on his face. He waited for a moment to allow the clapping to die away. When it finally did, he turned to face the new Secretary of Health and Human Services. "Alex? Alex. Good to have you on the Cabinet. I know that you're going to do great things for the pharmaceutical industry, for people of our nation. I know that the drug companies will make amazing advances during your tenure, because you understand what they need to succeed, and I know you'll help them get it."

"Yes, sir. Thank you, Mr. President," Azarro said, sounding flustered.

"Oh, Alex," Drumpf said, seemingly surprised that Azarro opened his mouth. "Would you like to say something to the group?"

"No, Mr. President. Well, yes, sir, I would. I just want to thank you, for leading our great nation … back to even greater greatness. Your leadership has been absolutely vital to a rising stock market, improving profits, and a positive climate in the country. You know, where I was born, in Johnstown, Pennsylvania, seventy miles east of Pittsburgh, most houses in the area, even today, have Drumpf campaign signs in their yards, on their walls, on billboards. America is becoming Drumpf Town, but today, right now, Johnstown is truly Drumpf Town, USA!"

"Wow, thank you, Alex." The President looked around at his Cabinet. "Drumpf Town, USA. I like that. That's really nice. I might have to steal that from you. D'you mind if I steal that idea? I like it. Of course, you won't mind. I'm the President. I can do what I want."

Most members of the Cabinet laughed at his joke. Even Scott and Amanda did, standing to either side of Martin. Martin smiled but couldn't muster the strength to laugh.

The President looked around some more. "Alex and Alex. I just realized; we have the Alex brothers. Alex Azarro and Alex Acoatta. That's fantastic—the Alex Brothers." Then the President's face grew serious.

"Everyone, the Alex Brothers just reminded me of something. Something that's very important. As you know, the liberal, fake-news media has called me racist, called me a bigot. You know that isn't true. I think my Cabinet proves it."

"Now," the President shrugged. "We do have our share of old, white, rich guys, that's true. But if you want to make America great, you need a team that is great—rich, powerful, experts in their fields. But look. We have the Alex Brothers, one Hispanic and one Lebanese. We have a black Secretary of Housing and Urban Development. We have three females in our Cabinet—each attractive, very attractive in their own ways, and one is obviously Oriental. This is a diverse Cabinet, and it is direct proof that I am not a bigot, not a misogynist. And it's really great for America."

Forty-five minutes later, the meeting was still going and Martin couldn't figure out what, if anything, of actual substance had occurred. He leaned over to Amanda and whispered, "Are all Cabinet meetings like this?"

Without looking up at him, she whispered back, "In what way?"

"In every way," he whispered.

She shrugged. "More or less. Yes."

REMOTE CONTROL

Martin sat in his tiny office in the bowels of the White House. He was bored; he had nothing to do. Amanda was on the computer, humming to herself as she typed something.

She was wearing her glasses that day, large black plastic circles that spread across her wide cheeks. Sometimes she wore contacts, but Martin liked the glasses.

'She's cute,' Martin thought, 'and probably smarter than me.'

On the desk sat a single phone, dark gray. It was ancient. Martin knew this, because a cord connected the handset to its base. The phone rang.

Amanda's hand sprung out, as if coiled and waiting, and picked up the phone before Martin was sure it was ringing.

"Chung," she answered.

Martin wasn't sure why she answered with only her last name. Most of the White House Staff used their first names, although some of the important ones used 'Mr.' or 'Mrs.'

"Mm mmm. Mm. Yeah. Okay." She hung up.

"His remote control is on the fritz," she said. "Take him a new one."

"Wait, what? Who? *Him?*"

"Yes, Him. Who else?"

"Why me?"

"Because we're low-level pukes, and that's what we do."

"But, why not you?"

"You're nervous, aren't you? Haven't you been into the Residence yet? Does he even know your name?"

Martin was nervous, although it bothered him to be called-out by her.

"He knows *my* name," she stated, almost triumphantly. "I made sure of that."

Martin raised an eyebrow at her.

"Ew! No. Not that way, asshole. But the whole point of working here is to put a bullet on the resume, maybe make a name for ourselves, move on. You can't do that if he doesn't know your name."

Martin knew, like most young Staffers, Amanda was a recent college grad trying to use her time in the White House as a stepping-stone to bigger things. Martin, on the other hand, wasn't sure what he was doing in the White House.

"I'm on it." He stood up and turned to leave.

"You better get moving," Amanda called after him. "You know he gets impatient."

.   .   .

Martin *had* been in the Residence, but only a few times. There was enough work elsewhere in the White House that coming here was rare. He was breathing heavily as he approached a Secret Service Agent he didn't know. The Agent eyed him suspiciously. Martin smiled awkwardly and held up his security badge in one hand and the large remote control in the other. The Agent nodded, and Martin continued past.

Finally, he came to the door. Another Secret Service Agent stood beside it and glanced at Martin. It was another Agent that Martin had not met yet. 'How many of you people work in the White House?' Martin thought.

"You want to take it in yourself or just give it to me?" the Agent asked.

"Uh. I'll take it in?"

The Agent squinted at him, then knocked twice on the door, and opened it. "Go on."

Martin gulped involuntarily. He stepped to the door and then through.

President Ronald Drumpf sat in the middle of a large gold-colored sofa. A tray holding a half-eaten dinner rested on the coffee table in front of him. The President was staring at two massive flat-screen televisions. His face was colored in the prismatic glow of electric light. The President loosely held a remote control, identical to the one in Martin's hand. He tore his eyes from the screens long enough to glance at Martin and then down at the new remote in his hand.

"CNN is absolutely shameful!" The President was almost shouting.

Martin couldn't tell if Drumpf was speaking to him or some-one else in the room. He quickly looked around; there didn't seem to be anyone else.

"Shameful! Their coverage is continuous fake news. I can't be-lieve they're still in business. The American people are getting sick and tired of their lies, their exaggerations. Is that the new one?"

Martin didn't respond to the question; he didn't even real-ize the President was speaking to him. He was staring at the two televisions. The picture on each was divided into three windows. One television was showing CNN in a large window, MSNBC in a smaller one, and a show Martin didn't recognize in the third. The second television was showing FOX News in its large window, MSNBC again in a smaller window, and a rerun of The Apprentice in the third. It seemed as if the sound for all six windows was play-ing concurrently.

"Excuse me. Is that the new remote control?"

Martin panicked. "Yes, sir, Mr. President. This is the new one. It should work properly, already, but I'm happy—"

"Give it to me." The President held up his hand.

"Yes, sir."

The President eyed him, and then shifted his gaze back to the televisions without dropping his arm.

Martin placed the remote in the President's outstretched palm.

The President took it and then expertly thumbed the volume up on one of the windows. Martin waited for a moment and then turned to go. He stepped to the door and reached for the knob before being interrupted by the President.

"You know. Hope used to bring me my remote. She'd help me if I needed it. She was loyal. Such a loyal girl. I miss Hope."

Martin turned back around. The President's eyes were locked on the televisions. Martin waited; he wasn't sure if he should stay or excuse himself. And he wasn't sure if he should respond to the President's comments about Ms. Hills—she had left only a few days prior.

"I never forget a face. Never. You look familiar to me. How long have you been with us?" Even while speaking to him, the President didn't look at Martin.

"Well, sir. I've only been here a few months. This is the first time that I've assisted you here."

"I thought so." The President thumbed the remote again, and Erin Burnett's voice drowned out the other sounds from the television. "Her. She's an attractive lady. Very attractive. What color do you think her eyes are? Blue? Or gray?"

"Uh, blue, I think."

"Blue? Maybe. She's attractive, isn't she? Too bad she's on CNN. I think she'd do much better on Fox. But, well, who wouldn't? Fox is a much better network. Expert journalists. Not like the hacks on CNN."

Drumpf shifted his gaze across all six pictures. "Only a few months, eh? Wonderful. How?"

"Sir?"

"I mean, how'd you get the job?"

"Oh. Sir, my father works for you at Mer-a-Lago. Bill Jermanski. He's a mid-level—"

"Phil? Phil."

"Bill, sir."

"Bill? Bill! Of course. I have a lot of good people working for me at the Club. The best in the business, at the best club in Palm Beach. Your dad must be one of the best. I mean, I wouldn't hire him if he wasn't."

"Yes, sir. You were chatting with him last December at the Club. And apparently he told you about me."

Martin paused, expecting a response. The President said nothing, just sat and stared at Erin Burnett on CNN.

"You told him that I should come up to Washington. That I'd be welcomed to work here in the White House."

"And here you are. Wonderful story. We're glad to have you ... "

"Martin, sir. Martin Jermanski."

"Marty Jermanski. Phil Jermanski. Do you go by Marty?"

"Bill, sir. But, yes, Marty's fine."

"Well, Marty. What do you think of CNN?"

Martin knew the drill. He had heard enough stories from other staffers and had overheard enough senior officials to know the correct response. It amazed him that senior administration officials could act like no one was around when speaking in front of lowly staffers.

"Fake news, sir. All of it. I don't think you should even waste your time watching them."

Drumpf laughed. "Good point, Marty. I probably shouldn't. But you have to keep an eye on what they're saying. If you don't, you won't be able to call them on their lies."

The President was momentarily distracted by something on one of the televisions – Martin couldn't tell which one. He waited patiently. Eventually, Drumpf noticed that he was still standing there.

"Thanks for the new remote, Marty," he said, without pulling his eyes from the screen. "This one seems to be working just fine."

"You're welcome, sir. Goodnight."

CELL PHONES

Martin had been excited when he received his "official" White House phone. It was an iPhone 8! Up to that point, he had still been using an old iPhone 4 from several years earlier. Of course, his excitement quickly wore off when he learned that he didn't have total control of the apps that he could install on the phone. In fact, the phone wasn't actually his. It was one of a pool of phones used by all junior White House staffers. On a monthly basis, he was required to turn it in and exchange it for a "clean" one.

The White House Communications Agency scanned each phone, for malicious software, for signs of misuse, and for other "Red Flag" conditions. Martin didn't know what those were; he didn't particularly want to for that matter. He learned that the more senior staffers didn't have to turn-in their phones as often as the junior ones. He also learned that those staffers had more freedom with respect to what apps they could install. But at the same time, *everyone* was required to follow the Communications Agency's policies.

Except, it seemed, the President. The man had no patience for the policies of the Communications Agency. More than one staffer saw the irony in this. The Communications Agency was actually a military organization, manned by personnel from all of the Armed

Services. The President showered praise on the military – except when military policies got in his way.

When it came to Drumpf's phone, the junior staffers had started a pool—the number of days the President would hold out before finally turning in his phone. Martin had never won the pool and began to lobby for an Over-Under bet. He was sure that his chances would be better with the Over-Under. But there were no takers.

"Your turn!" Amanda rushed into their office and stood over Martin. He looked up to see her waving a fresh phone for the President in her hand.

"No!" he lamented, dropping his head onto the desk.

"Oh, yeah! Get on it, bitch!"

He pulled himself up and crossed his arms. "Why do you get to call me that? I've never called you 'bitch.'"

"And you never will, bitch. Now move it."

He shook his head and stood up. He knew he wasn't going to win. Besides, although he would never admit it to Amanda, he enjoyed his interactions with the President.

"Fine."

"That's what I thought! Bitch!"

'*So* annoying,' he thought. He took three steps and then spun around. "Does the Chief of Staff know I'm headed that way? I'll never get in there unless he okays it."

"It was the Chief of Staff who called for the phone!"

"Got it."

On his way, Martin was informed that the President was in the Oval Office. The schedule didn't show any meetings or guests, but he knew to ignore the schedule. It was, at best, a close approximation of the day's events.

As Martin approached the entryway, Ben was on duty; he nodded to Martin and informed him that it was okay to enter the office. Then Ben looked down and saw the phone in Martin's hand. He chuckled slightly as he knocked twice on the door. "Good luck."

As Ben pushed the door open, Martin realized that he still wasn't sure if the Agents were aware of their nicknames. They had to be, right? They were the Secret Service, after all.

The President was sitting at his desk, leaning over with an elbow resting on the vast wooden surface. He was holding his desk phone in his other hand.

The Chief of Staff was standing slightly away from the desk, thumbing through a stack of papers. He looked up when Martin entered the Oval Office, saw the phone in his hand, and smirked.

Madeleine Watterhoot was standing close to the Chief of Staff. Martin had tried to talk her up the first time he met her. She had politely but firmly shut him down. He got over it pretty quickly; he was always on the lookout for the redhead from his very first day.

Martin approached the desk, then paused about fifteen feet from it. The President looked up, saw Martin, and started to smile.

"Of course, I understand!" The President almost yelled into his phone. "It'll be fantastic. The best!" Then the President saw the phone in Martin's hand. His eyes grew wide in mock fury. "You can tell her to go fuck herself. That is, if she'd be willing to. I know I wouldn't fuck that." The President kept on with his conversation on the phone even as he looked Martin up and down. Finally, he raised his right hand, pointed at the phone in Martin's hand, and gave Martin, and the phone, the finger.

Martin just stood there, waiting. He knew he might be standing there for a while. The President seemed to alternate between fury and joviality with whoever he was speaking to on the phone. Martin stopped paying attention to the conversation after about a minute and, instead, let his eyes wander. The Oval Office. It had seemed so impressive the first time he had seen it. Now, not so much, although the carpet under his feet did still feel particularly thick.

And then the Chief of Staff was standing right next to him.

"Martin."

"Yes, sir."

"I'm not sure how long he's going to be on. He's already ignored two prompts to get off the phone. I can't wait around all day."

The Chief of Staff pulled two folders from the thick stack cradled in his arm. "Give these to him, before you try to give him that phone. Just ask him to glance through them. And make sure you get his old phone away from him."

Martin looked over at Watterhoot. "Sir, what about Maddie? If you leave, she's going to ask me what they are. She'll insist on taking them."

Kellner shook his head. "Yeah, she'll push you around, won't she? Leave that to me."

Martin took the two folders and watched the Chief of Staff walk over to Watterhoot.

Kellner said something quietly to her that Martin couldn't make out. He then walked to the door, opened it and held it for her to step through, and moved to follow her out. Just before the door shut, Kellner nodded at Martin. "Good luck."

"Who the fuck does he think he is? He can't say that about me! Fuck!" The President's bellow caused Martin to flinch. Martin turned slowly.

The President waved him closer. "Well, you tell that son of a bitch that Ronald Drumpf, the President of the United States of America, will not accept that! Got it?"

Martin stepped closer, holding the folders in front of him.

"Ah, you know I love you. Of course, I do. Get that fixed, okay? Thank you. Thank you."

The President pulled the phone from his ear and started to put it down.

The voice of whoever was on the other end was clearly audible, still speaking, as the President dropped the phone onto its cradle.

"Fucking shit. Marty, we are surrounded by a bunch of idiots. Idiots!"

"Yes, sir, Mr. President." Martin expected the President to say something else. When he didn't, Martin continued, "The Chief of Staff asked that I—"

"He wants me to read whatever shit is in those folders, doesn't he?"

"Yes, sir."

"Where's Maddie?" the President asked. "Has she seen these?"

Martin shrugged and hoped it would be enough.

"He didn't ask you here just so you could hand me these folders did he? Why is he wasting your time? He can stand and wait, can't he?"

"He's the Chief of Staff, sir." Martin handed the two folders to the President, who immediately dropped them on the desk.

"Marty. The Chief of Staff is an impressive guy; he really is. Four star Marine General. Long, distinguished career. But I don't need a Chief of Staff. He just gets in the way, clogs the flow of information around here. Sometimes I think he's more pain than he's worth."

"It's hard to find good people, sir." As soon as he said the words, Martin desperately hoped that they wouldn't get back to Kellner. The President didn't seem to notice his discomfort and only nodded absently.

"You know, Marty. There didn't always used to be a White House Chief of Staff. For many, many years the job didn't exist. It might be time for it to go. If Presidents, many of them throughout our history, if those Presidents didn't need a Chief of Staff, I probably don't either. I should just fire him."

"Mr. President, I'm not sure that's a good idea." And as soon as he said those words, Martin even more desperately hoped he hadn't said them. The President looked at him and scowled.

"Is there anything else today, Marty?"

"Well, sir, yes—"

Just then, Martin heard a door open and spun to see who was entering the Oval Office. It was the President's daughter, Ivania. She breezed into the room, wearing a blue business suit, and only briefly glanced at Martin before settling her eyes on her father. A wide smile spread across her face.

"Hi, Daddy! How is the most powerful man in the world today?"

"Sweetheart, hello! I'm doing okay. Marty here is giving me some things to think about. How are you?"

Martin noticed that she seemed not to hear anything about him. 'Bitch.'

"I'm not having a great day, today, Daddy. I'm frustrated."

Martin realized that he wasn't going to get that phone from the President anytime soon. He backed away from the desk as Ivania moved to stand next to her father. He felt very much like a servant, disappearing into the background now that an "Important Person" was in the room.

"What is it, sweetheart?"

"Well, you know those projects that I am working on? The different product lines in China?"

"Sure."

"Well, the Chinese government seems to be stalling my trademark applications. You know that I can't go wide until we have those in place. I need those to be approved."

"I understand." The President fell silent, as if in deep thought. Martin wasn't sure if the President ever had a deep thought.

Then the President did something unexpected. He spun his chair around to face Martin.

"Marty. What do you think we should do?"

Martin panicked. Do? About what? The President's daughter was having trouble with some business arrangement. It had absolutely nothing to do with the affairs of the government. He racked his brain. And then be blurted out the first thing that came to his mind. "Trade for more?"

"Trade what?" the President asked.

"Sir?" Martin asked. 'Uh-oh.' Ivania was looking at him quizzically. She really was attractive.

"Marty." The President's voice caught Martin's attention. "What did you say?"

"Trade more?"

"Did you say trade war?" Drumpf asked.

'Did the President just say trade war?' Martin wondered to himself. "Uh, yes, sir." He wasn't exactly sure what a trade war was. Wars are bad, sure, but a war with trade? Probably not so bad.

"So you're recommending a trade war with the Chinese?" Drumpf asked.

"Sir." A vaguely affirmative response.

"A trade war to get the Chinese to approve Ivania's trademarks? It's brilliant! It just might work. What do you say, Ivania?"

"Well, Daddy, I'm not sure. But I'm not an expert on those things. You have experts that work for you."

"So I do. The best experts in the world." The President paused. He picked up his phone and then stopped. He looked over his shoulder at Martin. "Who should I call?"

"Well, Mr. President. I know that we don't have a Department of Trade Wars. But we do have a Treasury. Maybe them?"

"Mmm. Maybe," Drumpf said. He pondered for a moment and then put the phone back down. "But I can figure that out later."

Martin was eyeing Ivania again. And this time, she was looking back at him. The eye contact was mesmerizing.

"Is there anything else, sweetheart?"

The President's question snapped both of them out of it. Ivania gently cleared her throat, looked down on her father, and smiled warmly.

"No, Daddy. That's it. Thank you!"

She leaned in and gave him a big kiss on the cheek. "You're the best Daddy in the whole world." Then Ivania stood up, flashed Martin a quick look with an expression he couldn't read, and turned and marched from the room.

Martin watched her go. She certainly did fill that dress well.

"I'm a lucky man, Marty," Drumpf said. "A lucky man. She's gorgeous, isn't she? I mean, she's a real knockout. Don't you think?"

The male staffers had discussed the President's comments about his daughter. The main topic of discussion was always how to react to his comments. Was it okay to agree with him? Was it disrespectful? Could agreeing with him get a staffer in trouble? There was no consensus. Martin had to tread lightly.

"You're a lucky man, sir."

"Well, sure! But what about Ivania? You'd fuck her, wouldn't you? You'd probably love to."

Martin wasn't going to touch that one with a ten foot pole. He said nothing.

"Of course, you would. Who wouldn't? Beautiful, voluptuous, smart, sexy. There isn't a man alive who wouldn't hit that." The President shook his head with a satisfied grin on his face.

"You know, sir," Martin said. "There are some guys, homosexual, who probably wouldn't … be interested … in … your daughter."

The President turned and looked up at Martin. "I don't have a problem with the gays, Marty. There's nothing wrong with them. I've known many, for years. New York City is full of them. But even them, even they would want to fuck Ivania."

Martin felt the need to change the subject. Fast. Then he remembered the phone he had slid into his pants pocket. He was torn—happy to be changing the subject away from the President's daughter, but unhappy to have to bring up the phone.

"Mr. President."

"Yeah, Marty?"

"There's one other piece of business we need to discuss."

"Sure. Go ahead."

"It's time to exchange your official phone."

"Goddamnit, Marty! You know I hate playing these phone games. Can you explain to me why I need to trade phones with you? No one on the Staff has been able to explain it to me. Not a one."

"Well, it has to do with security, sir. There're all sorts of people and organizations who'd love to listen to what you're saying, listen in on the conversations that you have. Many of those people and organizations are not friendly to the United States."

"This isn't a Russia thing, is it, Marty?"

Martin knew to stay away from that topic. Nothing infuriated the President like Russia. He thought quickly.

"No, sir. It has nothing to do with the Russians." Who then? What could he say? "It's more to do with the North Koreans. The Iranians."

"Mmm."

The President seemed skeptical—as if those countries really didn't bother him that much. Martin tried some others.

"It also has to do with the Canadians, the Germans, and the Europeans."

"Ah!" The President nodded vigorously.

Martin made a note of his reaction.

"I think you're right," Drumpf said. "Why didn't they tell me it had to do with the Europeans? And those fuckin' Canucks. Now *that* makes sense to me."

"So here's your new phone, sir." Martin stepped closer and placed the phone on the desk in front of Drumpf. "Your passcode is the same. All functionality is the same."

"Got it. Thanks, Marty."

The President shook his head and reached for the pile of folders sitting on the desk. He grimaced and then opened the top one. He read for a few seconds and then sighed, bored already.

Martin quietly cleared his throat.

The President looked up. "Still here, Marty?"

"Mr. President, I need your old phone."

"What?" Drumpf looked down at the new phone on his desk. He pursed his lips. "I have the new one. I'll turn in the old one later today."

"Please, Mr. President."

"Okay! You can have it, Marty. You're definitely a go-getter. Here." Drumpf reached into his coat pocket and reached out with the phone in his hand. "Take it."

"Thank you, Mr. President."

Except Drumpf didn't immediately let go of the phone. He tugged it, almost out of Martin's hand. But Martin had been warned of the little game and held tight to the phone. Finally, the President laughed and let go of it.

Martin walked to the exit and was about to leave the room when the President called out to him.

"Marty! If you see the Chief of Staff, please have him come see me. I need to talk to him about trade wars. Thanks."

SURPRISE PHONE CALL

Martin was sitting at his small desk. Amanda had called in sick for the day, so he was alone. There wasn't much listed on the schedule for that day, so he didn't have much to do. Lonely and bored.

And then the phone rang.

Martin reached for it but didn't pick it up immediately. Sometimes slow and bored was good. The phone rang a second time.

He picked it up. "Jermanski."

"Mr. President," said the voice on the phone. "It's Steve."

"Sorry," Martin said, not recognizing the voice. "This is Jermanski."

"I've been trying to get a hold of you— Wait. Who?"

"Martin Jermanski," Martin said.

"Son of a bitch!"

"Excuse me?"

"That fucking operator," the voice said. "She knows how to connect someone to the Oval Office. I bet she thought it'd be funny to connect me to you."

"I'm sorry, but I—"

"Who the fuck are you, anyway?" the voice asked.

"Martin Jermanski. I'm a first year Staffer." First few months actually, but Martin didn't say that. The person at the other end of the line groaned audibly upon hearing his answer.

"Well, Jermanski," the voice said. "This is Steve Banyan, and I need to speak to the President."

The tone of voice told Martin that the guy thought 'Steve Banyan' would mean something to him. It didn't.

"Well, Mr. Banyan, I'm sorry that—"

"You do know who I am, don't you?"

"Ah, no," Martin said. "Actually, I don't."

"What kind of losers are they hiring over there?" Banyan asked. "When I ran the place, I would have had a cut on your hiring. Probably wouldn't have hired you."

Martin was starting to get pissed. But, in his short time at the White House, he had dealt with more than a few people like this 'Steve Banyan.' What did this Banyan guy mean about running the place? "Mr. Banyan," he said. "I'm sorry the operator mistakenly connected you to me. I'm sure there's a good explanation."

"Well, I doubt it. Maybe The Ronald doesn't want to hear from me today. He is there, right?"

"Yes, sir," Martin said. "According to the schedule."

"According to the schedule?! What kind of Staffer are you?"

Martin just bit his tongue and waited. There was a long silence. And then muffled sounds – Banyan talking to someone else on his end. Martin rolled his mouse back and forth to wake up his computer and then googled 'Steve Banyan.' A wikipedia entry. But before he could read the first sentence, Banyan started up again.

"Jermanski, I got some time to kill. So let's chat."

"Sounds good, sir," Martin said.

"So how long have you been at the White House?"

Martin looked down at his watch. Why did people do that when asked about dates?

"Several months, sir." He exaggerated.

"Well, that might explain why you don't know me," Banyan said. "I've been gone almost eight months. How's it going these days?"

"I'm about the lowest of the low around here. Probably not the best person to ask."

"Or maybe that makes you the perfect person to ask." A pause and then, "So have you googled me yet?"

"Actually, I was just about to," Martin said.

"Don't bother. I'll cut to the chase. The Ronald hired me to run his campaign. He won because of me; I won him the race. Once in the White House, he named me his Chief Strategist, which I did for about seven months before departing."

"Why'd you leave?" Martin really wasn't that interested.

"There were some ... disagreements between me and some of his other advisors. Someone had to leave. Enough people got into the President's ear—it was decided I'd be the one to leave. Do you know that when he started running, The Ronald didn't want to win, had no desire to become President? He was just looking for the ratings boost. He was hoping to cash in on the extra fame that the Presidential run would give him."

Did this guy know what he was talking about or was he some crackpot? Martin was content to sit and listen.

"It was actually brilliant. If you dig just below the surface, Ronald Drumpf was the epitome of that disgusting new type of 'star' – someone famous only for being famous. His businesses were all in the toilet, all of them. The Apprentice had been losing steam for years. The only thing left to do, for someone like Drumpf, with no real business sense but huge name recognition, was to run for President. From his perspective, there was no way to lose. Actually, there was one way for him to lose, and I'll get to that in a second."

Martin tried to scan the Wikipedia article about Banyan while he was talking but couldn't. The voice on the phone did not match the picture on Wikipedia, or any of the pictures that came up when he did a google image search.

"Look at it from his perspective," Banyan continued. "No matter how the campaign might go, the Drumpf name gets bigger and bigger. And he wouldn't have cared if it was negative publicity, because press is press. But then the craziest shit happened. He started beating those other assholes in poll after poll. He actually became the front-runner. Amazing."

Martin had never been interested in politics, but this story *was* interesting. How true was it?

"Sometime before he really started to take off, I realized that the son of a bitch just might pull it off. And I also realized that he didn't know a thing about politics, foreign policy, or the real problems that plague our country. I knew that he needed someone who understood all of those things and more. But not only did he not understand those things, he could seriously damage the country by winning and not having someone close to him. He needed a close aide to guide him, someone to teach him, someone to channel his impulsive, bizarre-o, narcissistic personality."

'Let me guess,' Martin thought. He knew where this story was heading.

"I looked around, and I didn't see anyone near The Ronald capable of being that person. *Certainly* not Lewandowski. No one. So I reached out to the campaign and offered my services. Drumpf was initially wary, but I was able to win him over fairly quickly. I think he looked at me and realized, this is someone who knows his shit, who can work with me in a positive way, and who can take this campaign across the finish line. And that is exactly what I did. We won. And we proved all of those fucking libtards wrong! It was a great day."

"That's pretty great, Mr. Banyan." Martin didn't know how else to respond.

"You bet it is! Pretty fucking great! But what's your story, Jermanski? What're you doing in the White House?"

Martin was not keen on answering the question. Especially since he really wasn't sure of the answer. He didn't think this guy would be impressed with 'I didn't have anything else going on, so my dad pulled some strings for me.'

"Well?" Banyan seemed to get impatient pretty quickly.

"Honestly, Mr. Banyan, I didn't have anything else going on, so my dad pulled some strings for me."

"No shit? Well, good for you! Who's your dad?"

"No one, really. Middle management at Mer-a-Lago. But he's known Mr. Drumpf for a long time."

"Well. Here's the fact, and it's true. Sad, but true. In this world, for good or bad, it's often who you know more than what you know. You can take it to the bank."

Banyan coughed. He didn't sound healthy to Martin.

"But back to what I was saying earlier," Banyan continued. "Remember how I said there was one way that Drumpf could lose? The one way he could lose was by winning!"

"Huh?" Martin didn't get it.

"Think about it. The best case for Drumpf would've been to take Hillary to the limit and then lose by a handful of electoral votes. He gets to say that he almost became the President of the U.S. of A. but doesn't actually have to deal with the drudgery and severe unpleasantness of the job. He's officially and forever off the hook. Can do what he does best, which is spin that loss into a bigger name for himself, a bigger Drumpf brand, and a whole lot more money coming into his company, his companies. And he can run his companies saying that he was this close, THIS close to winning."

Banyan was talking faster now. Martin had to ask himself again, 'Could it be true?' Banyan obviously believed it.

"Instead, what happened? He won and, by doing so, lost! Because now he has to be President. Has to figure this shit out. He needs to learn how our government actually works—which is a lot harder than just throwing huge stones at it and saying that none of it works—and then work it." Banyan paused momentarily. "Melanya was bawling, bawling! Even worse, he has to spend time actually being President when he would really, really prefer to continue his 'Ronald Drumpf, Mogul' act, which includes golfing, fucking prostitutes or porn stars whenever he wants, and ignoring his wife and youngest son. Don't get me started on 'Ronald Drumpf, Family Man.' Don't get me started."

"But I don't get it," Martin said.

"What don't you get, Jermanski?"

"Why work for him then? Why work his campaign or become his, his Chief Strategist?"

"They really are hiring idiots these days, aren't they?" Banyan muttered under his breath, although easily loud enough for Martin to hear. "Why? Seriously? Because you don't have to be the most powerful man in the room to get your way, to push your agenda, you only have to be the smartest. Because if you can outsmart the most powerful man in the room, you become the most powerful man in the room. And if the most powerful man in the room is the most powerful man in the world, you then become the most powerful man in the world."

"Got it," Martin responded. *That* made sense.

"You're damned right! But, listen. I've enjoyed our little chat today, but I have to run. Lots to do. Good luck, Jermanski."

"Thanks, sir. Take care."

As Martin dropped the phone in its cradle, he couldn't believe the conversation he just had. Sometimes lonely and bored weren't so bad after all.

Martin spent the next few hours reading up on Banyan, reading the wikipedia article, articles that it referenced, and then still other articles as he continued to Google. The guy's story seemed to check out, in general terms. And his personality on the phone seemed to match what he read about him.

Shortly before lunch, he received the phone call he was dreading. It was the summons to assist with document reconstruction. Even when no longer a part of the DRT, they still drag him back. It was the essence of his life as a staffer: scotch tape and the willingness to work until your eyes hurt and your fingers cramped.

As Martin hung up the phone and stood to join the other slave laborers, Banyan popped back into his head. Why had he bothered to talk to Martin at all? If he was so important, surely talking to a lowly staffer was a complete and total waste of his time.

INSIDE BASEBALL

It was the kind of morning on which Martin should not have to go to work: bright, sunny, vaguely-warm, and a Sunday. At least, it had been that when his alarm first woke him up. The clouds had come and gone and come since, as if they couldn't make up their mind. Cloudy or sunny? But he was at work regardless.

He was chosen to work the Annual Easter Egg Roll. Which really meant that, despite having worked at the White House for over two months, Martin was still a low-level staffer. Oh well, at least he wasn't taping together Drumpf's shredded documents anymore. As Martin stood with the others waiting to be told what exactly they would be doing, he realized that the South Lawn on an almost-sunny day wasn't the worst place to have to spend a couple of hours.

As expected, Martin and most of the others were runners, there to do the bidding of the event organizers. At that moment, he was merely standing and listening to the President remark on the day. He looked at the assembled children and wondered who gets invitations to bring their children to the White House for an Easter Egg Roll? What even is an Easter Egg Roll?

"…and all of the people that work so hard with Melanya, with everybody, to keep this incredible house or building, or whatever you want to call it—because there really is no name for it; it is special—and we keep it in tip-top shape," Drumpf said. "We call it sometimes tippy-top shape. And it's a great, great place."

Martin knew for a fact that the President wasn't a fan of the White House. Why didn't Drumpf say *that* in one of his speeches? He said all sorts of other crazy shit; why not say something honest about the White House? And everyone knew that Melanya Drumpf absolutely detested the place. Standing up on the balcony next to the President, Melanya didn't look too miserable that morning. 'That's good,' Martin thought.

"So I want to thank you all for being here," Drumpf said, approaching the end of his remarks. "The band, unbelievable. I love you people. I hear them a lot. They're as talented as anybody and any players anywhere. So thank you very much."

The band. Martin had to admit that being here on a Sunday morning wasn't great, but it was way better than being here, dressed in a military uniform, playing an instrument. Poor soldiers, or Marines, or whatever they were.

The President finished speaking, said a quick word to the Easter Bunny who was standing on the balcony with him, and then moved to exit. Melanya gently tapped the Easter Bunny as she passed. Martin wondered which staffer was given that duty. He was glad it wasn't him.

As the President and First Lady walked down to the lawn, the band played for them. Drumpf stopped to observe the band for a moment and then continued down to where the egg roll would occur.

Martin stifled a yawn. The egg roll was about to start, which meant that his time at work was past the halfway point.

The event was really more of an egg toss than egg roll. Some of the kids chucked their eggs almost the entire length of the track.

"You ready kids?" The President's role was to wait until each of the kids was ready and then start the roll by blowing his whistle. "Okay. You ready? Set."

Except not all of the kids were ready. Martin saw at least two who didn't have a spoon in their hand or an egg in front of them. That didn't stop Drumpf. He blew the whistle anyway. And it happened several times. Martin was sure that a few of the kids were ready to cry.

"What're you doing this afternoon?" It was Scott Bokor, who had slid up to Martin unnoticed. Martin had no plans.

"No plans."

"A group of us are getting together. D'you want to join us?"

Martin was suspicious. Over two months on the job, and he hadn't yet been invited to any social gatherings other than his one outing with Luke. It *was* April Fool's Day, after all.

"Sure."

After several rolls, the First Family moved over to white picnic tables where children were sitting coloring Easter-themed pictures.

"We're meeting at the south corner of the Eisenhower on 17th in about forty minutes. Haven't decided where we're headed yet."

"Got it. I'll be there." Martin still wasn't sure: Would they?

.   .   .

They actually were. Martin walked up to a group of ten or eleven. He knew most of their names but was certain that they didn't all know his.

"Who brought the newbie?"

Maybe the joke was on him after all. Best to stand silently and wait for an opportunity to say something.

"Been over two months," Scott said. "He's made it."

"If it isn't my bitch." It was Amanda. Of course, she would be there.

"Where to?"

"Somewhere where I can get a Twinpanzee."

"Seriously?" Scott asked. "You are such a beer fag!"

"What? I like my local brews."

"That's so poor."

'Holy shit! It's the redhead from my first day!' Martin hadn't seen her since that day. Why couldn't he remember her name?!

Martin wasn't a beer connoisseur; he was just going to let this conversation go by. And it was only just past noon—who starts drinking this early without a football game to watch?

"So whaddya think?" The question was directed at Martin.

"What do you mean?"

"You lasted longer than anyone expected you to," Adam's Apple said.

"Certainly longer than *I* expected you to." The redhead was talking to him! "I gave you a week, tops."

"Nice," Martin responded. "And yet here I am."

"So what do you think?" The redhead again, still talking to him.

Martin didn't know all of their names; he still couldn't remember hers. "You are?" With a slight smart-ass tone in his voice.

"Brianne. But you can call me ma'am."

"Oh really? Well, *ma'am*, I still don't get your question."

"Bitch!" Amanda now interjecting. "What don't you get? Why are you working at the White House? What do you think of it? What do you think of Drumpf?"

They were still standing at the intersection of 17th and New York, right outside of the Eisenhower. Martin was surprised to hear Amanda call him Drumpf in a loud, obnoxious voice in public. "Don't you think you should be a little quieter?"

"I'll be as loud as I want!"

"Someone shut her up." It was Martin's sentiment exactly.

The group started moving slowly. Martin found himself walking between Amanda and Brianne.

"So why are you here?" Brianne asked this time.

"I graduated college last year. The parents haven't been pleased with my career choices since. My dad works at Mer-a-Lago and spoke to Mr. Drumpf. The Ronald said that I should come and work for him. The rest is history."

"No shit!" Amanda again.

"Is your dad high in the organization?" Brianne asked.

Martin laughed. "No. Strictly middle management, and probably won't go further. He's happy. Still can't believe that I'm working here."

"What do you think of him?" Brianne asked.

"Mr. Drumpf?"

"Yes, Mr. Drumpf." Brianne feigned annoyance at having to answer the obvious.

"I don't know much about politics, or government. He seems to be similar to how my dad described him at Mer-a-Lago. He is who he is. What about you?"

"Brianne is a hard-charging, ambitious, powerful woman!" Rick, the staffer who was walking directly in front of Martin, turned around to interject.

Martin didn't know Rick well, but Rick certainly seemed to know Brianne. He decided that the guy was a prick.

"But if you ask her about her politics," Rick continued, "she can be a little cagey."

"That's the truth," said Jason, the staffer to Rick's right. "Cagey!"

"You're as much a bitch as Martin is, Jason!" Amanda said. "If Rick says it, you're going to repeat it."

'How old are these people? Perhaps I'm better off not socializing with them.'

"I'm not cagey," protested Brianne. "I just have a nuanced opinion of the President."

"What is that opinion?" Martin really didn't want to hear from anyone else; he just wanted to talk to Brianne.

"I think he was elected based upon a wide range of grievances that a large segment of the American population has had with the current state of the country."

"What does that mean exactly?" Martin asked.

"America elected him because they were pissed off with everyone else," answered Rick.

"But that doesn't tell me anything about what *you* think," Martin said to Brianne.

"He's doing what he thinks is necessary for the country," she said.

"I told you she was cagey." Jason had now turned around and was walking backwards in front of them.

"So what do *you* think?" Martin asked Jason.

"I have no opinion. I'm here to get the resume item," Jason said. "I'm gonna work hard for 18 months, maybe two years. Then I'm gonna get out."

"If you make it that long," Rick said.

"But why?" Martin asked, still talking to Jason.

"My parents are big Republicans, very active when they were younger," Jason said. "Wanted me to enter government. I'm here. Then I'll be gone."

Martin nodded at Rick. "Rick?"

"Drumpf is a fucking idiot," he said.

"I wouldn't say that too loudly," said Amanda, in perhaps the most normal tone of voice Martin had ever heard her use.

"It's true," Rick continued. "He talks a big game, about being the smartest in the room. But he can't read. He refuses to listen to briefings. He makes shit up."

"I'd lower your voice," Amanda again, actually seeming to be worried about the direction of the conversation. "You don't want that getting back to the wrong people."

Jason leaned a little closer to Rick. "Some of the wrong people might be in this group."

"Shit," responded Rick. "Nothing is going to happen. I've been here since the inauguration. I'm safe."

Amanda shook her head. "Say what you will about the President, but he has the right policies. You might not like his style, but he's fixing shit."

"How much shit is he going to destroy on the way to fixing other shit?" Rick asked.

Martin noticed that the rest of the group had fallen silent; all seemed to be listening to this conversation. He also found it strange that Amanda seemed on edge—something he had never seen in her before. And Brianne hadn't said a word since Jason said she was cagey; it seemed that he was right.

"So are there any other kinds of people here?" Martin asked.

"What do you mean?" Brianne asked.

"Well," Martin said. "It seems like there are three types of people." He raised one finger. "The ones working here for the job, to pad their resume, to please their parents." He raised a second finger. "Others apparently don't care for the President; I'm not sure why they're working here." He raised a third finger. "And others overlook Drumpf's issues, because they like what he's doing. Does that cover it?"

"There's one other group," Amanda said.

"Who?" asked Martin.

"The true believers," Amanda said, quietly and with a warning in her voice.

Martin didn't get whatever was going on with Amanda. He had never seen her so … careful. But he wasn't going to dwell on it. He was interested in continuing his conversation with Brianne.

"So which are you?" Martin asked Brianne.

"None of the above?" Brianne shrugged with a sly smile.

"Cagey," Jason said. "Just like I told you."

"There's actually one other group," Brianne said. "But they fit into all of the others."

"Oh yeah?" Martin asked. "Who're they?"

"They're the worst," Brianne said.

"Who?!" Martin asked.

"The backstabbers," Brianne said forcefully. "It doesn't matter which group they belong to, they're going to do the same to you every time."

Martin was surprised. Up until that point in the conversation, Brianne seemed chill. She didn't anymore. He wasn't sure where to go from there.

"Where're we going, anyway?" It was one of the staffers at the head of their small mob.

"What d'you mean? You were leading this little shindig." Another from the head of the pack.

Martin had lost interest in the little staffer crowd, except for Brianne. Perhaps he could interest her in slipping away?

"Backstabbers?" Rick asked, loudly. "Nothing to worry about. As long as you are in with one of the principals, you're covered."

"What happens when your principal is back-stabbed by another?" Jason asked.

"All I know is I'm safe," Rick answered. "I don't have a care in the world."

"What're you doing later?" Martin asked Brianne.

"We're all going to grab a bite," she said.

"No," Martin said. "I mean after."

"After lunch? You'll just have to find out."

Martin didn't. The staffer crowd stopped at a restaurant serving an Easter Brunch. The place was packed, and their group was split into three tables. Before he finished eating, Martin realized that Brianne had left. She didn't say goodbye.

ACE IN THE HOLE

The next Wednesday morning, Martin was running a little late. He had gotten in the habit of trying to beat Amanda in—it was easier to hold on to the computer than to try to pry it from Amanda's jealous grasp. But that day, he realized he was out of luck. He slid into the office and sat down across from her as she typed away on their lone computer.

She didn't look at him. Didn't greet him with the normal "Hey, bitch!" And she wasn't surfing porn. She was actually doing what appeared to be real White House business, which was unlike her for first thing in the morning.

"What's up?" he asked.

"Mmm," she responded, barely looking up.

"What's wrong with you?"

"Huh? Oh. You didn't hear."

"Hear what?" he asked.

"You know Rick, right?"

"Rick? You mean from Sunday afternoon? The prick?"

"Yeah, that Rick," she said glumly. "He was fired yesterday afternoon."

It wasn't that out of the ordinary. People came and went all the time in this White House. "So?" he asked.

She pulled her hands from the keyboard and sat up straight. "He was fired, because someone heard that he called Drumpf an idiot."

"Someone?" Martin asked. "Everyone in the group heard him call the President an idiot. And anyone who was on the street anywhere near us heard it, too."

"But Rick was one of the safe ones!"

"He thought he was," Martin responded.

"Rick worked closely with Steven Mills."

Martin shrugged. Yes, Mills was a very close advisor to the President, but that didn't necessarily mean that he would protect Rick.

"You're a bitch, you know that?" The normal Amanda was coming back. She stared at Martin for a second, put out by his nonchalance to the situation, and then went back to her work on the computer.

Martin couldn't get worked up about one staffer being fired, but apparently Amanda was shaken up by it.

"So what else is going on?" he asked.

"Oh," Amanda replied. "You got a phone call this morning. The phone had been ringing when I got in. Anyway, some guy named Steve asked to talk to you. Seemed full of himself."

"Did he give his last name?" Martin asked.

"No. I got the impression that he thinks you'll know who it was."

'Could it have been Banyan?' Martin wondered. He also found it strange that Amanda didn't recognize him. She had been in the White House during his tenure. But it must have been him; Martin didn't know any other Steves—none that would call him here.

The phone rang. Martin grabbed it before Amanda could react. Typically, her hand was much faster than his; she was able to get the phone every time. That morning, however, it wasn't.

Amanda looked up at him and then back at the computer. "Bitch," she muttered.

Martin was actually annoyed. That was the only reaction from her? Oh well. He held the phone to his ear. "Jermanski."

"Martin?"

"Yes."

"Steve Banyan."

"Good morning, sir."

"You're still there, I take it."

'I answered the phone,' Martin thought. 'Obviously.'

"How is life in the trenches?"

"For those deep in the trenches, it's about taping ripped-up documents together. For those of us who escaped that hell, it's more normal staffer stuff."

"Christ. That man's an idiot. It explains why all his businesses failed. You know, he would have never lasted at Goldman, or any other real business. It's easy when your name is on the marquee."

Martin just waited. No sense in commenting now.

"So listen, Martin. I have a proposition for you."

'Proposition?' Martin thought. How should he respond to that?

"Martin, you there?"

"Yes, sir, I'm here."

"Did you hear me?"

"Yes," Martin said. "I just don't know what to think."

"Of course, you don't. I haven't told you anything yet. But are you interested?"

"I guess it depends," Martin said.

"Who're you talking to?" It was Amanda, mouthing the words in as close to a whisper as she seemed able.

"Steve Banyan," Martin mouthed back, much quieter.

"Who?" She really wasn't very quiet.

Martin repeated himself a little louder.

"What does it depend on?" Banyan asked.

"You're full of shit," Amanda said.

"Uh, sir, several things," Martin said.

"You are so full of shit," Amanda said.

"Such as?" Banyan was losing his patience.

Martin couldn't think clearly enough, with Amanda across the desk, to consider the ramifications of any possible offer. He stood up and stepped away from the desk to put some distance between himself and her. In the process, the long phone cord knocked over her cup of coffee and almost pulled the phone from his grasp.

'Shit! Who uses corded phones anymore?!'

"Shit, bitch!" she shouted. "Watch the fucking cord!"

"Listen, Martin, maybe you're not the right guy," Banyan said.

"Well, sir," Martin said, shrugging a weak apology at Amanda. "I guess it depends on what exactly you want me to do, and what I'll get out of it."

"What you'll get out of it?" Banyan asked.

"You ain't gonna get shit, bitch!" Amanda, a little louder still.

"You're not alone, are you?" Banyan asked.

"No, sir," Martin said. "My office mate is sitting right across the desk from me."

"The one who answered the phone this morning?"

"Yes, sir."

"Is she hot?" Banyan asked. "She sounded hot. Are you hitting that?"

"You are so fucking annoying," Amanda said.

"No. I'm not," Martin said.

"Maybe you should be," Banyan said. "Does she know who you're talking to?"

"No," Martin said. "She doesn't."

"Doesn't what?!" Amanda asked, getting red in the face.

"Okay. Let's keep it that way," Banyan said. "Can you excuse yourself or go somewhere private?"

"Not on this phone," Martin answered.

"What on this phone?" Amanda asked.

"Ha! That's right," chuckled Banyan. "Terrible White House phones. Well, listen then. I'll talk, you listen. Don't say another word until I'm done."

'Sure,' Martin thought. 'I've been trying to talk as little as possible since picking up the phone.'

"I need an ear on the inside," Banyan said. "Someone to keep me in the loop. I still talk to the President, you know. We talk pretty regularly. But to be able to serve the President best, I need to know what the President doesn't. Who's supporting this policy or that policy. Who's arguing against a given policy. What their arguments are."

"Okay," Martin said.

"Are you going to tell me who you're *really* talking to?" Amanda was no longer even trying to be quiet.

"Only by understanding the various arguments, and who is making them, can I provide my best advice to the President," Banyan said. "Of course, I can't talk to most of the principals. In some cases, there's bad blood. In other cases, they'd think there's bad blood, even when there isn't. Anyway, I can help the President best if I understand the situation in the Oval Office." Banyan paused.

Martin wasn't sure if he should speak up, so he held his tongue.

"Bitch! Who the fuck are you talking to?" Amanda, now standing and raising her voice.

Martin had had enough. "Steve fucking Banyan!"

"Bullshit!" Amanda thundered back.

"Why'd you tell her that?" Banyan asked.

"There's no fucking way!" Amanda said, staring at Martin with wide, angry eyes.

"Didn't I tell you not to say a word?" Banyan was now sounding pissed. "That it would be better if she didn't know?"

"Fuck you!" Amanda was annoyed that Martin seemed to be ignoring her. She sat down hard, pulled her chair in loudly, and went back to work on the computer.

"She doesn't believe it, anyway," Martin shot back at Banyan. "It doesn't fucking matter!"

"Whoa!" Banyan. "Watch your mouth, kid!"

Martin spoke more harshly than he intended. "Sorry, sir."

"She must be a real piece of work," Banyan said.

"Sir?" asked Martin.

"Your office mate," Banyan replied. "Sounds like a real ball-buster."

Martin laughed. "Actually, she can be."

Amanda scowled at him over the computer.

"So what do you say?" Banyan asked.

"Uh. Sure, sir. Count me in." Martin still wasn't sure what he was agreeing to. He figured he could always back out later. And maybe he could use it to his advantage somehow.

"That's good, Martin. That's good. You're my ace in the hole." Banyan paused.

Again, Martin wasn't sure if he should speak up or not.

"Well," said Banyan. "I have to let you go. Keep your ear to the ground. Pay attention. I'll call you in a few days."

"Understood, sir. Thanks."

Banyan hung up without another word.

Martin did the same, and then sat pondering what had just happened. It was then that he realized he never learned what he was going to get out of the deal. 'Shit.'

"Are you going to tell me who that was?" Amanda asked.

"No."

"Fuck you, bitch."

The phone rang again. This time, Amanda's hand was quicker.

"Chung. Mm mmm. Yes. Okay." She hung up the phone. "Oval Office. Document detail. Go."

"Seriously!" Then Martin remembered his deal with Banyan. Perhaps a trip to the Oval Office to retrieve hand-shredded documents wouldn't be so bad. "Okay."

"Okay?" Amanda asked, incredulously.

Martin didn't even answer. He was already on his way.

·   ·   ·

Martin approached the entrance to the Oval Office.

"Packed house in there this morning," the Chin said.

"Thanks," Martin responded.

The Chin knocked twice on the door and then opened it for Martin.

The Oval certainly was packed. Martin stepped into the room to find almost two dozen people. Kelly Conville was sitting on the sofa, staring at a cell phone. Steve Mills, surrounded by several other staffers, was standing before the President's desk, talking to him. The Chief of Staff stood beyond the President; he alone seemed to notice Martin enter the room.

"Mr. President," Mills was saying, "I think this policy is going to ratchet up the discussion. It's going to force Congress to solve the issue once and for all."

"I like it, Steve. I think you're right. It's a crime what's been happening on the border, but I don't have to tell you that. How soon can we make it happen?"

"Well, Mr. President. Ultimately, it will be for the Attorney General to make official. It falls under his purview. If you give me the go ahead, I'll contact him. It'll probably take a few weeks for Justice to fully research and then prep for implementation. Maybe a little longer."

"I'm sick and tired of these things taking so long. Why does everything take so long? I've decided! It's done. Just ... Just make it happen!"

"Yes, sir. Mr. President. But—"

"I don't want 'buts.' I want you to get the policy implemented."

"Yes, sir."

"I know you're working hard, Steve. I really do. It's just that everything takes so long."

"We'll get it turned on as quickly as possible."

"I know you will. Thanks, Steve. Thank you very much."

Martin had no clue what policy they were talking about. He assumed that he'd be told if necessary. He waited by the entrance. People started to clear out of the room.

As the last ones filed past him, Martin approached the President's desk. The only other person in the room was the Chief of Staff who, at that moment, was standing near the President, reaching for some papers on the desk.

The President put his hand on the stack of papers and pulled them in front of him. "What do we have here?"

"Briefing notes regarding Mr. Mills' policy proposal, sir," the Chief of Staff answered. "I'll take care of those."

"That's okay, John. I got it." The President picked up the papers, gave them a brief glance, and then tore the entire stack in half.

"You don't need to waste your time," the Chief of Staff said, reaching to take the papers from the President's hands.

The President tore the sheets in half again and again and turned away from the Chief of Staff to put distance between him and the papers. He then dropped one of the two resulting stacks of Oval Office confetti onto the desk, far beyond the reach of the Chief of Staff, and tore the other pile of papers in half yet again.

"Mr. President, surely I can—"

"You know it helps to calm me, John. Thanks for your help."

Martin stopped only a few paces from the desk. The President looked up at him. "Marty! Good morning! What are you here for today?"

"He's here to pick up your papers, Mr. President," the Chief of Staff answered through gritted teeth.

"Fantastic! I'm almost done with them." He tore some more pieces of paper into even smaller pieces. He then stopped, picked up a few stacks of paper, held them several inches above the desk, and then dropped them. The neat stacks of paper scattered into a little mountain of torn paper. The President smiled and then pushed the little mountain toward Martin.

"Thank you, sir." Martin bent down and gathered the mountain into his hand, pulled it to the edge of the desk, and then dropped the paper into the garbage can. He watched the small pieces of paper fall and scatter further into a huge mess at the bottom of the can.

"We've made some important decisions this morning," the President said to Martin. "Some very important decisions."

"Yes, sir."

"Marty," the President said. "What do you think about immigration?"

Uh-oh. Martin stood up to find the Chief of Staff looking him straight in the eye. He felt that he was in a very unsafe place. "It's a complicated issue, Mr. President."

"It is complicated, Marty. Well, it's complicated for many people. But it's actually very simple. I've thought about it a lot. I have the solution. There are actually a few different things that we can do to solve the immigration issue. Most have to be done by Congress, but there are some levers I can pull."

Martin nodded. Sometimes the silent nod was the safest thing to do—especially with the Chief of Staff staring directly at him.

"It's an issue that we have to fix," the President continued. "I've been saying it for years; I campaigned about it, you know. But did you know that I can't solve the issue alone? The President, by himself, by myself, can't solve the issue. It actually requires Congress. Can you believe that?"

"I understand, sir," Martin said. "I'm sure that it's frustrating."

"Marty. You're a smart guy, you know that? Smart, smart guy. How long have you been with us?"

"Only a few months, sir. Not many at all."

"That's what I thought," the President said. "You know that doesn't matter, though."

"Sir?"

"Marty. I have several things going for me. You have to remember this. I'm extremely smart. One of the smartest men I know. I'm obviously a brilliant real-estate businessman. Both of those are important, but do you know what really makes me as successful as I am? It's my ability to read people. I can look at someone and size them up in an instant. And I knew, from the first day I met you, that you're one of the good ones."

"Thank you, sir."

"Not everyone that I have working for me is a 'good one' though. We had to let someone go yesterday. Did you hear about it?"

"No, sir." A blatant lie. Martin couldn't understand why he had just lied to the President.

"It was unfortunate. We had to let a junior staffer go. You probably knew him. His name was Rick. Rick something ... John?" The President didn't wait for the Chief of Staff to answer. "I think the stress of the job got to him. He said some very rude things."

"I'm sorry to hear that, Mr. President," Martin said.

Drumpf looked at him, seemingly not satisfied with the comment.

'Is the President upset with me?' Martin wondered.

"I mean, it's unfortunate that someone would behave ... would act in a way that required ... that forced you to have to fire him."

Drumpf looked at him a moment longer and then his face changed. Apparently, Martin's awkward comment was okay.

"Some people forget their place, Marty. I think this ... Rick, I think he forgot his place."

Martin only nodded, standing next to the President's desk, holding the President's garbage can in front of him.

Then the President abruptly turned to face the Chief of Staff, who was still standing at the far end of the desk. "John, I've made a decision."

"Yes, Mr. President?" It appeared that the Chief of Staff didn't like the sound of the pronouncement.

"Marty is one of the good ones."

"Yes, sir." Kellner's eyes were firmly fixed on Martin as he answered the President.

The President turned back to face Martin.

Martin could sense the President looking up at him, but he was having trouble breaking eye contact with the Chief of Staff.

"Marty?"

The sound of the President's voice broke through, and Martin tore his eyes from Kellner to look down at the Commander in Chief.

"I'm smart enough to realize that Rick probably wasn't the only person on staff who has secret opinions of me. There are probably people who far outrank you who dislike me and what I am trying to do for our great country. I'm also smart enough to understand that most people don't pay any attention to the junior staffers. I mean, let's face it, I have what, several dozen staffers that work for me? I don't know most of their names, maybe only a handful. You junior staffers just don't matter. Most of you do good work, I guess, but you're not really important. But because no one pays attention to you, you're invisible. You watch and listen, and you know things." Drumpf paused, still looking up at Martin. "You know things, don't you, Marty?"

'What kind of things?' was the first thought that Martin had. "Uh, yes, sir. Absolutely."

"I need someone like you, Marty. Someone I can trust. Someone who can keep me in the loop with what's going on around the White House, around the staff. What do you say?"

Martin didn't know what to say. Since he didn't know what to say, he said the one thing that seemed to work every time. "Yes, sir!"

"That's fantastic, Marty. Great! Really, really great. You're my ace in the hole."

OVAL OFFICE MEETING

Martin was waiting as the tall, black man strode into the small crook in the passageway that served as one waiting area to enter the Oval Office.

Martin smiled nervously and approached him. "Good morning, Mr. Roddmann. My name is Martin. There are a few things I need to tell you before you enter the Oval Office."

Roddmann nodded, already bored with the young staffer. He got the drill. After all, he'd visited Kim Jong Un, *in North Korea!* There was no protocol issue in the White House that could compare to the crazy that he endured meeting Kim Jong Un in Pyeongyang. The security and precautions taken by the North Koreans were top-notch.

"Please address Mr. Drumpf as 'Mr. President'—"

"Wait," Roddmann interrupted, "Seriously? I've known Ron for years. Before the Apprentice. Shit. Hell, we used to 'grab 'em by the pussy' together! We used to grab them together, but, hey, Marty, that's between you and me, you know?"

Martin felt the color drain from his face; he also felt smaller somehow.

"Whoa! It's okay, Marty! Just bustin' your balls, man. 'Mr. President.' Got it. What else?"

Martin continued his discussion of Oval Office etiquette but felt that Roddmann stopped listening almost immediately. As Martin talked, Roddmann peered about. He could only imagine what Roddmann might be thinking: The stories were true. The White House, or at least the little room where he was waiting to meet the President, was dingy. The walls weren't as white as they should be, and scuffed. The Ronald certainly didn't spend much time in *this* little room – he'd hate it.

"Hey," Roddmann interrupted. "Who's this guy? Secret Service, right?"

"That's right, Mr. Roddmann," Squint said. "I'm the Agent on duty right now."

Roddmann reached out to shake Squint's hand.

Squint looked at Roddmann for a moment and then shook his hand.

Roddmann shook enthusiastically and pointed at Squint with his free hand. "You shoulda seen the guards that Kim Jong Un has working for him. Those boys are some vicious-looking motherfuckers. They're ready to tear some shit up."

"I'm sure they are," said Squint. "But I think Mr. Jermanski has some more things he needs to tell you."

"Oh, shit! Martin," Roddmann spun and looked down on him. "Marty? I forgot you were there. What else you got for me?"

Martin hated speaking to someone who he knew wasn't listening to him. But he had to get through his spiel. "Well, one final comment about shaking his hand."

The word 'final' seemed to really catch Roddmann's attention.

Martin gulped to himself. "Don't reach out to shake his hand until he reaches out to shake yours."

Roddmann nodded.

"And try not to …" Marty paused. "Don't—" He let out a short breath. "Ah—"

"What?" Roddmann asked. "Don't what?"

"Shake his hand for too long. Or make a point of noticing that your hands are a lot bigger …"

"Wait," Roddmann said. "His hands?" Roddmann laughed.

Martin felt himself sweating.

"You mean he really is concerned with the size of his hands?"

"Well, no," Martin said. "It's just that—"

"No shit! I thought that was just some crazy, liberal-media bullshit. Okay." Roddmann made a point of lifting both hands, spreading his fingers wide, and then balling them into fists before dropping them back to his sides.

Martin couldn't take his eyes off of them. Roddmann's hands were *huge*. If it were possible, he felt more color drain from his already pasty face. He cleared his throat. "There will be a few other people in the meeting today."

That caught Roddmann's attention.

"Other people?" Roddmann asked. "I thought that I'd get to sit down with the President alone. Like the old days, with the strippers, the porn stars, the prostitutes." Roddmann laughed. "Shit, kid, sorry. You didn't hear that from me."

Martin waited for a moment. He tried to gather himself. "Also in the meeting will be U.S.F.K., a Four Star general."

"Wait," Roddmann said. "Who?"

"U.S.F.K. Oh, I'm sorry. United States Forces Korea. He is the General that commands all US military forces in South Korea."

"Four stars?"

"Yes, he is an Army General. And he might have one or two other officers with him. And the Secretary of State will also be present." Martin noticed that Roddmann was less than pleased with the latest information.

"Mr. Roddmann, is something wrong?"

"No, man. Nothing," Roddmann said. "I was hoping to shoot the shit with my boy, Ronald, you know? I wanted to tell him about my time with Kim Jong Un, maybe smoke a joint or two. Relax. But this doesn't sound like that."

"I'm afraid not today," Martin said. Squint was smiling behind Roddmann's back. "And there might be some others present as well. The President's National Security Advisor is in today."

"You mean the guy with the—" Roddmann stroked his upper lip.

"Moustache? John Belten, yes, sir."

"The Stache!" exclaimed Roddmann. "That's right. But the Prez needs some black guys in the White House. Where're all the brothers?"

Martin wasn't sure if he was being serious or not. He didn't know how to answer the question.

"Hey," Roddmann said. "Do you think I could get a permanent position here? The Prez and I get along really well."

Again, Martin didn't know how to respond. While he was trying to think of an answer, Roddmann shook his head.

"Naw, man," Roddmann said. "Look around at this place. Kinda dingy. Not worth it."

"You should see my office," Martin said.

Roddmann didn't seem to hear him. "Hey, Marty. It's Marty, right? What about Ivania? Where is her office? I heard she had an office here in the White House."

Martin knew well enough not to answer that question. It would be easy to tell Roddmann that the First Daughter's office was actually really close by.

"It's gotta be close by, right?" Roddmann asked. "I mean, The Ronald trusts her and her husband more than anyone else in the building, right?"

"Well, yes, sir. Ms. Drumpf's office is located—"

"Mr. Roddmann," a voice behind the NBA star caused him to turn. The Chief of Staff approached the basketball player and stuck out his hand. "The President is almost ready to see you." Kellner shot a glance at Martin. "I know that you've previously met Ms. Drumpf. Perhaps you'll have the opportunity again, but she's not available today."

Just then, Squint opened the door to reveal the Oval Office and The Ronald talking to a group of men. Another staffer made eye contact with the former basketball player and motioned for him to enter the room.

"Jermanski," the Chief of Staff called. "Why don't you join us, in case Mr. Roddmann needs anything."

Martin was surprised but didn't turn down the invitation. He followed the Chief of Staff into the Oval Office and closed the door behind him. He knew to stop just inside the room, against the wall and beside the door.

"Ronald!" Dennis Roddmann strode into the Oval Office like he owned it and spread his arms wide. Several people spun to see who broke White House protocol with his first spoken word. Most of those people made it clear merely by their body language that they felt he had crossed a line.

Martin didn't think Roddmann would get the hint. Or care, even if he did. He didn't seem the sort to concern himself with crossing lines.

"Dennis! It's fantastic to see you," Drumpf said. "I'm so glad you could make it."

"It's hard to turn down an invitation from *the most powerful man in the world*." Roddmann purposefully emphasized the words, fully understanding the effect it would have on the President.

Drumpf stood a little taller, broke into a broad grin, and stuck out his hand to shake. "Dennis, that may be the case. But I still need your help. I'm glad you came. You've met the little Rocketman, a couple of times I think. Aside from the Secretary of State, no one else I know and trust can say the same thing."

"I'm happy to help in any way I can, sir."

Martin couldn't believe that Roddmann actually used 'sir'.

"Fantastic. Well, let's get to it. But first let me introduce you to everyone else." The invitations lasted for several minutes. In each case, the President made it a point to explain his own personal brilliance, calm demeanor, and wit while offering back-handed compliments to the others in attendance. Finally, the group sat down in comfortable chairs around a low coffee table.

"Dennis, one last thing," Drumpf said, pointing to a Naval Officer in a black suit and holding a black briefcase. "See that? That's the *football*. Those are the nuclear codes."

Roddmann raised his eyebrows and nodded with the standard 'I'm impressed' look.

"But let's get to it," Drumpf said. "Dennis, I want you to begin. I've been speaking to the rest of my staff for quite some time on this important topic, quite some time. Here's my question: What does K.J.U. want?"

"Mr. President," Roddmann said. "K.J.U. wants a few things, but there is one thing he wants more than anything. It's no different than what any of us want. He wants *respect*. From you, from the South Koreans, from the world. He also wants respect from Vladimir Putin."

A few eyebrows raised at the comment, but no one commented.

"He wants assurances that he won't be invaded. And he would very much like to travel to the United States to watch some NBA games in person."

"NBA games?" The Secretary of State huffed and then rolled his eyes.

"Yeah, NBA," Roddmann insisted emphatically. "He's a huge fan."

"Okay. Hey. Conflict." The President raised his hands as if he were physically holding Roddmann and the Secretary of State apart. "You know I like it, but now isn't the time. So you think that he just wants respect?"

"Mr. President, listen: He wants to be treated like the leader of a powerful nation. That's why he built his nukes – to prove to the world that he's powerful."

"Respect. I can understand a man who craves respect." The President sat back and pondered for a moment. Then he nodded, almost to himself. "Respect is a tough thing. You have to earn it. You have to deserve it. I understand respect. I'm not sure the little Rocketman deserves respect."

The National Security Advisor was about to speak when Roddmann cut him off. "Ro— Mr. President. I've been to his capital. I've been to one of his houses. I like him, and I think he does deserve respect."

"Mr. President. The question isn't whether or not Kim Jong Un deserves your respect or not," the National Security Advisor said. "The real question is whether he respects you. Does he respect you? Does he respect America? Does he respect our ability to continue down the present road of negotiations and eventual disarmament? Those are the questions that should concern us."

"John, you and I see eye-to-eye on the Rocketman," Drumpf said. "That's why I asked you to join the team. You know it is. But I also know that Dennis Roddmann is a smart guy. Mike is a smart guy. Both have met him. And they both told me almost the same thing. And it's a fact. It's a fact. A man who craves respect will do things to earn that respect—things he might not otherwise do. We can use that."

Several of the men in the room nodded in unison. There seemed to be general agreement. The President was satisfied with the direction of the conversation.

·   ·   ·

The meeting lasted close to an hour. Martin had long since stopped paying attention. His mind wandered except for the occasional instance when Roddmann and the President's other, more conventional, advisors disagreed with each other. Martin would tune in to the conversation long enough to realize, again, that he wasn't really interested.

And then movement caught his attention.

The President stood and everyone at the table stood with him. "General. Thank you for your time. I want you to know that I've learned a lot from our chat today. And Dennis. Dennis, my man! It's been a real treat to have you. A real treat."

The President turned back to the General. "I'll have my people contact your people to arrange that … that other discussion."

"Yes, sir, Mr. President. I look forward to it."

Martin couldn't be sure, but it appeared that the General rolled his eyes.

"Jermanski," said Kellner, indicating the General.

Martin took the hint and raised a finger to get the General's attention. "General? Right this way."

The General followed Martin out of the Oval Office.

"This way, sir. I'll walk you—"

"No need, son," the General said. "I've been here before; I know the way." He began to walk away and turned to another officer walking with him. "My people? Your people? He does understand that I am part of *his people*? He understands that, right?"

Before the General turned the corner and moved beyond his sight, Martin saw him shake his head.

MEETING WITH THE CHURCH

Martin stood at the formal entrance to the White House. He, Madeleine Watterhoot, and one other staffer were waiting to welcome a group of visitors for the day's lunch meeting. At exactly ten minutes prior to the meeting's scheduled time, a line of vehicles pulled to a stop in front of the entrance. Martin and the other staffer stood back as Watterhoot walked to the lead car and greeted the passengers that gingerly climbed from it. Slowly, the passengers from the second, third, and fourth cars climbed from their vehicles and congregated in a large group.

After a few minutes of small talk, the assembled group began to move toward the entrance. Martin waited as the group moved past him. He was to be the last in line, to assist any stragglers and to 'push' the group to ensure they made it to the dining room on time.

Martin stood with his hand vaguely pointing in the direction they were to walk. The majority of the visitors ignored him as they strolled past; one or two glanced his way. As was typical as a junior staffer, he was mostly invisible to the visitors. He was also apparently deaf.

"I have grave concerns about our visit this morning," one of the visitors, an older gentleman in a light gray suit, said to the man he was walking beside. "This man, this President, is not our man."

The man to whom Light Gray Suit was speaking, dressed in a darker gray suit, only shook his head. "Everybody in the group understands your concerns. You voiced them quite forcefully at the hotel last night, and then at dinner, and then this morning. We share your concerns; you know that."

"We risk losing our moral authority," Light Gray Suit insisted.

"Moral authority?" Dark Gray Suit asked. "We can maintain ours even as he has none."

"Can we?" Light Gray Suit challenged.

"We prayed for a tool, a tool that we could wield to correct the injustices done over the past many years," Dark Gray Suit answered. "The Lord gave us Ronald Drumpf, and he is correcting those injustices."

"Drumpf is as bad as everything that's said about him. At least Obama was a decent man."

"Decent? Maybe. But he consorted with sodomites, baby-killers, morally bankrupt sycophants," Dark Gray Suit said. "Obama, the man, *may have been* a decent person. And I'm not sure that I agree with you about that. But his policies and beliefs came directly from the mouth of Satan."

Light Gray Suit didn't seem to like that answer, but he only shook his head.

Martin was surprised that the men were talking aloud, seemingly not even trying to keep their voices down. They certainly weren't trying to hide their conversation from him.

"We've talked about this at length. Now is not the time to beat this dead horse," Dark Gray Suit said. "The deal has been made; the dice have been cast."

"Is it a deal with the devil?" Light Gray Suit asked, sounding almost as if he was in pain.

"Now, now," Dark Gray Suit said. "You are a Bible scholar of the highest degree. You know as well as I do that the Lord has always worked through imperfect servants. It's His way. He has done great things throughout history, and only once was His servant on Earth perfect. The Lord has used adulterers, murderers; Ronald Drumpf has never killed a man."

"Not that we know," Light Gray Suit responded.

Dark Gray Suit laughed. "You go too far. The deal is done, and you're well aware of it: Drumpf gives us what we want, and to this point he has done so repeatedly, and we ignore his ... indiscretions."

"What if we get everything that we want, but as a result, the flock is broken?"

Before Dark Gray Suit could respond, they arrived at their destination. The two men were the last two to be ushered into the dining room. As they took their seats, Martin stopped at the door and surveyed the scene.

The President sat at the center position of the long table; the Vice President sat to his right. The gathered assemblage of men sat across from him—they were all white; the majority were almost as old as he; and most were as heavy as he. Most smiled at the President. Some, a little two widely, but Drumpf was probably incapable of noticing.

The President was at ease, comfortable with this group. He leaned forward conspiratorially, "I want to thank you for taking the time to have lunch with me today. It means a great deal to me, a great deal to the American people. The bond that we share is vital to the restoration of America as the greatest nation on the planet. I know what your concerns are, I understand your needs, and I think that we've done a good job for you so far, a great job. My administration has done more to respond to your concerns than any other in American history. And we're only getting started."

The men seated around the table all nodded.

"We have more to do, and we will continue to take actions that address your concerns," Drumpf continued. "We plan on rolling out some additional reforms in the coming weeks and months that should make you very happy, very happy. I don't want to say too much, because we still have some issues to work through, but I promise you that you will like what we're going to do."

Drumpf looked around and nodded at the men nodding at him. Then he turned to the Vice President. "Mike, a brilliant Vice

President. He is doing great things for you by the way. Great things. Mike, do you have any comments?"

"Well, Mr. President," Spence said. "First and foremost, I want to thank you for your leadership, for your vision, for having your hand on the tiller of our great nation. Great changes have come to the nation, and that is your personal doing. I also want to thank you for taking the time to meet with this august body of men, spiritual and sanctified men who represent so many Christians across our great nation. Your willingness to hold this lunch, here in the nation's house with these men, with no desire for anything in return, with no ulterior motive, is truly a great thing. It is rare that an office-holder would take the time out of his busy schedule to meet with religious leaders. That speaks volumes about your morals, your Christian upbringing, and the importance that you place in faith and our Lord, Jesus Christ."

"Thank you, Mike," Drumpf said. "Those are very kind words. And I appreciate it; I truly do."

"Well, Mr. President," Spence said. "It is rare in our nation in recent years to have a leader willing to speak against the forces of Satan."

The men all nodded their heads. A few uttered quiet "Amens."

"A leader who puts the needs of our Christian brothers and sisters where they belong," Spence continued. "And to our guests today, I just want to thank you for making the trip to our nation's capital for the purpose of this meeting. Your willingness to engage with the political leadership of the nation is important for your flocks, and it's important to us here in Washington, DC."

"Indeed," Drumpf interrupted. He had seemed to grow bored during the Vice President's pronouncements. "Gentlemen, I know that you have concerns that you are prepared to discuss with me today. And I am looking forward to hearing your concerns, to understanding the issues that you see in your congregations. But before we discuss those issues, there is one thing I want to discuss with you."

The President leaned back in his chair, lifted his hands in front of him, and then placed them on the table's edge. "Your support will be vital this Fall, absolutely vital."

"You have nothing to worry about, Mr. President." The man sitting directly across from Drumpf answered brightly; his slight southern twang was a pointed contrast to Drumpf's Queensian accent. "Our combined congregations, our flock, fully support you and the Republican party."

Drumpf leaned back. "The Republican Party needs your help. Me, not so much. I'm not up for re-election this November. The Republicans, some are running scared. Some are just quitters. Some have given up. But for those in the fight, they need your help."

"Mr. President." A thin, pasty man a few spots down the table and across from the President, tentatively raised his hand. "First, I want to thank you for your unwavering support. Your leadership has truly been heaven-sent. I, and most in my flock, believe that with all of our hearts and minds. You are bringing our Savior back to center-stage, where he rightfully belongs. I think I speak for all of us when I say the evangelicals in our great nation are fully behind you."

Two men responded with a "Hear, hear" and a few others responded with enthusiastic "Amens."

Drumpf nodded sagely, as if he expected everything that was said to him.

Pasty Face continued, "We will support the Republican Party as they do battle in the polls. But some of us have concerns. Some of the Republican candidates do not seem fully onboard with your teachings; some are heretically speaking against you. What would you have us do?"

Drumpf considered this for a moment. He seemed to consider his words—something that Martin didn't think he had ever seen before.

"I understand your concerns, and they are real concerns. But here's what I think," Drumpf said. "A Republican is better than any other candidate. A Republican who fully supports me is better than a Republican who doesn't. A Republican who doesn't support me is better than an independent—do those even exist anymore? And an independent is better than any Democrat."

The entire group nodded, as if Drumpf's words were wise beyond belief. Martin thought his comments were little better than common-sense.

"I understand, Mr. President," Pasty Face responded. "And thank you."

"One other thing," Drumpf said. "I'll endorse candidates. Pay close attention to Twitter, to my girl Sarah Saunders, to Mike. There shouldn't ever be a doubt about who I support."

Several of the men smiled enthusiastically.

"And I have one last thing before hearing your thoughts," Drumpf said. "You all here today know the value that I place on religious faith, on faith in your Lord."

'Wow,' Martin thought. 'Did he say 'your Lord' on purpose?'

"I want you to know that my beautiful wife Melanya—and she is extremely beautiful, isn't she? And gorgeous, talented, intelligent—is a rock in my faith. Her faith is as great as anyone I've ever seen, and I lean on her faith in trying times."

"In fact," Drumpf continued. "All three of my wives, all beautiful—in their younger days, were women of faith. I've always attempted to surround myself with faithful women, extremely faithful, as you understand. Each of them helped me to grow in my relationship with God. Just as those of you who are married lean on your wives for support. Although I don't think any of your wives are as beautiful as mine, as hot. I've seen pictures of most of your families. Some of you have hot daughters, for sure, very, very beautiful. But my wives have been, without a doubt, more beautiful than yours."

"And all three of them have had great faith in God, and tremendous humility and kindness, and helped me to keep my faith in the Lord. So please keep Melanya in your prayers, just as you keep me in your prayers. Pray for her to remain as beautiful as she is today. Pray for her to grow more beautiful! And as faithful. But let's talk of your concerns now."

Another man raised his hand. Martin guessed he was in his mid-forties. He wore an expensive suit; his graying hair was perfectly coiffed.

"Mr. President," Expensive Suit began. "You know, better than anyone, the danger to our faith that is illegal immigration. The Mexicans, the Central Americans, Heaven forbid the South Americans – they come into our country; they steal our jobs; they rape our women. Most of them are Catholics you know, of the *worst* sort. But we thank you, for your wisdom, your leadership, your faith, in leading the fight against their attacks on America. Your foresight and strong stance on this issue is vital to keeping our nation great."

A white-haired gentlemen, narrow from his collar down, politely raised his hand. The President nodded at him. The man cleared his throat and began to speak in a quiet voice. "Mr. President. Your election has been a Godsend to the nation. Without doubt, you have single-handedly steered the great ship of America away from the shoals of sinfulness and idolatry and back toward the calm waters of faith, humility, and fear in the Almighty God. Your firm hand on the tiller of our nation has returned us to a righteous path, a path from which we have strayed in recent decades."

The man paused and then spoke again, in a louder voice. "And while immigration is an important issue, there is only one true issue that my brothers in faith feel most strongly about. Sexual deviance, homosexuality, and the heart-breaking murder of millions of children each year—in our nation alone. It is high time that the great curse of Roe V. Wade be struck from the pages of history. It is high time that the Supreme Court put faith above the modern, and sinful, idea of choice." He pounded the table with his hand and raised his voice further. "The rampant sexualization of our society, the pornography, the denigration of chaste and decent women – these things need to stop! And we know, we are sure, and we will tell our flocks the truth of your strength and faith in the face of these evils, that you are the leader that this nation needs to help us do just that!"

A few men applauded the speaker, and then more, and soon the entire room was applauding him and then turning their praise toward the President. Drumpf sat back and basked in it.

When the room finally calmed, the President leaned forward in his chair, turned to make eye contact with each man at the long polished table, and said, "I am with you in this battle. We, together, will solve this problem. I assure you."

The conversation lasted another thirty minutes. It alternated between the various men at the table kissing Drumpf's ass and him making grand pronouncements and occasionally saying things that Martin believed were completely inappropriate toward a group of religious leaders. It seemed that the men at the table were tripping over themselves to outdo each other and pay Drumpf the strongest compliment.

As the meeting approached its scheduled completion time, a man who hadn't spoken at all raised his hand and was called on by the President. "Mr. President, I know that our time is almost over. I was wondering if we might pray for you before we go."

"I would be honored," Drumpf responded.

Dark Gray Suit stood up. "Perhaps instead, Phillip should lead this prayer. Phil, if you please."

Light Gray Suit looked up in surprise and then nodded firmly. The man who initially volunteered to pray shrugged slightly.

The men at the table all stood and moved to stand in a tight circle around the President. The President bowed his head and closed his eyes. Almost as one, the men rested their hands on his back, his shoulders, and even his head.

Martin, who was watching intently, saw Drumpf open his eyes in apparent surprise. Drumpf looked back and forth without lifting his head. His annoyance was clear, but he held himself in check.

"Dear Heavenly Father," Light Gray Suit began. "Father above all and Lord of all that was, is, and will be. Protector of unborn children. Guardian at the walls of our nation. Creator of the Universe. You, Lord, who are so much more than any of us and yet who loves each of us, we thank you on this day. We thank you for giving us a political leader who clearly places your teachings above all—above his own interests, above Earthly riches, and above the slings and arrows of those who act in Satan's honor. We thank you for arming this man with wisdom, strength, and perseverance to fight on your behalf and on behalf of your most ardent followers. We thank you for the gift that his ascendance has been to our nation and to the world. Dear Father, we ask that you shield this man from the lies of the opposition, from the falsehoods spread by Satan's servants, from the weakness and treachery in his own ranks. We ask that you lay your hands on him and continue to guide him, as you have most evidently done since his first day in office. Lord we ask that you continue to speak through him, through his words, deeds, and leadership."

Martin was not very religious. His parents had gone to church regularly when he was in elementary school, but that ended sometime when he was in the seventh grade. He wasn't sure if he had been to church since, aside from a few weddings. But he was surprised by Light Gray Suit's prayer. Did the man actually believe everything he was saying about the President? And if the man believed in an All-Knowing God, did he actually believe that God believed those things he was saying about the President?

Light Gray Suit continued to pray, and Martin found himself more and more blown away by his comments. And then it abruptly ended. The circle surrounding the President broke up. The men were smiling and cheerful, and the President shook each of their hands.

Martin knew that the first thing the President would do after saying goodbye would be to immediately wash his hands. Martin was sure that the hand-shaking was driving the President crazy, but he was doing an impressive job of hiding it.

The glad-handing lasted a few minutes and then the President left, leaving Martin and the other staffers to walk the men back to their waiting vehicles.

Once again, Martin brought up the rear, and once again Dark and Light Gray Suit were the two closest to him.

"What have we done?" Light Gray Suit lamented.

"What we've done? What you've done! I'll tell you," said Dark Gray Suit. "You prayed for Drumpf with one of the most powerful prayers I've ever heard said over a politician. The Lord was certainly moved by your words today, and the President will be a better man for it."

"He disgusts me," Light Gray Suit said. "The way that he spoke of our wives and daughters; it was sickening."

"Come now," said Dark Gray Suit. "They were only words. And we'll never allow any of our lady-folk to meet the President. I wouldn't allow that man anywhere near any of my flock."

OFF THE RECORD

"Have you heard?" Jason asked Martin. They were getting lunch a couple of blocks from the White House.

"Heard what?" Martin responded.

"A couple of reporters are interviewing staffers."

"What?!" Martin tried to insert as much sarcasm in his voice as possible. He knew of several staffers who spoke to reporters from various outlets. He knew that most of the principals did the same, and probably more often.

Jason sensed the sarcasm and frowned. "Fuck you, man. No, they're not trying to get dirt on the administration. Well, we don't think so—"

"Who's 'we'?" Martin asked.

"Doesn't matter. They're asking questions about the staffers themselves."

'Intriguing,' Martin thought. He didn't want anything to do with it. "What kind of questions?"

"Why don't you come to one of the meetings?" Jason asked. "You can let them ask you themselves."

Still not interested. "Where are they from?"

"Does it matter? Newsweek? Politico? I don't know."

"Does Newsweek even still exist?" Martin hadn't seen or heard of it since his parents stopped receiving it in the mail. "Are you sure 'they' are even talking to staffers?"

"Yeah. It's two guys."

"Well, that makes it official then."

"I'm meeting them tomorrow night with a group of four or five," said Jason. "I figured you might want to join us."

"So what are these guys' names?"

"Dan and Ben, I think. Dan and Bill? Bill and Mark. No, Dan and Ben."

"No idea where they're from?" Martin asked.

"I think Politico, but I'm not sure."

"Which way do they lean?" Martin asked.

"I thought you didn't pay attention to politics at all."

"I don't. But if I'm going to talk to a reporter, I'd like to know if he's going to be friendly or hostile, or just lie through his teeth."

"I think they lean a little left," said Jason.

"Safe to talk to them?"

"A whole bunch of people already have."

"Do any of the higher-ups know?" Martin asked.

"I don't think so."

Martin was certainly intrigued. Maybe he'd go and just listen to the conversation. "Yeah, but what kinds of questions are they asking?"

"Supposedly, they're asking about 'the life of the staffer' and such. Our social lives, our love lives, where we live, where we hang out."

"Bullshit," Martin commented.

"What do you mean?"

"Why would they, or anyone, care?" Martin asked. "Seriously, who cares about the lives of White House staffers?"

"Don't be a buzzkill."

"But, again, who cares?"

"Apparently, Politico does," Jason said. He took a few bites of his meal.

Martin had lost interest in the topic.

"Well," asked Jason. "Are you going to join us?"

Martin finished chewing and swallowed his last bite. "Since my social life is currently *off the hook*, I may as well. Where are we meeting?"

"Not sure," said Jason. "I'll call you."

.   .   .

"Yeah," Jason was saying. "It's hard to get laid in the city."

Five guys sat around the table. Three staffers and the two reporters. The conversation had been going for about a half an hour, and Martin hadn't yet said very much. He was leery.

The third staffer was Hawk Nose, from Martin's first visit to the PPO. Of course, he now knew that his name was Brent.

"Yeah," Brent agreed. "But that has nothing to do with you being a Drumpf staffer."

Everyone laughed at the joke, even Martin—although he was disappointed in himself for doing so. It was too easy.

Both reporters rubbed him the wrong way. Ben, dark-haired, wore a thick five o'clock shadow. That alone annoyed Martin, but he understood why Ben did it. Without it, Ben would look like he was twelve. And Dan had what Martin referred to as a 'shit-eating grin.' Not only that, his head was misshapen—it was widest at his temples and narrowed from there down to his jaw. Martin actually felt bad for the guy.

"What would you say, Martin?" asked Brent.

"Uh. About what?" Martin's mind had wandered. He had stopped listening to the conversation several sentences prior. He couldn't concentrate while looking at Dan's head.

"Shit, man," Jason moaned.

Brent and the two reporters only laughed.

"About your time in DC," Brent said. "Socially. Sexually. In any other way?"

"Well," Martin said, speaking directly to the reporters. "I've only been in town a few months. I was warned early on not to mention my ties to the Administration. I try not to bring it up."

"Any horror stories?" Ben asked.

"Actually, no. Not personal ones," Martin said. "Certainly not like these two." He raised his bottle in their direction in mock salute.

The group laughed. Martin was hoping to deflect the conversation away from himself. For whatever reason, he felt paranoid about the whole thing. The other two seemed all too happy to answer every question with a long story; Martin didn't get it.

"I was actually punched once," Brent said. "Some bitch, who wasn't even the girl I was talking to, found out that I worked in the White House. She interrupted my conversation to cuss me out. Next thing you know, she's throwing a right hook at my jaw. That shit fucking hurt!"

"I heard about that," Jason interjected. "She was, what? A hundred pounds soaking wet? She tore you up!"

"Fuck you, man," Brent responded. "Although she did have a mean hook."

"Anything like that happen to you?" Dan asked.

"Nope," Martin said. "But I think that has more to do with Brent's face than anything else. That face just begs to be hit." Martin caught himself starting to stare at Dan's head again. He laughed and hoped that they'd think he was laughing at Brent.

The conversation continued for quite a while, the two other staffers sharing stories that they'd heard second and third hand. Dan and Ben listened intently. Eventually, Dan spoke up, "One of your peers told us that he was yelled at walking out of work."

"Oh, yeah," said Jason. "I've seen that happen to people; it's never happened to me, though."

"Why do you think that is?" Ben asked.

"Sign of the times, I guess?" Jason shrugged.

"So where do you guys all live?" Dan asked.

Martin didn't understand the fascination and slowly withdrew. Eventually, his phone came out, and he was surfing the internet. And then he received a text. It was from Luke.

Martin realized that he hadn't talked to Luke, or Mike, in a few weeks. He shuddered at the thought of the DRT. He opened the text to find a photo. It was a picture of him and Gabrielle standing in the bar the night he had met Luke. He had no idea that Luke had taken a picture of them.

Martin read Luke's text: 'Just came across this. Had completely forgotten about it. You ever hear from her?'

Martin typed back: 'No. But thanks for the photo. This is great!'

Martin stared at the picture. Gabrielle was hot. He had forgotten how attractive she was.

And then the two reporters announced that they were out of time. The five of them stood.

"Do you guys know when the article is going to come out?" Jason asked.

"Not exactly; that's out of our hands," Dan answered.

"Do you have our names spelled correctly?" Brent asked. "Do you have all of our phone numbers and email addresses?"

'Calm down, guys,' Martin thought. 'They're reporters.'

They shook hands around, and the reporters left.

"That was pretty sweet," Brent said.

"Wait, what?" Martin asked.

"Shit," Brent said. "They seemed interested in talking to us. Us!"

"Yeah, well, just so they don't use our names," Martin said.

"What do you mean?" Jason asked.

"You did fill out the same paperwork that I did when you were hired, didn't you?" Martin asked.

"I'm sure we did. Why?" Brent asked.

"Well, the NDA," Martin said.

"NDA?" Jason asked.

"Seriously? I'm new around here," Martin said. "And I'm not that smart. Surely, you guys know. NDA! Non-Disclosure Agreement!"

"Well, sure. Yeah. NDA," Brent said.

"Oh, yeah. NDA," Jason agreed.

"I signed one on my first day, when I sat down with Helen and filled out that mountain of forms," Martin said.

"I didn't really pay attention to what I was signing," Jason offered.

"I only knew about it, because my dad signed one a long time ago," Martin said. "He even mentioned to me before flying to DC that there might be one."

"It had to be okay to talk to them," Brent said. "The White House arranged for some people to meet with them."

"Really?" Martin asked. "I hadn't heard that."

"Give me some credit," Jason said. "I'm no fool."

"That's questionable," Martin said. "What d'you think's going to happen?"

They both stared at him blankly.

"If these guys actually write an article, which, okay, let's say they do," Martin said. "You'll get to read it, and it might include a quote from one of us or it might not. If it does, yay! If it doesn't, oh well. But then what?"

"You're such a buzzkill," Brent said.

"Let me enjoy this," Jason said. "Please?"

"Don't not enjoy it on my account," Martin said. "Go crazy."

SECURITY CLEARANCE

Martin was verifying that the Cabinet Room was ready for the up-coming Cabinet Meeting. It wasn't really a job. The hospitality staff, including people who had worked in the White House for many years and some who came from Mer-a-Lago itself, were more than capable of setting up the tables, with the Presidential silver, name plates, hors d'oeuvres, and pens and pads of paper meticulously placed. Martin was there only because he was told to be. The others in the room would have resented his presence, except he knew enough to stay out of their way and was friendly to them. He looked around; there was literally nothing for him to do.

The meeting was scheduled to begin in twenty minutes, which meant that the first arrivals would begin showing up any minute. Some would stand around and chit-chat. Others would sit down immediately and demand their coffee, made in just the right way. Still others wouldn't show up until seconds before the President did. Martin had been fascinated while watching his first two or three, but now the meetings seemed to blend together. It rarely seemed to him that anything of substance was ever discussed. The President was much more interested in the latest headline, the latest broadcast.

"Marty!"

The voice snapped him out of his daydream.

'How the—?' "Sir?"

It was the President! Martin knew that Drumpf had a habit of ignoring his schedule and wandering the White House alone, but he had never been caught by it, until now.

"Marty. It's good to see you. Are we ready?"

"For the Cabinet Meeting?" His eyes darted around the room. Everything *seemed* to be in order. The room was empty except for the President and him.

'Where did everyone else go?' Martin thought.

"Well, yeah," said the President.

"Yes, sir!

"Fantastic. Fantastic. Glad to hear it. It's going to be a good meeting today. We have lots to discuss. We might even be discussing some classified information."

"Yes, sir," Martin said. "I'll be stepping out just before it starts. I haven't been given a clearance."

"What? How's that possible?"

"Well, sir. I was never told to apply."

"Apply? Well, they do seem to have a lot of rules about that … That's too bad, though. I really wanted you in there today."

Martin didn't know how to respond. The President wanted *him*?

"Fuck it. Marty, stay for the Cabinet Meeting. We'll get the clearance straightened out later."

"Sir?"

"Don't worry. I can do that. You'll have to fill out some paperwork, I'm told. Declare your finances. Report any foreign connections."

Drumpf chuckled to himself. "Finances. You don't have any finances, do you, Marty? Your dad works at Mer-a-Lago. I know how much he makes. Well, I don't, but I could easily find out. Good man, your dad. Good man. It's probably not enough to have *finances*, not like my family and a lot of the Cabinet have finances. So that shouldn't be an issue."

"Foreign connections? Do you have any of those, Marty?"

"Um, no, sir?"

"I didn't think so, but you could. But certainly nothing that would get you in trouble, do you? But it wouldn't matter. All that matters is that I want you in there. You probably won't get to talk, not during your first meeting. But you'll be able to stand off to the side and listen."

"Yes, sir."

"You know, Marty. I have the best Cabinet in history. The best, absolutely. They are intelligent, hard-working, rich people. Very rich, on average. I think it is the wealthiest Cabinet in history. I'm told that historians have written histories about past Cabinets. I haven't read any, but that's what I'm told. Someone mentioned to me the other day that Lincoln's Cabinet was a good one—a whole book written just about his Cabinet. Well, they're going to write a book about my Cabinet one day. Best in history, obviously. Because I picked them." The President paused and looked around. His mind seemed to wander.

A long moment passed and then the President turned back to Martin. "But you know, Marty. Sometimes they need some help. They're not very creative. Can't keep up with me. They're pretty smart—but not as smart as I am. Probably not as smart as you. That's why I want you in there. I think you'll be able to help them out. I'll need you to help them."

Martin didn't know what to say. He felt like it was a common occurrence.

"Have you graduated from college?" Drumpf asked him.

"Yes, sir."

"Perfect. I could tell. I knew it. Although there are plenty of smart and capable people who haven't. You don't need a college degree to succeed in this world. But for a lot of people, it helps. Some of us don't need it, but we get one anyway."

"Mr. President."

Both men turned. It was the Chief of Staff, just entering the room.

"Mr. President, the Cabinet members are arriving now. The first should be here in a few moments. Is there anything you need before we kick off today?"

"Yes. I want Marty here to stand in. I want him present."

The Chief of Staff seemed annoyed by the suggestion, but it didn't seem that the President noticed.

"Do you have your clearance?" The question was posed directly to Martin.

"No—"

The Chief of Staff didn't even wait for Martin's full response. "Mr. President. We'll have to adjust the agenda for the meeting. You know that we will be discussing—"

"I want him in there. And I don't want to change the agenda. I know about his clearance. I don't care. You can fix it after."

"Mr. President. The press is beating you up about clearances here in the White House. They're beating all of us up. We can't afford to have—"

"I don't want to hear another word about it. I'm sure you can get it taken care of."

The Chief of Staff opened his mouth and then shut it. He glared at Martin for a brief moment and then smiled. "Got it, sir. Mr. Jermanski will have to sit down and fill out some paperwork this afternoon, but that can wait until after the meeting."

"Fantastic! Okay. See, Marty? Your first Cabinet Meeting!"

Actually, it wasn't his first Cabinet Meeting. He had been present for several. But it *would* be his first classified meeting.

The President had left Martin standing awkwardly next to the Chief of Staff; he had moved to greet some of the members of his Cabinet as they entered the room.

The Chief of Staff imperceptibly leaned sideways toward Martin. "Don't fuck this up, kid," he growled. "The President can't go to jail for this. But if you screw up, you could."

·   ·   ·

When the Cabinet meeting was complete, Martin couldn't tell what was classified and what wasn't. It all seemed the same—boring, mundane, and a waste of his, and all of its participants', time. He left the Cabinet Room and decided to swing by the Oval Office before heading back to his own.

Chip was standing outside the Oval Office. The female staffers gave Chip his nickname—they found him to be extremely handsome, and he did fill out his suit well. If that didn't make sense, they nicknamed another Secret Service Agent Dale, because he was, in their opinion, as good looking and well-built as Chip.

"Afternoon," Martin said. "Do you know if anyone was by to pick up the President's papers today?"

"Don't think so, Marty," Chip said. "I don't believe the President even came to the Oval before the Cabinet meeting."

"Got it. Busy in there now?"

"No," he said and then knocked on the door.

Martin opened it and then stepped through.

The President was sitting at his desk talking to Kelly Conville and the Chief of Staff. Watterhoot was standing close by as well, but she didn't seem to be a part of the conversation.

"Sarah's the best," the President said. "She's doing a tremendous job, tremendous. If it weren't for her doing great things, my job would be a lot more difficult. Of course, I could handle it without her, but she helps a lot."

Martin approached the President's desk. As he drew closer, he could see that there were no papers in the garbage can. At the moment, there was also nothing on the President's desk.

"There's one area where I wish Sarah was a little stronger," the President continued. "She's just not that attractive. I mean, look, I get it. You don't have to be attractive to be good at your job. But it certainly helps. Especially, as my Press Secretary. Hearing that bad news, hearing the hard answer, being told something that you don't want to hear is always better if the person doing that is attractive. I think it would be better for the American people if Sarah was more attractive."

Martin turned and moved back toward the exit.

"She's doing good work, Mr. President," Conville said.

"You're right, Kelly," the President said. "She is, and I love her. I really do. I love her almost like a daughter. In some ways, she reminds me of Hope Hills. I miss her, you know. She was a fantastic help, during my campaign, in the White House, everywhere. She could always tell what I needed, and then she'd get it for me. Or have someone get it for me. And Hope was a beautiful woman, a beautiful woman. Almost as beautiful as Ivania. Perhaps even as beautiful as Melanya. Hope was capable, talented, hardworking, and beautiful. She was really beautiful. Really beautiful."

Martin stopped at the exit and looked back at the three. They didn't once acknowledge his presence. Low-level staffer, indeed.

"Are you concerned that she's planning to leave, sir?" Kellner asked.

"Of course, I'm concerned," the President said. "Aren't you?"

Martin stepped out and pulled the door shut behind him.

$\cdot \qquad \cdot \qquad \cdot$

Martin was sitting at his desk, scrolling through work emails on his official phone when there was a knock at the door.

He and Amanda both looked up at the same time.

It was a female staffer, twenty-seven Martin guessed, who he had never met. She looked pissed.

"Hey," Amanda said. It was the closest thing to a friendly greeting he had ever heard from her.

The staffer looked at her and returned the "Hey." Then she turned to Martin.

"I'm not sure why I was told to bring this to you," she said. "You should have been told to come to us, but anyway. Here's your SF-86." She dropped a thick folder of papers onto the desk in front of him.

"What's an SF-86?" Martin asked.

"What's an…?" Angry Delivery Staffer muttered. She looked at Amanda. "Can you please help your clueless office-mate? I don't have the time for this shit."

"Sure thing," Amanda said as Angry Delivery Staffer turned and left.

"So someone decided it's time to give you a security clearance, eh?"

"I guess so," Martin said.

"Yeah," she said and shook her head. "So that form, your SF-86, needs to be completed, probably immediately. It's a pain in the ass. It'll probably take you the rest of the afternoon. Luckily for you, the President's playing a late round today. I doubt there'll be anything else for us to do."

LOYALTY ATTACK

The President and trusted military advisors sat in the White House Situation Room. The Vice President was present; the Secretary of Defense was present; the National Security Advisor was present. Several civilians also sat around the table – men and one woman who were not known by the President. The topic of the day was North Korea. The brief was purely informational, to update the President on the latest thinking regarding the reclusive leader, his military, and his nation.

The plan had been, as was the case in all meetings such as this one, for the Secretary of Defense to thank the President for taking time out of his busy schedule to meet with them that day and listen to the assembled Korea experts. The President had stepped into the room, taken his seat, and started talking almost immediately.

"Bull Dog! Bull Dog. Glad to be here today. I know you have some experts lined up for me to talk to. Is this them?" The President looked around at the civilians he didn't recognize. His eyes lingered on the sole female in the room, brunette, middle-aged, at one time attractive but not keeping herself up well. That was the President's split-second appraisal, and then he glanced at the others. Those who had spent time with the President could sense his disappointment. "Jim tells me that you're the experts on North Korea. I'll tell you

– I'm not too shabby myself. I understand the little Rocket Man. I do. And I understand his little country, probably better than you do. I've already spoken to some of my people. Our General from Korea. He's not Korean – the American General *in charge of* Korea. Had a good conversation with him. I also spoke to Dennis Roddmann. He's been there; he's an expert."

"And, of course, the Secretary of State. I know that it probably surprised all of you when you heard the news that he had travelled to Korea this past Easter. Well, it was a bold move, and it was my decision. My idea even. And it was a great idea. We gained a lot out of that initial meeting. There's more to do, but we gained a lot. But I'm sure you're all aware of that. You've probably been studying my plans for Korea – how else would you become experts, right?"

"I assure you, Mr. President," the Secretary of Defense interrupted, "that our guests today have studied Kim Jong Un and the DPRK for years. We have a panel of experts, from academia, from private think tanks, and from elsewhere. I thought it important, as we continue to progress with developments on the Korean Peninsula, that you hear some of what they have to say."

"Jim, you're right. Absolutely." The President turned back to the civilian experts and cocked his heard toward the Secretary of Defense. "The best Secretary of Defense that this nation has had in, well, certainly my lifetime. Brilliant man, outstanding General, esteemed warrior. He was my first choice. And I got him." The President trailed off, momentarily, and seemed almost lost in thought. "But who's first, Jim? Which *expert* gets to start the discussion?"

"Well, thank you, Mr. President. First, I'd like to introduce Mr. ... " Almost immediately, the President's eyes began to gloss over – the Secretary's introduction surely missed. "... which is a respected think-tank with offices here in Washington, DC and elsewhere. His organization prides itself on the quality of its research and non-partisan views."

"Non-partisan?" The President perked up at the word.

"Yes, Mr. President." A bespectacled man with graying hair spoke up. "We pride ourselves on our strict research methodologies and even-handed policy recommendations."

The President frowned. "But you're a think-tank, right? Who tells you what to think? Which side do you root for?"

The man seemed confused. "Sir?"

"You know, I'm non-partisan. I've been a Republican; I've been a Democrat; I've even been an Independent. And I always thought for myself. You have to, to succeed in life as I have. All businessmen have to think for themselves, that's the only way to make money, to become rich, famous. But you people in academia, in think-tanks—you don't think for yourselves. Someone always tells you what to think."

"Sometimes, yes, and sometime, no, Mr. President." The Secretary of Defense interrupted again. "His think-tank is home to many experts. I brought him here today, because *I* trust him and his research."

"You trust him, Jim? Well, okay. Let's hear it, then. Go ahead, Mr. –" The President couldn't remember his name.

The expert didn't let it phase him. "Thank you, Mr. President. As the Secretary of Defense said, I…"

The President looked down at the briefing folder in front of him. He opened it, only half-interested in its contents. Enclosed were several sheets of paper. He flipped through them. At the top of each was the expert's name, followed immediately by the name of the organization that the person represented. There were a few sentences about the organization and just below that was a section titled "Key Conclusions and Take-Aways" in large, bold font. Under that heading were four or five bulleted statements.

The President was disappointed. There was nothing interesting here. He looked up at the man speaking to him, nodded as if listening, and then glanced over the man's shoulder at the digital clock hanging on the far wall. They were only six minutes into the scheduled ninety-minute meeting. He looked back down at the briefing sheets and scanned the Key Conclusions from three of them. Then something caught his eye. He read the sentence and then read it a second time. "The threat of a loyalty attack is low but should not be discounted."

"Excuse me," the President interrupted without looking up. "A 'loyalty attack,' what is that?"

The man speaking, whose briefing sheet was not the one that mentioned loyalty attacks, seemed flustered. "Sir?"

The President looked up, first at the man and then at the others. "Who wrote about loyalty attacks?"

"It's possible that more than one wrote about the concept," the Secretary of Defense spoke up, "but I believe you mean—"

"Yes, Mr. President." Another man spoke up. Thin, balding, and sitting ram-rod straight. "I believe you're referring to my paper."

"Yeah, sure. Tell me about loyalty attacks."

"Well, Mr. President. A loyalty attack is when a member of a military, para-military, or police force attacks 'the enemy' as a way to demonstrate his or her own loyalty to the regime."

"I don't follow. How is that different than any soldier in the military?"

"The difference, sir, is that the soldier in question is not following orders, but making the decision himself to attack."

"But wouldn't attacking when you aren't ordered to do so actually be disloyal?" The question was the first time since the President entered the room that the Vice President spoke.

"Well, yes and no. Yes, in that the soldier was choosing to attack on his own and ignoring his military superiors. But, also no, because from his perspective, the attack is purely to demonstrate his loyalty to the greater regime."

"Wonderful," the President said almost inaudibly to himself. Almost.

"There are any number of imaginable reasons why someone would conduct a loyalty attack." The expert began again, using a professorial, lecturing voice. "These types of actions don't fit with our American, Western understanding of military culture, but we shouldn't discount the behavior in troops who have been raised in an extreme cult-of-personality setting."

The Secretary of Defense interjected, "Our understanding of the true feelings of low-level personnel in the Korean military is incomplete, but there is anecdotal evidence from North Korean defectors that—"

"So, you're saying that a soldier in the North Korean Army might try to attack a South Korean or even American solider *just to prove* his loyalty to Kim Jong Un?" The President leaned forward in his chair, intrigued by the idea.

"Yes, Mr. President." The man was obviously torn. His desire to continue was evident—it wasn't often that the President of the United States seemed genuinely interested in your personal research. But the man was receiving a decidedly different vibe from the Secretary of Defense—a cool stare and slightly clenched lips.

"Wonderful." The President said the word aloud. More than a few eyebrows in the room rose in response. "When might such a thing happen?"

"Say, for instance, that a soldier, brain-washed since he was a child to revere the Kim family, was in some minor trouble – a disciplinary infraction or some failure to perform. To make up for that previous failure, that soldier might conduct a loyalty attack."

"Like what? You mean shoot a gun? Fire a missile?"

"Hard to say, Mr. President."

The man paused. The situation was disconcerting. The President was obviously interested in the topic, perhaps too much so. He was leaning forward in his chair; his eyes were narrowed; he wore a slight smirk. The Secretary of Defense, however, was now visibly frowning. His eyes were also narrowed, but his emotion was quite different.

He gulped ever so slightly. "Fire an artillery piece. Shoot a torpedo. It could take any form."

"Would he get into trouble with his military superiors?"

"I would assume so, Mr. President."

"And he would *still* conduct the attack?"

"Yes, sir."

"That's true loyalty! Wow! Jim, that is loyalty." The President turned to the look at the Secretary of Defense. He was smiling. "Are our military personnel that loyal?"

"Mr. President? No, sir," the Secretary of Defense answered. "They are *more* loyal than that. They are so loyal that they would never consider doing such a thing."

The President seemed crestfallen. "Well, what would happen if someone did such a thing?"

"Sir. No soldier, sailor, airman, or marine in my Armed Services would contemplate such an act. And if they did, they would be apprehended and prosecuted to the fullest extent allowed by the Uniform Code of Military Justice. And the punishment would be swift, and it would be severe."

The President now seemed genuinely disappointed. "You're sure?"

"Absolutely, Mr. President."

The President slouched slightly in his chair, turned back to the man, and then glanced again down at the briefing sheet. "You say that it 'should not be discounted.' Why do you say that?"

"Because we just don't know what might happen. And if it did, it could be bad."

"Well, what is the worst case? What could happen?"

"A worst case might be an errant artillery attack on the Gisma."

"Gisma?" The President was puzzled.

"Gisma? The G.S.M.A., Mr. President," the Secretary of Defense answered. "The 'Greater Seoul Metropolitan Area.' Seoul and the areas immediately around it."

"Ah. Gisma, of course. I knew that. Thanks, Jim." To the Secretary of Defense, and then the President turned back to the man. "And why would that be bad?"

"North Korea has several thousand pieces of powerful artillery just over the border, north of Seoul, aimed directly at the capital. If one were to be 'accidentally' fired at Seoul, there are three possible outcomes. The first is that North Korea immediately apologize, inform the world that it was a mistake, and attempt to diffuse the situation – highly unlikely. The second is that other artillery units would then, for fear of having missed a command or misunderstanding the situation, join in and cause an artillery chain reaction

– very bad for Seoul and potentially destabilizing. The third is that South Korean forces respond immediately, before cooler heads can prevail, and launch a full-scale counter offensive. All from a single soldier, or unit, deciding it best to launch a single artillery shell."

"Wow. So you're telling me that a soldier, while trying to prove his loyalty, could actually start a war in Korea."

"Possibly, sir."

"That is loyalty right there. Loyalty." The President shook his head in appreciation and seemed to fade into thought. Glancing up, he looked at the digital clock again, its large red numbers not having moved as far as he hoped.

"We have much more to discuss, Mr. President," the Secretary of Defense said. "Let me introduce you to our next speaker—"

The President didn't really care about the next speaker. Those who knew him could read his body language. The expert briefers could not and so dove into their presentations with gusto.

SECRETARY OF DEFENSE

"Martin, right?"

The Secretary of Defense knew many of the young White House Staffers' names, even those with whom he rarely interacted. Martin was always impressed by it.

"Yes, sir," Martin responded.

"Ordinarily, I would walk our guests out, but I have another meeting in a few minutes and won't be able to get there on time. Can you please get them to their cars?"

"Absolutely, sir." Martin was certain that the SecDef was fudging the truth a little. He usually did *not* walk his guests out – that's what staffers were for, after all. But Martin understood that the comment made those guests feel important, probably more important than they actually were. And Martin got the distinct impression, based upon the President's exit from the Situation Room, that Drumpf did not think the guests were important.

The lone woman in the group turned to one of the others and said quietly, "He really doesn't get it, does he? Did he pay attention to a word you, or I, said?"

"I thought they were just stories," the man responded in a whisper that was louder than the woman. "Maybe he is an idiot. It's fucking scary."

Martin was only slightly shocked at the open criticism of the President, but then again, nobody bothered to censor themselves in front of the staffers.

The woman didn't appear to like the man's vulgarity, but that didn't stop her from agreeing. "I just can't believe it. If he's not going to listen to us, why have us in the room?"

"Because, Margaret," the SecDef interjected. "Because *I'm* going to listen. And I value your opinions. And expertise."

"Jim, I don't know how you work for that man."

"*That man* is the President of the United States of America. That man is the rightfully elected leader of our great nation. I work for that man, yes, but I also work for our nation. And it's an honor to do so."

"Maybe so," another one of the experts joined the conversation. "But how can you stomach him? How can you put up with him?"

"He's so gross!" Margaret said.

"You all do remember I'm a Marine." SecDef smiled, not in a knowingly-clever-way, but in an earnest, I-want-to-convince-you way. "It's much harder to tell a mother, or a wife, or a child that her son or husband or father, or daughter for that matter, has died. And I've done my fair share of that. There's nothing about this job as hard as that."

The 'experts' stood still, momentarily chastened by the comment.

And then the SecDef broke into a sly smile. "Except for life in this city."

Every member of the small huddle, even Martin who wasn't actually a part of it, laughed at the quip. It was an easy joke, but it prevented what could have been an awkward ending to their meeting.

'The man is smooth,' Martin thought to himself.

The SecDef glanced over at Martin. Martin took his cue.

"Gentlemen, ma'am. If you'd follow me. We'll get you out of here and back into the springtime sun."

"Thanks, again, Jim." One of the men shook the SecDef's hand one last time. "And he is a fucking idiot."

SecDef grasped the man's hand longer than was appropriate and pulled him close. "Bill, I've known you for over twenty years now; we served together. But don't ever say that in this building. Don't ever say that in front of me. And if you want the President to listen to anything you have to say, don't ever, ever let him hear you say that. Don't even let him imagine you saying that, because I won't be able to get you back in the building."

Martin only barely heard the last two sentences, as he had directed the other visitors to follow him and had turned his back on the conversation to show them out. He didn't hear Bill's response, but he did hear his footsteps as he rushed to catch up to them.

"I know Jim values our opinions, but if the President doesn't, is it even worth it coming here?" one of the men asked the group.

"Maybe we should have this discussion in the car, and not here in the White House," Bill said.

Martin chuckled. It seemed like Bill took the SecDef's hint.

"Excuse me."

Martin felt a tap on his shoulder. He turned to see that it was the third man who had tapped him.

"You've worked in the White House for quite a while. What's it like working for President Drumpf?"

'Danger, Will Robinson,' popped into Martin's head. He had never been put on the spot by a visitor to the White House before. He struggled to think of something to say that wouldn't come back to haunt him

The experts all laughed. He must have made a face that they noticed.

'Shit!' Martin thought. "Sir. It's an honor to serve the American people."

"Good answer, young man," the lady said, and to the other experts, "You shouldn't corner him like that. You're going to get him in trouble."

"I feel like all of us are in trouble," the third man said. They all laughed again.

They emerged into a bright spring afternoon. Two sedans pulled up to the curb.

"Ma'am, sirs. These cars will take you back to where you need to go. Have a good afternoon."

The experts climbed into their cars, and the cars pulled away.

'That was close,' Martin thought. As he stood there and watched the cars disappear into the Washington, DC traffic, Martin stopped to wonder what, if anything, he did think about serving in the Drumpf White House. He had been working for almost four months in the administration. He realized that he hadn't really developed any strong opinions one way or another.

'It's strange,' he thought, 'working in the White House, but all staffers from all times probably think so.' It was certainly different from any job he ever considered having.

He took one last deep breath of fresh air and then turned to re-enter the West Wing. It was time to head back to his small office, sit down in his uncomfortable chair, and do the business of the nation.

·   ·   ·

Martin decided to stop by the Oval Office before returning to his cramped office in the basement. At the very least, he'd be able to enjoy the sunlight for a few more minutes before returning to the dungeon.

Approaching the Oval, Martin saw that Phil was on duty. It was always nice to see him.

"Oval's closed," Phil said.

That was a surprise. Martin had checked the schedule before coming. It had been empty.

"What's going on?" Martin asked.

"Conference with Mogul's personal lawyers," Phil said. "And Watterhoot's orders."

"Since when do you take orders from her?"

Phil just smirked, as if to say, 'You know we don't.'

"They're discussing the Meiller investigation," Phil said.

'Don't want anything to do with that,' Martin thought. "Got it, thanks."

Martin turned and headed back toward his office. It was the one topic that the President never discussed in front of Martin. The staffers-are-deaf-and-invisible view didn't apply to the Meiller investigation at all. To Martin's knowledge, there were no other topics that simply were not discussed in front of staffers. Meiller's investigation was the one, and Martin was glad for that. It could throw the President into alternating bouts of rage, misery, and paranoia. Strong Presidential emotions were always dangerous for the worker bees.

GAME OF THRONES

"Jermanski," Martin said into the phone. He listened for a moment, a perplexed look spreading across his face.

It was obvious that Amanda picked up on his confusion.

"Okay. I understand," Martin said into the phone and then hung up.

"What was that about?" Amanda forgot to add 'bitch.' She must have been genuinely curious.

"I don't know."

"What do you mean, you don't know?"

"I'm not sure. I've been invited to the eleven o'clock in the Oval Office."

"That makes no sense!" said Amanda.

"I know it!"

"Well, what do you mean, invited?" Amanda asked.

"Literally, invited. It was Rob, sounding extremely formal."

"You're telling me that Rob called you to invite you to a meeting in the Oval Office?" Amanda burst out into laughter.

Martin actually chuckled in spite of himself. "What is it?"

"It's genius!" Amanda laughed some more; she couldn't help herself. "Ah, shit!" She scowled and then laughed some more.

Martin had no clue what was going on. "What?"

"Ah, fuck," Amanda shook her head. "I may as well tell you. I gave it away now."

"What?!"

"It's a prank! Classic!" she said between bouts of laughter. "Although it hasn't been used in, shit, months. I wonder whose idea it was…"

"What do you mean?"

"Rob pranked you," Amanda said, as if speaking to a child. "You haven't been invited to any Oval Office meeting."

"He sounded pretty serious." Martin wasn't sure whether he should believe her or not.

"Listen. It happened to just about everyone, all of the junior staffers, back in the Priebus days. Barely a day went by without some staffer finding herself in an embarrassing situation. And they were always put in that situation by the other staffers!"

She definitely sounded convincing. Martin thought for a moment and then picked up the phone. He punched in a quick number.

"Yeah, this is Jermanski. Is Rob there?" Martin listened for a moment. "Really? I like, literally, just got off the phone with him." He listened some more. "Okay, thanks." He hung up.

"He wasn't there, was he?" Amanda.

"No," Martin answered.

"Classic move. Now you'll wonder." Again as if speaking to a child, and then Amanda frowned. "Shit! I ruined it. I should've kept my mouth shut."

Martin was wondering. He looked up at the wall clock. Seven minutes to eleven. He stood up. "I'm going to take a little walk."

"I bet you are, bitch! They got you, hook, line, and sinker!" Amanda laughed more. "Go check!"

Martin had already left their office and was walking toward the Oval.

"Just do it in a way that doesn't embarrass you," Amanda called out, loud enough for him to hear several paces down the hallway.

Martin moved quickly for most of the trip and then slowed to a nonchalant amble as he drew closer. He attempted to feign indifference. Then he put on a businesslike frown. Then he tried to wipe the frown from his face. He wasn't sure if he succeeded.

"Martin!" It was one of the other staffers, coming in the opposite direction. "I saw your name on the eleven o'clock. What gives?"

'Was this guy in on the joke?' Martin wondered. "What do you mean?"

"Of all the attendees, you are by far the most junior."

"Oh. Well, what can I say?" What *could* he say?

The only answer was a puzzled look, and then they were past one another. Martin checked his watch. Three minutes. He needed to either march straight into the Oval Office as someone who belonged or decide right then to turn around and return to his own shabby, little office.

He drew closer. He felt his face grow hot. He didn't know what to do.

Down the hallway and around a slight corner, the door to the Oval was open. Chad was standing next to it. People were filing in.

Martin continued to approach. 'Shit, shit, shit.'

He and Chad made eye contact. 'Chad is a good guy,' Martin thought. 'He'll give me some kind of signal.' Martin stepped closer.

Chad gave him no signal. 'Shit.'

'Nothing? Come on, Chad,' Martin wanted to scream. And then he was past the Secret Service Agent and in the Oval. He looked around and breathed a sigh of relief; he realized there was still time to excuse himself if necessary.

The Chief of Staff! Martin was sure that Kellner would signal him in some way, whether he should stay or go. The man didn't need words to get his point across.

Martin tried to make eye contact. It shouldn't have been so difficult. Kellner scanned the room before every meeting—it must have been a Marine thing.

Why didn't Kellner look at him? Wait, yes! No. Kellner looked right past him. 'Seriously?' Martin could only think of the line from the Princess Bride: 'Inconceivable!'

"Ladies and gentlemen," one of the principals began.

The President was staring off into space, seemingly bored.

Martin swung his eyes back to Kellner, and they made eye contact!

Kellner gave him no signal. Nothing.

"Thank you for being here this morning," the principal continued.

Martin looked to his left and right. Maybe he was mistaken; maybe Kellner and he hadn't made eye contact.

Martin began to slide toward the door. It was only a few paces behind him, because he hadn't moved too far into the room when he arrived. He bumped into someone. "Sorry."

The principal was talking again, but Martin was more interested in affecting his escape. He made it to the door. And then he made eye contact with Kellner again; he was sure this time. And Kellner gave him the 'what-do-you-think-you're-doing?' face. Martin stopped in his tracks and then took a step away from the door. Kellner gave him the slightest nod.

Maybe he *was* actually invited. 'Shit. Maybe I should pay attention.'

"As you all know, the midterms are coming up at the end of the year. It's an important time for the country, a very important time," Drumpf said.

Martin wasn't sure how long the President had been speaking.

"It's a great time to be President," Drumpf continued. "Our fellow Republicans, however, might not enjoy how things go."

"Sir. It could be dangerous for you if enough Republicans lose in the midterms," Mark Skort, Director of Legislative Affairs, said. "If the Democrats win control of the House and narrow their deficit in the Senate, they may try to push ahead with—"

"Don't say that word!" Drumpf interrupted. "Do not say it."

"Mr. President," Steve Mills interjected. "We have to be ready for every eventuality."

"Nothing can happen to me," Drumpf said shaking his head. "My base wouldn't allow it. Can you imagine what would happen if... Do you know how they would react?"

"That might not necessarily be a good thing," said Skort.

"Mr. President," said Andy Breiburg, Director of the Domestic Policy Council. "I think there's something that you haven't considered."

"I'm sure I have," the President shot back. "I'm extremely intelligent." He paused, and his eyes roamed across the room. "But what is it you think I haven't considered?"

"Mr. President," Breiburg continued. "Who stands to gain the most from your possible im—"

"Don't say that word!" Drumpf almost shouted.

Breiburg cleared his throat. "From a possible shift of power in Congress?"

"The Democrats, obviously," Drumpf deadpanned.

"Well, yes, sir," Breiburg responded. "But who else?"

The President didn't answer.

Martin braced himself. Breiburg was right on the border of lecturing to the President. That always ended poorly.

"Who would benefit the most if you were to... have to leave office?" Breiburg asked.

"Hillary?" Drumpf asked, growing exasperated with the questions, but seemingly willing to play along.

Several people in the Oval Office laughed. Clinton was always an easy target. Breiburg even laughed but then cleared his throat and waited for the chuckles to subside.

"Actually, sir, I was referring to your Vice, Mike Spence."

The room instantly became silent.

Even Martin was shocked; he looked around to try to gage the reaction. Frowns, stone faces, a few seemingly interested in hearing more, but no agreement. 'Does Breiburg really think he can say such a thing and keep his job in the administration?' Martin wondered. He turned to look at the President.

Drumpf sat in silence, pondering the statement. He looked into space, made the standard Drumpf-'Meh' face, and then focused his eyes back on Breiburg. "I didn't expect that. Tell me more."

Martin glanced around the room again. 'Who,' he asked himself, 'in the Oval Office would report this back to the Vice President? Surely, Spence has spies here.'

"Sir, Spence was on the road to being a one-term Governor. His views, while we agree with them, weren't helping his popularity in Indiana. In fact, the Indiana Republican Party was openly defying their Governor. You saved his career."

The President smiled at the last comment.

"He was going to lose his re-election bid. If you hadn't chosen him to be your Vice President, his political career would have ended, and he would have returned to being a lawyer or television talk show host or whatever it is he did before he entered Congress back in 2001."

Martin scanned the room. Still mostly stone faces, but a few more seemed interested. No one appeared openly hostile.

"It was as if you had reached down from on high and plucked him from a future of obscurity. You saved him!" Breiburg paused; he was trying to choose his next words carefully. "Now, having Spence on your ticket certainly helped your election, especially with the 'value voters.'"

Martin glanced at Drumpf. The President typically didn't like other people receiving any credit for his successes. But Drumpf was obviously intrigued by Breiburg's argument.

"But your choosing him was much more valuable to Spence than he's been to you." Breiburg's voice changed; he seemed to stand a little taller and speak a little louder.

It seemed to Martin that Breiburg's confidence grew. He was genuinely curious to see where this was going to lead.

"Now look at the situation from his perspective," Breiburg continued. "He's been loyal to you and can continue to be loyal to you, but if you were to be…removed from office, he'd become President."

Drumpf was fully on board the argument at this point. His eyes squinted in his 'deep-thought' expression. He was nodding absently.

Breiburg was obviously relishing the President's attention. "From sinking into obscurity in his podunk state to becoming President of the United States in just over two years, without having to be elected, without doing a thing on his own. He becomes the next Gerald Ford!"

"Gerald Ford?" Drumpf sat up straight. "What the hell does the aircraft carrier have to do with Spence? It's that goddamned electronic thingy…What's it called? They should have used steam. The Navy screwed up on that one, I can tell you that. They need Albert Einstein to get that thing to work."

"Uh, yes, sir. The Navy may have made a mistake," Breiburg said, not quite sure how to continue. "But I was referring to President Gerald Ford, who became President after Nixon resigned, following his impeachment."

"Goddamned it!" the President yelled at Breiburg, who visibly cringed. "Do NOT say that fucking word in my Oval Office!"

"I'm sorry, Mr. President. It slipped. It won't—"

"Mr. President," Mills interrupted. "Despite the poor choice of words, Andy's point is valid. Under the right circumstances, the Vice President could be a threat to you."

"But he's the Vice President," Drumpf protested. "Mike's a decent guy."

"There are lots of people who are *decent*, sir. Some Democrats are decent, maybe even some *liberals*. But decent does not mean not a threat."

"You two. You might be on to something. So what if Mike is a threat? What do we do?" Drumpf looked around at the entire room. "Can I fire him?"

"Sir, I don't think that's possible." It was Kelly Conville.

Martin hadn't even noticed her. Had she been there the whole time?

"Kelly, why not?" Drumpf seemed annoyed. "Does anyone know for sure?"

"Sir," said the Chief of Staff. "The Vice President doesn't serve at your pleasure, which means you can't fire him. The closest you could do is choose a different running mate for your reelection campaign."

"John, is that true?" the President asked. "Of course, it is. You wouldn't tell me if it wasn't. But it's a stupid rule. Are we sure that it applies to me?"

"Yes, sir," Conville said. "It applies even to you."

"Yeah, but my base would defend it," Drumpf insisted. "They'd defend the decision. We need to have Shawn talk about it. He can get out in front of it; we can even make it seem like it was his idea."

Several people in the room were shaking their head 'no,' but none of them seemed willing to open their mouth.

The Chief of Staff breathed an exasperated sigh. "Mr. President, that wouldn't be wise," Kellner warned.

"Dammit, John," the President blurted. "It's still a good idea."

"We can't remove him from office, unless we found reason to have Congress impeach him," Conville said. "Or we could force him to resign."

"Dammit, Kelly," Drumpf fumed. "Do not use that word in this office!"

"What would even be an ..." Drumpf started and then stopped himself. "What could he be removed for?"

"Sir, none of our legal experts are here today—"

"Who called this meeting without inviting the lawyers?" stormed the President, looking around angrily. "Where's Dan? Where is he?"

"I'm not sure where Dan is, sir, but we can have an answer for you by tomorrow," Conville said in a soothing voice. "I'll take care of it personally, Mr. President."

"Listen, people," Drumpf was obviously annoyed. "There is a White House Counsel. His name is Dan McGohn. He's extremely important to me. Who called this meeting without Dan?!"

"Mr. President," Kellner said. "Dan has been in communication with the Meiller team; it's been occupying a lot of his time."

The President just shook his head and fumed. "Okay. Fine. Fine. Dan needs to talk to those treasonous idiots. I get it. But back to Mike. What about him resigning? Do you think he would, if I asked him?"

About five different people answered the question with a brisk "No, sir."

Drumpf sat back in his chair, not expecting that response to his question. "Wow. Okay. So what do we do then? No...removal. No resignation. What?"

Martin looked around the room again. He couldn't believe the conversation. *Surely* someone here would blab to Spence.

REELECTION STRATEGIES

"We need to take the midterms seriously," Breiburg said. "We need to go on the offensive. We need to support the Republican candidates, actively campaign for them. Only by keeping the Republicans in power can we prevent … threats to your presidency."

The President seemed convinced. "But what about Spence?"

"If you're safe," Breiburg answered, "then he isn't a threat. He can remain the V.P. until the end of your first term."

The President stared long and hard at Breiburg. It seemed to Martin that he had said the word 'impeachment' one too many times. If he wasn't careful, he would be gone long before the Vice President.

"And you can decide then," Kelly Conville interjected, "whether or not to keep him as your Vice President."

"I can choose another running mate," Drumpf stated, repeating what Kellner had told him only a few minutes prior. "And I have two years to figure that out."

"Just don't choose Sarah Palin," Conville offered.

Several people in the Oval Office laughed at the joke. Even Drumpf smirked at it.

"I can't," responded the President. "She's my Ambassador to Nambia."

Several people in the room laughed at what they believed was a joke. Others, including the President, didn't see the humor. Very quickly, those that were laughing stopped.

"Mr. President," a principal began.

But the Chief of Staff, to the President's side and just behind him, firmly shook his head 'No.' Martin was confused; did Kellner know what the principal was about to propose?

"Yes?" Drumpf asked.

Kellner continued to shake his head and shot the principal a very clear message with his eyes.

"I'm sorry, sir. Nevermind."

"What? Nevermind? I've never heard that from you before."

"Sir." Kellner decided it was time to move the discussion forward. "The purpose of this meeting is to plan your election-related activities leading up to the midterms."

"Good point, John. Thank you. Yes. Does anyone have any ideas?"

"Mr. President," Conville spoke up. "Most states have primaries starting in the early part of the summer. One priority needs to be choosing who you plan to support in each of those primaries and then putting the word out."

"Of course," the President responded, not very impressed with the suggestion.

"Sir," Steven Mills spoke up. "We need to stick to our guns on those policies that your base is pleased with. Immigration. And others. Some legislative victories would help, as well."

"Kelly, Steve, I love you. Both of you. I do," Drumpf said. "But those are obvious suggestions. Someone give me something strong. Does anyone have any suggestions worthy of the Drumpf name?"

"More personal interviews, sir?"

Martin didn't see who made the suggestion from his spot near the wall. But he did see John Kellner shake his head negatively.

"What do you mean?" Drumpf asked.

"An interview, or interviews, with friendly personalities for you to showcase what you've done for the nation. A chance for you to speak directly to your base, the whole nation, explaining what voting Republican in the midterms means for the country."

Kellner continued to shake his head 'No' out of view of the President.

Then Drumpf turned to the Chief of Staff, who perfectly timed stopping his head. "John?"

"It's risky, sir."

"Risky?" the President asked incredulously. "There's no interviewer I can't handle. It's a great idea. I won the election by speaking directly to the American people. I should speak to them more. I haven't done it enough, lately." The President nodded his head. "It's brilliant. I'm glad I thought of it."

"I'll prepare a list of interviewers for you to choose from," Conville offered.

"Thanks, Kelly. Look, I already know what I want. It has to be a 'she'. Young. Blond. Attractive. Smart, but not too smart. A firm conservative." The President paused. "Actually, the conservative part isn't as important as the rest. Doesn't really matter."

"Toni Lahren?" someone suggested.

"No," Conville responded. "Has to be someone more established."

"Is Lahren the one that—" the President began to ask.

The Chief of Staff gently cut him off, "Yes, sir."

Martin was curious to know what the President was going to ask. Kellner shook his head slightly.

"We'll get you a list, sir," Conville stated.

"Got it. Okay, so what else?"

"He could write a book," Martin said quietly, loud enough only for the people around him to hear. Unfortunately, it seemed that the Chief of Staff heard as well; he shot Martin a dagger of a look.

A few of the people that heard Martin nodded their heads.

Martin, encouraged by their agreement, asked rhetorically, "What if he released a book this fall, just before the midterms?"

More heads nodded. And the Chief of Staff again eyed him dangerously.

But Drumpf had obviously not heard the suggestion. He looked around in frustration. "You are supposedly my core group, my key advisors. Does anyone else have any ideas?"

"Perhaps you could write a book?"

It was Martin's idea! And it was stolen, just like that. (Actually it was his mother's idea, before he even moved to DC, but who's going to quibble?)

"Say that again?" asked the President.

"Yes, sir. A book. Released just before the midterms. Everybody knows that you became an international phenomenon after you released *The Art of the Deal*. Perhaps it's time for another book."

The President broke in to a huge grin. "Now that's a brilliant idea. A book. I could write a book and release it just before the midterms."

It seemed to Martin that the President just stole the idea that was stolen from him. Everyone in the White House knew that the best ideas came directly from the President's mind. 'Karma's a bitch,' he thought.

"Well, it's gotta have a catchy title and a good cover," Drumpf said. "Of course, it'll have the Drumpf name on it. That will guarantee sales. Think of the sales!"

"Sales are not the concern, Mr. President," Steven Mills spoke up.

Drumpf frowned immediately and squinted hard at his advisor.

But Mills continued before the President could protest. "We know your name'll drive sales. Everyone understands that. No name has ever driven success like Drumpf."

The President seemed to relax a bit.

"The message is more important. It has to be your best book yet. It has to be honest, down to earth; it has to tell your story, even to people who may not want to hear it."

The President's hackles were rising again. "Down to earth? There is nothing about Drumpf that is down to earth! And my story? Who wouldn't want to hear my story?!"

"You're absolutely right, as always, sir," Mills began to back-pedal. "There's nothing down to earth about your name. But you need to speak in a way that those Americans who are down to earth … So that they get it, so that they can understand your greatness."

The President calmed again.

"We need those people, few as they are, who don't like you to hear your story. We need to convince moderates, even liberals, that you're best for the nation. That Republicans are best for the midterms."

"Steve. The people who are too stupid to see that now, I don't think we'll be able to get through to them," Drumpf pushed back. "The Hillary-lovers, the Benghazi-deniers, the Bernie-ites. They wouldn't know the truth if it punched them in the face."

"With the right book, sir, they could," Conville said. It seemed she just had to jump in. "With the right co-author, they could. With the right message, they *would*."

Drumpf sat considering her words. He didn't seem convinced.

Martin grew frustrated. The President was actually considering his idea, and he wasn't going to get the credit for it.

"Who's going to write the thing?" Drumpf asked.

"I'll get you a list for that, too," Conville answered.

"Kelly, how many lists are you getting for me?"

"Well, sir. A list for interviewers. And a list for authors," she answered.

"Are you also going to get me a chopping list, Kelly?"

Several people in the room laughed at the President's joke. Martin didn't. It wasn't that funny.

Conville didn't get the humor either. "Do you need me to, sir?"

Drumpf laughed. "Ah, Kelly. You know I love you. I really do."

"Daddy!" Ivania called out. "I think you *should* write a book; it's a great idea and will only burnish the brand. 'Art of the Deal.' 'Art of the Comeback.' It should be called 'Art of the…' something."

"Ivania. You're right!" Drumpf agreed and then opened his arms wide to the entire room. "She's beautiful, everyone, isn't she? And brilliant. My daughter is a true American treasure. We're lucky to have her in the White House."

One or two people clapped briefly, and then several others joined them. For a moment, the entire Oval Office, including the President, was clapping for his daughter. Martin clapped as well, although he wasn't sure why. At the very least, it was better to be part of the crowd than not.

"So what should it be?" the President asked.

"Art of the Midterms!" someone called out.

Drumpf responded with his classic 'What? Are you kidding me?' look. "We can do better than that! Surely."

"Art of the Election!"

Drumpf shrugged. "That's better, but we've already won. And the media has already written all about how I won. Most of it was lies, fake news, unfair and slanderous. But it's been written."

"You could set the record straight, Mr. President," Mills offered.

Drumpf considered it.

"We could gather a list of title suggestions from the entire staff," Conville said.

"Are you going to put that list together for me, as well, Kelly?" Drumpf asked with a grin on his face. "But she's right. We don't need to come up with a title right now. There's plenty of time for that."

'Art of the Presidency,' Martin thought to himself. It was the obvious title. He considered opening his mouth, but then reconsidered. There was no way he was going to spill that one in this group. Art of the Presidency. It had a nice ring to it. He really liked it.

Perhaps he could mention the idea to the President casually, when picking up shred or at some point when they cross paths. Martin also knew he'd have to make the President believe that it was *his* idea. That was the only way to accomplish anything.

He could suggest the title and then offer to write it as well. Unless there was someone on Conville's list who was a known or better author. He had to get in the President's ear sooner rather than later.

"But listen, everyone. I think this has been a great meeting; it's been good to talk to you all today, to hear your thoughts. You've done good work, you, Steve, you, Kelly, with your lists, everyone."

Martin didn't know it at the time, but he would soon learn that this was the President's way of cutting the meeting short. Regardless of what the agenda said, or the President's official schedule, when the President was done, the meeting ended.

People who were sitting started to stand. Those who were already standing began preparing to leave the Oval Office.

Apparently, the President wasn't done talking. "I have to tell you, though. I'm still not sure the Democrats are a threat to me in the midterms. Or after. I just don't see it. My approval ratings are fantastic. We're making progress on a host of issues. America is great again."

Some people sat back down. Others fidgeted. One or two listened with rapt attention. Martin was ready to go. He still wasn't sure if he had been pranked or not. Was he supposed to have attended the meeting?

"Do you still want those lists, sir?" Conville asked the President.

"Sure, Kelly. I'll look at them. I read everything you put in front of me, you know." Drumpf smiled, as if he made a joke. "But one thing that we will continue is our rallies. And many of you help organize those rallies, and you do great work. They are how we get our message out to the American people. I talk to them face to face. And they love it. They LOVE it! They eat it up!"

The President seemed to run out of things to say. The Oval Office fell into an awkward silence.

After a moment, the Chief of Staff cleared his throat and then spoke up. "That's all for today, ladies and gentlemen. Thank you. Have a good afternoon."

Doors opened, and people began to file from the office. Martin watched as some of the President's closest advisors approached his desk. Ivania. Steve Mills. Conville. For a brief moment, Martin considered walking up to the desk to offer to write the book. He didn't.

THE INTERVIEW

Martin and a small group of the President's staffers, including Amanda, were gathered in a small studio. They had verified the décor, based upon the President's very specific wishes, and verified that the President's seat was a few inches higher than the interviewer's. The President was set to arrive at any time, meet with his hair and makeup team, and start the interview as quickly as possible.

The decision had been made to tape at least one interview with a friendly "personality." This was to be the first of those interviews.

"Have you seen his hair and makeup done?" Amanda asked.

"No," Martin said. "This is my first time anywhere close to the President and a television interview."

"That's the thing. Almost no one has," Amanda said. "Bet he comes in, and everything's done."

"That might explain why I can't get a hold of his hair or makeup teams," Martin muttered.

The next person to enter the room was the interviewee, a twenty-nine year old blonde woman, dressed to perfection. Martin found her to be decidedly attractive.

Amanda approached her and thrust out her hand. "Ms. Cornacre, good afternoon. My name is Amanda Chung; I'm one of the

President's staffers. He's set to arrive momentarily. Do you need anything?"

Cornacre seemed surprised that someone was speaking to her. "I'm sorry," she said, looking down at Amanda and her outstretched hand. "Who are you?"

Martin cringed. Although her back was to him, he could sense Amanda's instant rage. But he was impressed by her control.

"Yes," Amanda said. "I'm one of the President's assistants. We've already arranged the studio, but I wanted to know if there is anything you need, before he arrives."

"Oh. Well," Cornacre said. "Amanda? No. I don't think there's anything you can do for me." She turned her back on Amanda and walked to speak to the tech staff.

Amanda spun on her heel and marched back to Martin. Her teeth were clenched; her eyes were wide; and her fists were rolled into white-knuckled balls. Martin had never seen her so angry.

"Fucking bitch," she muttered. "Learn some fucking manners, you fucking fake-blond, pretend-conservative, cock-sucking television whore."

Martin bit the inside of his lip. He wasn't sure how Amanda would respond if he failed to stifle his laughter.

The President entered the room only a moment later. As Amanda had predicted, his hair and makeup were already done. He walked directly to his seat and sat down in it without saying a word to anyone.

Cornacre, who had been talking to sound and video since Amanda had greeted her, left them and walked to the President.

Drumpf immediately stood up and smiled widely. "Leslie, right? It's so good for you, to meet me."

"Mr. President!" Cornacre began. Whereas she had seemed a flaming bitch toward Amanda, her entire demeanor was different toward the President. She returned his smile with a wider one; her eyes seemed to sparkle unnaturally. "It is so nice to meet you!"

Martin only shook his head. He'd never received that treatment from any female but had seen it often enough. Amanda, standing beside him, groaned loudly.

"I'm sure that it is, Leslie. You're not going to be too rough on me this afternoon, are you?"

"I would only be rough with you if you wanted it, sir," Leslie replied with a sly laugh.

Amanda made a loud gagging sound.

Martin shushed her. She was *extremely* loud.

"I'm sure you would, Leslie," Drumpf said. "You're a very beautiful young woman. Very beautiful. How long have you been appearing on television?"

Martin was sure that the President knew the answer to his question. Actually, Martin knew that the President had been briefed on it—whether he actually knew it or not was up for debate. But it had been part of the vetting process that the higher-ups used to determine the interviewer.

"Four years now, sir," Cornacre replied. "But you are, by far, my most prestigious interview."

At the mention of her four years on television, Martin thought back to the Oval Office discussion where it was decided that Ms. Cornacre would be chosen to interview Drumpf. Someone had joked with the President that he had been giving interviews since Leslie was in diapers, and actually longer.

The President had said, "I bet she was a beautiful little baby, in her diapers."

"She's fucking disgusting," Amanda said under her breath.

"You know, Leslie, most interviewers tell me the exact same thing. It's not surprising. But let's get this thing started. We can talk more afterward."

"Of course, sir, of course," she said. "I'd very much like that."

'She's pouring it on pretty thick,' Martin thought. He didn't look at Amanda standing next to him for fear of laughing at what he saw. But he could sense the disgust and contempt radiating from her.

The interview started only minutes later.

"As you know, I am very lucky to be sitting with the President of the United States tonight, Mr. Ronald Drumpf. President Drumpf has graciously agreed to answer questions that might be a little off-topic, perhaps a little strange to those familiar with more mainstream reporting. We have—"

"Thanks, Leslie," Drumpf interrupted, seemingly oblivious to the fact that she was not close to being finished with her introduction. "I wanted to come and speak to your audience today for a number of reasons."

"First, let's face it: I'm the greatest modern President that the nation has ever had. And that's not speaking just for our great nation. I am the greatest elected leader in the world—bar none. Not only that, I'm the greatest President in, well, since I've been alive. Perhaps even longer. Has there ever been a President as interesting, or as successful as me? I tell you: No! For thirty years—even longer!—the Drumpf name has been synonymous with strength, wealth, success! Success! The Drumpf name is a winning name. And I'm a winner.

"So, of course, I'm sure we'll talk about me for a bit, but we also need to talk about Hillary. You know, Hillary is not Presidential. She didn't deserve to be President; she was never going to win. Now, Leslie, I've known Hillary for a long time, many years. I know her to be many things, but she is not Presidential. When Americans think about their Presidents, they want them to be attractive. Hillary, and I love her, known her for many years, is not a very attractive person. The American people and they are the best judge, would have never elected her. She's not good looking enough."

"Agree or disagree with his politics, Barack Obama was a handsome man. He was; he is. But Hillary isn't. And can you imagine Madelaine Albright being elected President? No! Of course not. Qualified? Probably. Capable? Yes. But the American people would *never* elect Madelaine Albright—she is *not* a good looking lady. And for the same reason, they would've never elected Hillary Clinton.

"Lastly, I'm sure that your audience…" Drumpf paused and looked around at the studio in which they sat. It appeared as if it was the first time that he had actually taken the time to look around.

The studio was well-lit, immaculate in the 2010's style of sleek minimalism, identical in that way to many of the studios that the Ronald sat in. Several cameras pointed at him from all angles. Bright lights, blinding, so Drumpf squinted to see the studio.

Martin was paying close attention to the President. Several days prior, he had complained that all studios used lighting that was too hot, that made him sweat, that risked ruining his immaculate hair. In choosing this studio, they had selected one that used only LED lighting, in an attempt to keep the President cool. He couldn't tell if the President noticed or not.

Martin was also concerned that the President would notice that there was no studio audience, something that Drumpf had asked for. There had been no time to arrange it.

"I'm sure that your audience will be interested in some of my policy ideas." The President paused, and Leslie opened her mouth to speak. But if she was hoping to re-assert her control of the interview, Leslie was going to be disappointed. Drumpf started up again quickly. "You know, I've taken some heat from you, a lot from the rest of the media, about some of my policies, about how they differ from typical Republican policies. As we approach the midterm elections, I hope to clarify some of my ideas. It's important that the American people know what they'll get when they vote for Republicans this fall. Let's do our part to help them out during this interview."

Drumpf paused again, briefly, and glanced at his interviewer.

Martin thought that he could tell what the President was thinking: 'Long blond hair. Extremely attractive.'

"Leslie?" Drumpf playfully chided her when she didn't immediately respond. She was supposedly an experienced interviewer, but the President was a more-experienced interviewee.

"Yes, Mr. President. I think the audience would be interested in all of those things, and perhaps other topics as well. I know that you are aware of the nature of my show. Surprises do sometimes happen."

"Leslie, I've been interviewed by Howard Stern on his show. I don't think anything here will equal what I've seen, what I've done, on his show," Drumpf said. And then his wide smile twisted into a leer. "Although, maybe you'll surprise me?"

Cornacre seemed to ignore the comment.

"Mr. President, it's true that you tend to refer to yourself as 'The Ronald', is it not?"

"Yes, Leslie. I'm known as 'The Ronald' in many places. It's who I am. Ronald Drumpf, 'The Ronald.'"

"Can you tell us about the time that you sued McDonald's, claiming that their 'Ronald McDonald' character infringed on your name?"

"Leslie, listen, you know that just isn't true. It's not true. I never sued McDonald's. Look, I *love* McDonald's hamburgers. The … The Whopper is my favorite. And Ronald McDonald is one of my favorite clowns!"

"But Mr. Drumpf—"

"Hear me out, Leslie. It's rude to interrupt. I can assure you that I never sued McDonald's. And I can tell you why: One. I only choose to sue when I'm going to win. I'm the best, and I have the best legal team. We only sue to win. I have won every suit of which I was a part. Every single one. I'm a winner, Leslie, and I only win when I sue. If I won, I'd certainly tell you about it. You know that I am not shy about telling you anything. Just ask me—I'll tell you anything."

"Two. McDonald's is an American institution. It is truly one of the great American success stories. Ray Kroc was a great businessman. It would be foolish to sue such a storied company. And I'm not foolish. My legal team, for the money that I pay them, they aren't foolish. They're the best."

"Have I ever told you about the time that I met Ray Kroc? Great businessman; great American. And I gave him a tip or two. You know that McDonald's is mainly in the real estate business.

Everyone thinks it's in the hamburger business, but it's really a real estate company. And if there's one thing that I know, it's real estate. It was in the late 70s. Ray Kroc came to me with some questions about McDonald's operations, and store placement. Now I don't know hamburgers, but I do know real estate. I gave him a tip or two, some advice, answered some of his questions. From that conversation, he built several new McDonald's at locations that he hadn't previously considered. And they took off. They took off! They became some of his best-selling, highest-performing franchises."

"But I'm also sure that you know, Leslie, that I love McDonald's food. I love it. All of it! Their fries, their burgers, their milkshakes! Love it all."

"Mr. President. Is it true that one of the main reasons that you eat McDonald's foods is that you are paranoid of other food? That you are afraid that someone might try to poison you?"

"Fake news, Leslie, fake news. That's an urban legend spread by the liars in the liberal media. And by that author in his hateful, poorly written book. I like McDonald's, because it tastes good. And like me, McDonald's is an American icon. McDonald's IS America. Just like Ronald Drumpf is America."

"Speaking of America. Do you know that I have several officers, from our Armed Forces, the greatest Armed Forces the world has ever seen, but several officers who work very closely with me? They carry the 'football.' You know the football – it's actually a briefcase, and it contains the launch codes to our nuclear arsenal. One of those officers, a naval officer, a submariner, brilliant guy, he told me something the other day that I had never heard before."

"When the commanding officer of one of our Navy ships comes onto the ship or leaves the ship, there is a sailor who announces it. So, let's say the name of the ship is the 'USS Enterprise.' When that commander gets to his ship, the sailor will announce, 'Enterprise, arriving.' Fantastic, isn't it? But that announcement isn't only for the commander of that ship, but also for other visiting dignitaries. Do you know how that sailor would announce it if I arrived?" He paused, waiting for her to answer the question.

"Uh, no, Mr. President. I don't." She was slightly flustered. He didn't notice, or at least didn't care.

"That's okay, Leslie. Neither did I. But I'll tell you. When I go to a ship, that sailor would announce it by saying, 'United States, arriving!' United States – that's me! He would announce it by calling me 'United States.' So like I said – McDonald's is America. Ronald Drumpf is the United States, is America!"

"But remember. Ray Kroc and I were good friends. He asked me if I like his food. Of course, I said, yes. That was when we talked about locations for restaurants, when I gave him my expert recommendations."

Cornacre shifted in her seat and leaned forward slightly. With a very serious expression on her face, she said, "Mr. President, what do you think of your portrayal on Saturday Night Live?"

"Saturday Night Live? Look, Lorne Michaels and I go way back. I've known Lorne for years. Many, many years. It's impossible to be a celebrity in New York City and not cross paths with each other. And I consider him a friend, okay? A good friend. And as you know, I hosted Saturday Night Live back in 2015. And I was one of their best, funniest hosts ever. And that episode had some of the highest ratings that Saturday Night Live ever experienced. I really enjoyed my time there – although some of those actors could probably learn some things from me. Some aren't as funny as I am. Not even close. And I told Lorne that. I tried to give him some advice, advice to make the show even better. I don't think they took any of my suggestions, which is a shame … "

"But, listen. What they've been doing lately is shameful. It's not funny. It's terrible. It's disrespectful and inappropriate. Although, I will admit that their Steve Banyan—Death—that was pretty funny. But whoever is impersonating me – Alec Baldwin? Alec should know better. He's really just ruining his career. No one in Hollywood is going to want to hire him after this."

"You do know that the show has a long history of impersonating Presidents?" Cornacre asked. "Dan Aykroyd lampooned President Carter. Several people did the same for Ronald Reagan. Dana Carvey acted as George H. W. Bush. Will Ferrell did Bush."

"Listen. Most of those actors were funny. Those skits were funny. Dana Carvey was hilarious. But Alec Baldwin just isn't funny. He's not funny at all. What is that face he makes? He doesn't even look like me. It's disgraceful, really. Disgraceful and sad. It's a shame, actually. He was funny on Thirty Rock, but he's not funny now. It's too bad, too bad."

"I do have to say that my favorite Saturday Night Live actor to impersonate a President was Will Ferrell. Will is a funny, funny man. Funny, and he was in a movie many years ago. Well, he's been in a lot of movies, I guess, but he was in one years ago. It was the ice skating movie. He played the ice skater. Do you know why I like that movie so much? I like it, because I gave Will some ideas that he used in that movie. Some of the funniest parts of that movie came from me, my mind. He got the idea from me."

"You mean 'Blades of Glory,' Mr. President?" she asked.

"'Blades of Glory!' Yes, that was it. You remembered its name – I'm impressed. The ice skater in 'Blades of Glory' owned a brush. He was very attached to that brush. He loved that brush, was very proud of it, because he used it to brush his hair, which was fantastic, by the way. He kept the brush in a special box, didn't let anyone else touch it. Will got the idea for that brush from me. Will and I met a few years before that movie, and I was sharing with him some of my hair care secrets. I told him about my hair, my brushing, and the special brushes that I use. I even showed him some of my brushes. He loved it, loved them all. Years later, he told me that my brushes were the inspiration for his brush in that movie. True story. You can ask Will himself."

"Maybe I will, Mr. President. I'm a fan of Will Ferrell's. If I ever meet him, I'll ask him about the brushes. Now I'd like to change topics slightly."

"Sure, Leslie. Anything!" Drumpf's eyes seemed to wander down her figure.

"Disgusting whore!" Amanda whispered a little too loudly.

Martin shushed her and then asked, "Who?"

"Who do you think? That blonde bimbo of a 'television personality.'"

Martin shushed her again. "Amanda, not so loud! You mean Cornacre?"

"Yes!"

"Mr. President," Leslie began. "There was a lot of chatter during the campaign and in the early days of your administration about the size of your hands. What would you say to all of those people?"

"Leslie. I can tell you, from personal experience, that many women find my hands to be the perfect size. I've touched many women with these hands, shaken many of their hands, kissed many of them—their hands." Drumpf held up both hands and spread his fingers wide. "The hubbub about my hands was pure liberal media, fake news, biased nonsense designed to weaken my image. The liberals were worried about my strength as a candidate, as a man, and they wanted to emasculate me; they wanted to pussify me. Let me tell you, you can't pussify Ronald Drumpf. It's impossible."

"I completely understand, Mr. President," she smiled widely. "And I appreciate you clearing the air on that issue."

"Let's cut there," the director stepped into the camera. "Leslie, Mr. President, let's take five minutes. Makeup! Quick touch-up, please. Refreshments! Can we get them some water, please?"

"I'm gonna lose my breakfast!" Amanda complained.

"Do you think they need both of us here, anymore?" Martin asked her.

"No, they probably don't," she answered. "So I'm outta here. Have fun! I can't take this bullshit anymore."

Martin was subject to another hour of bullshit that day in the studio and then returned to his office in the White House for even more bullshit.

REELECTION REVISITED

"I've watched the footage; it was a tragedy," the Chief of Staff said.

"It was horrible, painful to watch," said Breiburg.

Kelly Conville nodded. "It'll be traumatic for some people."

"It was traumatic for me," Kellner agreed.

Several key members of the staff were huddled in Kellner's office. They were discussing the latest national tragedy.

Martin had walked by and tried to slip through the small crowd of staffers standing in the hallway outside of the Chief of Staff's office. He paused to listen in, joining several other junior staffers doing the same.

When Kellner noticed him, he shook his head and said, "Why the hell not? You may as well listen also, Jermanski." And then Kellner addressed the whole group. "Listen, everyone. It's a trying time, but we can get through it. We just need to make sure that we operate with one voice."

"It certainly wasn't his best performance," Conville agreed. They were, of course, speaking about the President's interview with Ms. Cornacre.

"We have to decide when it's going to air," said Breiburg.

"Maybe first, we need to decide *if* it's going to air," said Conville.

"I've already decided," said Kellner. "It's not going to. We'll schedule some other interviews, with better-known personalities, people less ... desirable, from the President's perspective. He'll want the interview to air. The only way to do otherwise is to replace it with others."

"He won't be happy," Conville said.

Kellner shook his head. "Okay, people. One more general announcement, and then you're all going back to work."

That got everyone's attention—even those who weren't really paying attention in the first place.

"I know many of you hate it when I tell 'In-the-Military' stories, but I'm going to tell another. Our number one job is to keep the boss safe. Sometimes, that means keeping him safe from himself. And this isn't an unusual or strange concept—this is widely understood to be the normal way of business in the military. There, we call it 'loyalty up the chain of command.'"

Kellner looked around. He seemed to be gauging his audience.

"Only if he is safe, only if he feels safe, will he be able to concentrate his efforts on his number one priority—the nation. Today, this means ensuring that the Cornacre interview never sees the light of day. I didn't like a former President talking about his boxers on MTV, and I don't like our President speaking with Ms. Cornacre about ... well, anything. Does anyone have any questions about this?"

"One more thing," Kellner continued. "There are rumors of various people writing more books about the administration, some very well-known and others less so. Not uncommon, but there is the potential for some authors to stretch the truth to make a sale; that potential could lead to the administration looking bad. If you're contacted by anyone seeking to interview you, I trust that you'll do the right thing, for the administration and for the nation."

Again, he looked around. And waited. When no one spoke up, Kellner said, "Okay. Go out there, do great things for the nation, and stop hanging around my office."

The crowd began to thin; Martin waited. It would be easier to get where he was going once the hallway was empty. Then he saw her.

Just a few steps ahead of him stood Brianne. He hadn't seen her in weeks and had started to believe she no longer worked for the administration.

"Brianne!" he called.

She looked over at him and smiled. "Hey, Marty. Long time, no see. How goes it?"

"Good," he said. "Really good. Where have you been?"

"Where've I been?" She laughed. "You know that the work of the Personnel Office never ends. Hiring, firing, tracking, 'HR'-ing. That's what we do."

"I know, but I never see you."

She eyed him quizzically. "That's because you're already hired, there's no need to fire you, I can track your work from afar, and you haven't lodged any HR complaints."

'HR complaints are a thing?! In this White House?' "You've been tracking me from afar?" he asked.

"Don't get too excited. I track everyone from afar."

"Do you have a minute? I have a question or two."

"HR-related or personal?"

"Well, I was thinking HR-related, but I'm sure that I can come up with a personal question or two."

The hallway had completely emptied. They were alone just a few feet from the entrance to the Chief of Staff's office. She looked around, "Let's keep it HR-related and find someplace else to talk."

It took only a moment to find an empty office to duck into. Brianne let Martin enter first and then, much to his chagrin, left the door open behind her. "We can talk quietly in here. No one's going to spy on us. So what's up?"

"What's up with Mike and Luke?" he asked.

"You told me you weren't going to ask any personal questions," she said defensively.

"What? No, I'm not asking a personal question. Why were they left in the DRT for so long? I think they're still there, even now."

"Oh," she said. She seemed caught off guard. "You know— We can't talk about personnel decisions. It's against the rules, and it's unethical."

"Listen," he said. "Every time I'm in the PPO, those guys crack jokes about Mike and Luke. Whatever it is, it's an open secret. Except no secrets are open to me. Just tell me what's up. I only spent a few weeks in that office, and I thought I was going to die. They started there last fall sometime, and they're still there."

Brianne pursed her lips. She frowned. "Listen, if I tell you, you have to keep it a secret, okay?"

"Of course," he assured her. "Who'm I gonna tell?"

"Ok, look. They were both hired—separately, but around the same time—early last fall. Like you, they were initially put in the DRT, while a decision was being made where to put them permanently. It was then found out that both of them had, in the past, posted very negative views about Drumpf to social media accounts. Repeatedly."

"Okay," he said. Martin learned on his very first day that was a bad thing.

"There was some back and forth about what to do with them," she continued. "Some wanted them fired, immediately. Others thought that was unfair. Ultimately, they were confronted and given a choice—to stay on in the administration with the understanding that they could earn their way out of the DRT with enough time in service or leave immediately. They both, for various reasons, chose to stay on."

"They've been there—what? Eight or nine months? When does their time end? And then, if they make it out of the DRT, where would they work?"

"They both have very impressive resumes," she said. "Out of the DRT, they'll move into much higher, and much more important positions."

"Yeah, but when does that happen?"

"Right now, unless someone changes their mind, at their one year mark," she said.

"Shit," he said. "One year in the DRT. Is it worth it?"

"I don't know, but they seem to think so."

"Wow, okay. Well, thanks for telling me."

"You cannot share that with anyone, understand? Not a single person."

"Okay. I get it."

It was a lot for Martin to digest. At the same time, he very much wanted to try to spend more time with her. 'What's a good personal question I could ask her?'

"Listen, Marty. I've been here before, with a couple of staffers."

"What do you mean?" he asked.

"It's pretty obvious. You're not much for hiding how you feel. Listen, I don't date staffers. Well, I don't, now. I've dated a few in the past, and it always ended badly."

"That obvious?" he asked.

She nodded.

"Okay. Got it," he said. "But why did you think it was a personal question when I brought up Mike and Luke?"

"Mike was the last staffer that I dated."

WARREN G. HARDING

Martin was headed into the Oval Office when he passed the National Security Advisor leaving it.

"He's in a rare mood today. Good luck!"

Martin frowned. Having only been a regular in and around the Oval Office for a few weeks, he hadn't quite figured out whose impressions of the President he could trust. Some of the senior staffers and higher-ups would tell him that the President is in a fine mood when, in fact, he was anything but. Others would claim that his hair is on fire, and Martin would find him downright jovial.

It also often happened that the President was not in the office by the time he got there. The President had a habit of completely ignoring his daily schedule. Martin wasn't even sure why some poor staffer had to produce the thing each day.

"The President in?" Martin asked Phil, standing in the antechamber to the Oval Office.

"For now. What're you in for? The Chief of Staff likes to know."

"Typical daily morning run. Picking up his papers. You know the drill."

That brought a rare smile to Phil's face, and the Secret Service agent chuckled slightly to himself. "Not as well as you do."

Martin stepped to the door, knocked twice, and let himself in. The President was at his desk speaking on the phone; a group of high-level staffers was scattered about the Oval Office. As always, Watterhoot was standing close by. The Chief of Staff saw Martin first and nodded.

Martin approached the desk; there was no sign of any ripped up documents. Drawing closer, he glanced in the President's garbage can. There it was – a pile of torn-up paper, sitting neatly at the bottom. Happy to find the main prize of his trip that morning, Martin nonetheless felt a twinge of guilt. He pitied the poor staffers who had to tape it all together again. At least it wasn't him anymore!

He bent down to retrieve the contents of the can.

"Martin!"

It was Mr. Drumpf. So intent on his prize, Martin didn't notice that the President had ended his phone conversation. Drumpf was looking right at him.

"Yes, sir?" Martin stood up. "Good morning, Mr. President."

"Nice to see you, Marty."

"Nice to see you, too, sir."

Martin quickly glanced at the Chief of Staff, who was watching him closely.

"What're you here for, this morning?" Drumpf asked him.

"Just picking up the morning papers, sir," Martin nervously answered. "We have to keep your garbage can clean." He cringed inside. 'What a stupid thing to say.'

Martin bent down and picked up the can.

"Hold on, Marty," the President said.

Martin stood up, holding the garbage can in front of him.

Drumpf reached for his glass, fancy White House crystal holding chilled Diet Coke. "The Coke is flat. I'm just going to…" The President leaned over and reached forward with the glass.

Martin instinctively pulled the garbage can away from the President. And then he stopped himself. Drumpf was looking up at him with a raised eyebrow. Martin moved the garbage can back, to right in front of the President.

Drumpf looked up at Martin and then down into the can and dumped the beverage right onto the pile of shredded papers.

Martin felt his eyes grow wide. The President had a big, satisfied grin on his face. Martin dropped his gaze into the can. It was only half a glass of Coke, but it sloshed around the bottom of the can, soaking the base of the pile of papers. 'The poor staffers.' He tried to tip the can slightly, so that the Coke pooled in one corner and didn't wet any more of the paper bits. It seemed to work! And then his heart sank as the pile of papers collapsed into the little lake of Coke in the bottom of the can.

All Martin could think of was the poor staffers, trying to separate the wetted and Coke-stained papers to dry them and then attempt to reassemble them into whole pages. Did the President understand what he had just done? He looked up at Drumpf, who was still looking at him with the smile on his face. 'Yes,' Martin thought. The President most certainly did understand what he had done, and he was taking great pleasure in it.

Martin spun on his heel and moved quickly toward the Oval Office exit. Perhaps he could make their life a little easier if he got the can to them before all of the papers were soaked.

As Martin approached the door, the President called out, "Marty! I have a question for you."

'Oh shit,' Martin thought. 'He's on to me.' He slowly turned around. Most of the current inhabitants of the office were now looking at him.

"Yes, sir?"

"Who do you think the best President was?"

Martin blinked. What? He looked down in the garbage can. More little bits of paper were soaking up the brown liquid. The best President? Martin wasn't much for Presidential history. Not only that, Martin wondered if the President was fishing for a very specific answer. He felt the color drain from his face.

"Yeah, Marty. Who was the best President?" Drumpf repeated. And then laughed. "Other than me, Marty."

Oh. Well, taking himself off the table solved Martin's second problem, but it did nothing for his first: He was an idiot when it came to the Presidents.

"Abraham Lincoln," Martin blurted out. Surely, that was a safe answer. *Everyone* said Lincoln was a good President. Drumpf didn't respond, so Martin assumed he should try again. "George Washington?" Also a safe answer. He was the first, right? He had to have been good at the job.

"Someone other than the Big Two, Marty. Seriously, who do you think was the best? Again, other than me, of course."

Martin looked down in the garbage can again. 'Shit.' The Diet Coke puddle was almost gone, which meant that the paper bits had soaked most of it up. There were still a few dry pieces of paper. But Drumpf was looking at him; Martin could still feel his eyes on him. 'Best President?'

Then Martin remembered something that he had read just the evening before. In case of just this situation, he had googled "Best U.S. Presidents" and "Worst U.S. Presidents." He had quickly scanned various webpages, top ten lists, and read some articles. But they were all jumbled up in his head. 'Who was the best President?!'

Martin looked up to see the Chief of Staff approaching him.

The Chief of Staff took the garbage can from his hands and whispered to him, "Do not answer that question." He then stepped past Martin and out of the Oval Office.

"Marty! Come on! What do you think?"

Martin felt a pit forming in his stomach. The President was pressuring him for an answer. The Chief of Staff just directed him not to answer and then left the room. And Martin couldn't remember who was considered a good President and who wasn't.

"Harding?" He blurted the first name that came to mind.

"Harding? Who?" the President asked.

"Warren Harding," Martin said. He was a businessman, Martin vaguely remembered. And he was a strong supporter of the Navy. He seemed like a good choice.

"Warren Harding," the President considered the answer. "Mmm. I'll have to think about that. Thanks, Marty."

Martin felt a surge of relief flow through him. And then he looked at the assembled other staffers and aides in the Oval Office. Some were looking at him with disgust. Others were plainly confused. Not a single one looked happy. 'What's the big deal?'

"Tell me about him," the President insisted. "What do you know about Warren Harding?"

'Oh shit. Not much.' What did he remember? "Well, sir." A brief stalling tactic. Martin took a few steps back toward the desk while gathering his thoughts. "He was very popular while he was President. Extremely popular." The President nodded, a slight smile forming on his face. "He was a businessman prior to becoming President and a supporter of business." The President's smile grew a little wider. "He was a big proponent of the Navy. Oh, and he also voted to enter World War One."

The President nodded as his smile grew larger. "A businessman who was strong on national defense. I think I would have liked him."

"If you'll excuse me, Mr. President."

"Huh? Oh, sure, Marty. Thanks. You've given me a lot to think about."

"Yes, sir." As Martin exited the Oval Office, he felt better. The President seemed pleased with his answer. Hopefully, the Chief of Staff wouldn't find out about it. Now he had to find that garbage can and deliver it to the lowlies.

•   •   •

Two days later, Martin returned to his office after his lunch break to find Amanda in the office looking agitated.

"What's up?" he asked her.

"The Chief of Staff is upset, something to do with the Business Roundtable meeting this afternoon."

"Most of the arrangements were verified this morning. The Congressmen and staffers will be arriving," Martin said and then looked down at his wristwatch, "in about an hour. Members of the Advisory Group about twenty minutes after that. The room is already set up. Food service is set. The President's papers were prepared and delivered to the Oval Office this morning. What could he be upset about?"

"Something having to do with the room itself," she responded.

"I checked the room earlier," he said.

"Maybe you need to check it again."

"There are other people who can do this," Martin growled in frustration. "How about *you* check the room?"

"What?!" she asked in mock anger. "I'm not the bitch in this relationship." As much as her 'bitch' schtick was annoying to Martin, he actually preferred it to her concern about the Chief of Staff. He sighed and turned and walked from the office before even sitting down.

Martin arrived at the conference room to find everything in order. The table was set, nametags laid out; the cooks were just finishing setting up the hors d'oeuvres on the side table. He assumed that the correct number of chairs were positioned around the table. None of these things were his responsibility, but he checked them anyway.

After checking the individual items, he moved to the center of the room and spun a slow circle, taking it all in. There wasn't a thing that was out of place.

"Jermanski!"

'Uh-oh.'

"Jermanski," barked the Chief of Staff, a second time.

Martin spun to face Kellner, entering from the opposite entrance.

"Sir?"

"Are you responsible for this?"

As Martin was about to ask to what he was referring, the Chief of Staff raised his arm and pointed at the far wall of the room. Martin turned and saw a painting hanging in the center of the wall. But that wasn't a big deal; there was *always* a painting hanging there.

Then Martin looked closer. It was a different painting than had been hanging there just before lunch. It was a portrait. He took a step closer. It was a portrait of Warren G. Harding!

Martin felt a lump form in the pit of his stomach. He turned to face the Chief of Staff, who was now standing directly beside him with a deep frown on his face.

"Do you know anything about this, Martin?"

Martin opened his mouth and paused, unsure of what to say.

"It turns out that the President, without telling me, directed that this portrait be hung here in time for the meeting this afternoon, to be hung here to show his support for the members of the Business Advisory Group." Kellner paused and shook his head. "Do you know who that is?"

"Isn't it Warren Harding, sir?"

"Yes, actually, it is. What do you know about Warren Harding?"

"He was President back in the twenties. He'd been a businessman before running for President. He was big on national defense?"

"That's basically correct. But do you know what's interesting? That's almost *exactly* what the President told me about Harding."

Martin only nodded stiffly.

"Do you know anything else about Harding?"

"No, sir. Not really." Martin could feel Kellner's eyes boring into his.

"Let me enlighten you. He is believed to have had a least two affairs, possibly more; various members of his Administration were found to have conducted a whole variety of illegal and unethical activities; there is circumstantial proof that he was aware of at least a few of them and did nothing."

"I didn't know ..." Martin's voice trailed off.

"The President—"

"John! Marty!" The President, jovial and loud, burst into the room. "I see that you've noticed the change. What do you think?"

Martin smiled weakly.

The Chief of Staff growled low in his throat, loud enough only for Martin to hear. And then in his normal voice, "Mr. President. I'm not sure that this portrait sends the right message."

"Harding was a tremendous President. One of our nation's best! It's a shame there aren't more portraits of him hanging around."

"Sir, President Harding oversaw some positive developments in our history, however—"

"Exactly! He was an amazing businessman. He was a keen supporter of the Navy. I don't know if he supported your Marine Corps, John, but he definitely supported the Navy. You know, the Navy was transitioning away from coal during his time. He was instrumental in that change."

"Yes, sir. He was … instrumental … as you say."

"Then it's settled then!" The President's smile only grew wider. "I think his portrait is a worthy addition to the room, especially for the Business Advisory Group meeting this afternoon." He turned to Martin. "What time does the meeting kick off, Marty?"

"In about thirty minutes, sir."

"Excellent. Excellent. I'll be back around then. Thank you." The President turned to look at the painting and smiled, then he left the room as quickly as he had come.

"Did you have anything to do with this?" Kellner was examining Martin closely.

"Well, sir, uh, I—"

"Never mind." Kellner spun on his heel and took three steps toward the exit before turning back to Martin. "Get that fucking painting out of here. Now."

"But, sir, the President—"

"I don't care. I'll take care of him. You just make that portrait disappear. Got it?"

"Yes, sir."

Kellner was about to leave when he paused and looked at Martin one last time. "You don't know anything else about Warren Harding, do you?"

"No," Martin said. "Not really, sir."

"He's widely considered to be one of the very worst, and most corrupt, Presidents in U.S. history."

THE PROPOSAL

"Good morning, Mr. President."

"Morning, Marty!"

"Sir, I was wondering if you had a moment."

"Sure."

"I wanted to talk to you about that book idea."

"The book? My book? Kelly hasn't mentioned it in the last several days. Any idea why?"

"No, sir." Martin had actually heard that she had reached out to several authors, and none had been interested in the job. He was not going to tell Drumpf that. "I think she's swamped with all of the interest; she wants to get the right co-author."

"The co-author doesn't matter! I'll write most of the book. I've written several, you know. I'm an outstanding writer. The co author is just around to brush up the writing, to give it that extra punch. Mainly to assist during those times when I get too busy."

Martin sagely nodded his understanding. Silence was occasionally the best reply.

"My son could act as co-author. And I'm not talking about the older two, if you know what I mean. Although, perhaps the older couldn't. Neither of them have a head for writing. It takes a special kind of person to be a writer. Can you imagine those long hours sitting at a keyboard? Although some people write long hand. I'm one of those; I much prefer to write with a pen on paper. I do my best thinking then."

"I understand, sir," Martin paused. 'Should I go on? Oh, what the hell.' "You know, I was an English major in college. I did a lot of writing."

"Really? I didn't know that. What kind of writing?"

"All kinds, sir. Essays, stories, poems."

"Poems? Really? Poems are for pussies," Drumpf said, a frown creasing his forehead. And then a dirty smile spread across his face. "Unless you're trying to get some. Some women eat up poetry; they love it! You ever use poetry to get a girl?"

"Maybe once or twice."

"You dog! I believe it. You're a pretty good looking guy, Marty. Your face and some poetry—I could see it. Me? I'm not much of a poet. But I've always had money. Money will buy more pussy than poetry ever will. Don't forget that. Money can buy you most things; it can certainly buy you pussy."

"I'll try not to forget, sir."

"Do you know any decent authors to add to Kelly's list?"

"Actually, sir. I was thinking of throwing my name in the ring. I think I should write your book."

Drumpf looked at Martin for a moment and then burst into laughter. "You want to help write my book?"

"Yes, sir. I would." He said it simply, as if it were the most obvious thing in the world. He tried to sound confident, despite the pit in his stomach. He wasn't sure he succeeded.

But Drumpf noticed. He stopped laughing. He looked at Martin for a long time. Then he asked, "How's your dad doing?"

Martin was surprised by the change of subject. He tried not to show it. "Still at Mer-a-Lago. Still enjoying the work. He always likes to remind me how you've taken good care of us."

Drumpf narrowed his eyes slightly.

Martin had never seen the look before, at least not directed straight at him. 'What's the President thinking?'

And then Drumpf's eyes softened. He smiled. "You think you want to try? The book, I mean."

"Yes, sir."

"Kelly still needs to give me a list of possible titles. Her and her lists…" Drumpf shook his head.

"Actually, sir. I have a suggestion for the title as well. You don't want an author who hasn't thought about the title."

"Really? What is it?"

"*The Art of the Presidency*," Martin said.

"Mmm. *The Art of the Presidency. The Art of the Presidency.* I like it. I like it a lot."

Martin was excited but tried not to show it. The President liked his idea!

"I guess we can tell Kelly to stop looking for an author and to stop trying to figure out a title," Drumpf said as he thought about the title. "*The Art of the Presidency.* That's a brilliant title. It rolls off the tongue, doesn't it? Art of the Deal. Art of the Comeback. Art of the Presidency! This might be my best idea! Well, for today. I'm an exceptionally creative thinker, you know. Most ideas I have are brilliant."

As soon as the President latched onto the idea, Martin began to worry. Would the entire thing be stolen from him? Or would Drumpf allow him to run with it? He cautiously opened his mouth, "It is, sir. And I think I can write the book with you."

Drumpf laughed; it was an 'oh-you-foolish-boy' laugh.

Martin immediately realized that he was in a negotiation, and an important one. Supposedly, if you believed the President, Martin was negotiating with one of the best negotiators on the planet. He wasn't sure what to say. Was the President waiting on him to say something?

"Tell me, Marty," the President began in a sly voice. "What do you bring to the table that an outside, established author doesn't?"

Martin paused and thought hard. He knew the next few moments would be crucial. "Well, sir." Stalling for more time to think. "I've been in your White House for several months now. I know you; I know how your White House works." Martin started off slowly, but he spoke faster as his confidence grew, "I've seen your successes, and I think I can describe how you achieved them." 'Make it all about Drumpf,' Martin thought to himself.

The President, who had been leaning forward over his desk when he asked the question, began to lean back as Martin spoke.

Martin didn't know if that was a good sign or not. "You've given me access to your meetings; I can give an up close and personal account of what's happening here."

Drumpf looked calm throughout, even appearing to accept what Martin was saying. And then his face changed sharply. He almost snarled, "Don't pull a 'Fire and Fury' on me! I won't have that happen again!"

"Sir, no! Not at all!" 'What the hell was Fire and Fury'? "You'll be writing the book; I'll just be helping you brush up the writing and give it the extra punch."

As quickly as the rage had spread across his face, Drumpf seemed to calm down. Apparently, Martin's assurances worked. Drumpf smiled. "Sure, Marty."

Two knocks at the door and then the Chief of Staff came into the room. He was surprised to see Martin.

But before Kellner could open his mouth, the President cheerfully greeted him, "John. Marty and I were just discussing my book."

Kellner flashed Martin a look. "Really? I trust it was a good conversation, Mr. President. But I didn't see such a discussion on your schedule."

"No, sir. It wasn't," said Martin. "I was just in checking on the President's papers and the topic came up."

"Came up, eh? I'm sure that the President has other issues to deal with."

"Yes, sir." Martin quickly moved toward the exit.

As Martin pulled the door open to excuse himself, the President called out, "I'll think about it, Marty. Let's talk in a few days."

.   .   .

Martin made his way back to his office and considered his conversation with the President. It seemed to go well, but it was touch-and-go for a moment. 'What the hell was Fire and Fury'?

"Great! You're here," Martin said to Amanda as he swung into their office.

She looked up at him with her head cocked to one side. Her eyes narrowed. "You've never said *that* before. What's with you?"

"You've been here longer than I have," Martin started. "You know things."

Her demeanor changed instantly from confusion to hardcore Amanda. "You better believe it, bitch! I know all sorts of shit."

"What is 'Fire and Fury'?"

"What? The book?" Amanda asked.

"I guess?"

"You didn't hear about *Fire and Fury*?"

"No," Martin answered.

"Pretty sure it came out in January, just a few weeks before you started," she said. "It was all over the news. How could you've not heard about it?"

"Shit," Martin said. "I don't know. Can you just tell me about it?"

"It's a book, written by some journalist who spent months in and around the White House, last year. Spilled all sorts of dirt. All of the higher-ups were furious. It told some good stories."

"Were any of them true?" Martin asked.

"Shit, yeah! A bunch of them were," she said and then shrugged. "Some were exaggerations."

"Were you working here when the journalist was around?"

"I was. Saw him a couple of times, never spoke to him though. Why?"

"The President mentioned it this morning. He was pissed."

"Why'd he mention it?"

'Shit,' Martin thought. He didn't want to tell Amanda about him possibly writing the book. He lied. "He was talking to the Chief of Staff when I was in picking up his papers and mentioned it."

Amanda eyed him suspiciously. He wasn't a good liar, and she seemed to sense something was off.

Martin sat down, opened a folder, and paged through a stack of papers, trying to look busy.

In a few seconds, Amanda went back to typing on her computer. Martin wanted to ask more questions about *Fire and Fury* but wanted to avoid any more questions from her. Instead, he grabbed his phone. Fifteen minutes later, after learning about Michael Wolff, reading several news articles about him and his book, and reading a few book reviews, Martin ordered the book from Amazon.

.   .   .

That evening, Martin decided to call his parents.

"Martin? You're calling me, again? Wow!"

"Ha ha, mom," he said. "I call you occasionally."

"Occasionally is one way to describe it. But usually, I call you."

"Not cool, mom. But listen, I have some news."

"Should I get your dad?" she asked.

"He might be interested."

"Okay, hold on." She covered the phone with her hand, but it didn't prevent him from hearing, "Bill! It's Martin! Get on the phone!"

His dad picked up the second phone. "Hey, Marty. What's new in DC?"

"Well, do you remember the day that you guys recommended I come to DC?" Martin asked.

"Yeah," his mom said. "It was a Sunday afternoon; it was after the Jaguars game."

"Yup! Do you remember what dad gave me and what you said to me, mom?"

"I showed you that letter from The Ronald, right?" his dad asked.

"True, but you also gave me a copy of *The Art of the Deal*. And you, mom, told me that I should write the sequel."

Neither of this parents said anything.

"Do you guys remember that?" he asked.

"Yeah," his dad said at the same time his mom said, "Sure."

"Well, I'm going to," Martin said.

"Going to, what?" his mom asked.

"I'm going to write the sequel!"

"What?" his dad asked.

"Yeah. The Ronald has been thinking about things that he can do to support the Republican Party this fall during the midterms," Martin explained. "Someone—me!—made the suggestion that he should write another book. He loved the idea. So today, I volunteered to write it with him. And he accepted the idea!"

"Oh, my God!" his mom screamed.

"Wow!" His dad actually sounded genuinely excited. "Really?"

"It's going to be called *The Art of the Presidency*, and I'm going to start working on it immediately."

"Holy shit!"

"Bill!"

"Sorry, honey. I mean, holy cow! Marty that's great!"

It had been a long time since Martin had heard his dad be excited about anything other than a Jaguars game. It felt good.

"Martin. Are you sure?" his mom asked. "Why would he choose you? Aren't there other authors, proven authors, who could write the book with him?"

"Come on, honey," his dad answered. "We've talked about this before. It's just like The Ronald. Marty. This is great."

"Thanks, dad."

"The Ronald can sometimes be…unorthodox in his management style," his dad continued. "He's put people in charge of businesses that had no business being in charge. And they've done well." His dad cleared his throat. "Most of them have, anyway. He goes with his gut when he makes business, and personnel, decisions. If he thinks you're a performer, he'll give you responsibility. He picks people he trusts. Sounds like he trusts you, Marty!"

"It is such an opportunity!" his mom gushed. "Are you excited?"

"Of course. It's exciting, but it's also going to be tough."

"Whatever you do, do not let him down," his dad warned. "If you fail, or piss him off, you'll be out of a job in a heartbeat."

"Oh, I know, dad. I've seen that happen with the staff a few times."

"Ha! I bet you have!"

"Martin. We're so proud of you!"

"Thanks, mom."

"Marty. I'm proud of you."

Martin was surprised by his dad's comment. It had been a long time since he heard that from the old man. "Thanks, dad. That means a lot."

FIRE AND FURY

Three days after first mentioning *The Art of the Presidency* to the President, Martin came back to his apartment to find a package from Amazon. Opening the box revealed a softcover version of *Fire and Fury*. He read for a hundred pages and then had to put it down.

If the book was to be believed, Wolff had access to people and situations that Martin never did or would. How was he supposed to write a book with the same kind of oomph? And Wolff had been a journalist and had authored several books previously. Martin hadn't authored a thing.

Martin dejectedly wandered to his bookshelf and picked up the copy of *The Art of the Deal* his father had given him back in December. Tony Schwartzman. He realized that he didn't know a thing about Tony Schwartzman. Time to Google him.

'Holy shit,' Martin thought. 'Schwartzman obviously does not like Drumpf.' He sounded almost guilty about having written the book with him. Although, if Schwartzman was to be believed, *Art of the Deal* was almost completely written by himself.

More interesting to Martin was Schwartzman's comments about Drumpf's negotiating skills. Apparently, they've split all the proceeds for the book 50/50, which has earned Schwartzman millions of dollars since the book was released. 'That would be nice,' Martin thought to himself.

Martin picked up *Fire and Fury* and continued reading. It almost read like a novel. 'Can I write a book like this?' Martin thought.

Two things about the book really jumped out at Martin.

It seemed that Banyan wasn't lying when he told Martin that the The Ronald didn't want to win the Presidency. Or perhaps both men were telling the same lie. Martin couldn't be sure. Maybe Banyan got the idea from the book? But that didn't make any sense…

The book described, fairly accurately, how the President dealt with people and situations. It was obvious to Martin that Wolff had to have spent some time in the White House or at least talked to many people who did. It was uncanny.

Martin read some more and then grew bored. Many of the people described in the book were long gone from the White House. Obviously, the First Lady and First Daughter were still around, but many others had moved on. And Martin just wasn't interested in reading a book that seemed to describe his daily existence.

Then a cold pit formed in his stomach. If he wasn't interested in reading *Fire and Fury*, would anyone be interested in reading *The Art of the Presidency*? That is, if he could even write it. The President was convinced that everyone would read it, because of the Drumpf name, but that wasn't comforting to Martin.

While considering his ability to write *The Art of the Presidency*, Martin's official phone began to ring. 'Shit.' His phone had never rung when he was at home before. He grabbed it but didn't recognize the number.

"Hello?"

"Jermanski. Banyan."

"Hello, sir," Martin said. 'How'd he get my phone number?'

"You're probably wondering how I got your phone number," Banyan said. "I can get any number. Just remember, for about eight months last year, I was the most powerful man in the world. That was me! And you never know, it might be me again someday."

"Okay, Mr. Banyan. What can I do for you today?"

"I know I haven't called you late in the evening before, but it's been several weeks since we've talked, and I wanted to touch base."

"Understand," Martin said.

"Honestly, I probably didn't need to call," Banyan said. "It's been a pretty good month from where I'm sitting."

"Oh?"

"Shit, yeah. Bunch of lefty pinkoes resigned from the EPA. Drumpf is working to remove the Hondurans, who should have been deported years ago. He spoke at the NRA—minor point, but good. He's withdrawing us from the Iran Nuclear Deal. A staffer even poked fun of John McCain. Seriously? Can it get any better?"

"It can always get better," Martin offered.

"True. That's true. There was one item that caught my eye that I don't understand."

"What's that, sir?" Martin asked.

"Why'd the White House eliminate its Cyber Security Coordinator? Was that really Belten's bright idea?"

"He was the one who pushed for it, sir. I wasn't around for most of those conversations, but Belten wanted the post eliminated."

"That's fucking stupid. He's opening the door for the Chinese. The Russians and the North Koreans, as well. The U.S. has got to get better on cyber. If we don't, we're going to lose the next shooting war before it even begins. You know that we're at war already, right Jermanski?"

"Sir?"

"War. Yes. At war right now. With the Chinese."

Banyan paused. Martin didn't know what to say, so he said nothing.

"Okay. Let me put it another way. The Chinese are at war with us; they've been at war for decades now. Unfortunately, we're too stupid to fight back. You can't win a war you're not even fighting, and we're not fighting right now!"

'That's depressing,' Martin thought, but he still had nothing to say in return. He said nothing.

"You still there, Jermanski?"

"I'm here, sir."

"Did anyone argue with Belten on the cyber issue?"

"Yes, sir. Several people, but he convinced the President."

"Typical."

There was a long silence. Martin just waited. Finally, Banyan spoke again.

"I guess that covers it. Anything else worth mentioning?"

"No, sir."

"Keep it up, Jermanski. Thanks." Banyan hung up.

The conversation was typical of the last few that they had. Martin was surprised that Banyan kept calling him. He didn't think he ever gave Banyan any interesting or valuable information. He wasn't sure that he even understood the game that Banyan was playing.

'That's probably not a good thing,' Martin thought.

SECRET SUMMIT PREPARATIONS

Martin was better prepared this time around. He was standing in the antechamber to the Oval Office waiting for the 'secret' guest.

The schedule showed the President meeting with advisors to discuss the upcoming summit in Singapore with Kim Jong Un; several names were listed as attendees. Martin was told that morning that there would be others in attendance in addition to those on the list. One name in particular was whispered to him. He couldn't imagine any other President inviting this person to such a meeting.

Most of the others had already arrived and were in the Oval Office. The President hadn't come over from the Residence yet, but that wasn't necessarily uncommon.

About five minutes before the meeting was scheduled to occur, one of his fellow staffers approached Martin.

"They have you waiting out here for him?"

"Yeah," Martin replied.

"We just got a call. He's running late."

"Does the Chief of Staff know?" Martin asked.

"You know he has a way of finding things out, but I don't think so."

"Okay, thanks," Martin said and then turned to the Secret Service Agent on duty. Lex, so nicknamed due to his shiny pate, shrugged and opened the door to the Oval.

Kellner was just beyond the open door, rapidly approaching it.

"Jermanski," the Chief of Staff said, "He's running late. Might as well get in here."

"But, sir," Martin protested. "Shouldn't I just wait out here for him?"

"No. The President seems to think you might be useful."

"Hello, everyone!" It was the President, cheerfully entering the Oval Office via the other entrance. He was early.

Kellner winced slightly then barked at Martin, "In here. Now."

Lex cast a sidelong glance at Martin, and then Martin sprang through the door and pulled it shut behind him. And was immediately surprised to see several people who weren't on the list in the room. Secretary of State. Secretary of Defense. The Chairman of the Joint Chiefs of Staff. A handful of other military officers.

Martin missed a few comments from various people as he took in the room. He started to pay attention just as the Secretary of Defense began to speak.

"Mr. President. No one in this room doubts your readiness for the summit, however, we feel very strongly that you can never be too prepared."

"Bull Dog," the President replied, and then turned to one of the military officers closest to him and said, "God I love that name! You know the country is in good hands when your Secretary of Defense is called 'Bull Dog.'" And then back to the Secretary, "Listen, Jim. I understand this guy; I get him. I've watched videos."

"Sir," began the Secretary of State. "You and I have spent hours talking about Kim Jong Un and North Korea over the past several weeks. And I know that you understand the issues, you understand the man, you understand his nation. But we have gathered additional information that we feel is important for you to understand. As Jim said, you can never be too prepared."

"Listen. I know everything that I need to know about the man. I called him 'Rocketman.' Do you know why I did that? To see how he would respond. And when he responded, I learned things about him. Important things. Things that I will be able to use when we sit down." The President had been standing behind his desk. He paused momentarily to sit down.

"You can learn a lot by sitting and watching someone. He's a large man, pretty thick in the middle. Do you know what that tells me? He loves to eat. I can use that. He wears glasses. Do you know what that tells me? His eyes aren't so good. I can use that. His hair is always perfect. His fingernails always clean. Those tell me things about him. All of it, all of it, I can use. When we sit down, I'll know exactly who I'm talking to."

"Sir," Matthews chimed in. "We've received recent intelligence that might change some of your calculations. Things that no one knows; things that have actually surprised some of our analysts."

"Jim. I don't trust analysts. You know that. Some companies pay lots of money to hire 'analysts.' What does that even mean? What do they do? I've never had analysts working for me. A waste of money. I can *analysis* everything that needs it. I don't need to hire experts. Well, except for accountants and lawyers – everyone should hire accountants and lawyers. But beyond those, there's no need."

"You did find the concept of 'Loyalty Attack' interesting at the briefings that I arranged several weeks ago."

"Loyalty Attack," the President said. "Loyalty attack? Oh, yeah, I did. It's a very interesting concept, very interesting idea. But you also said that no one in your Armed Forces would do such a thing for me."

"That's true, sir," the Secretary of Defense agreed. "But the point is that we are able to bring people to you with ideas that you haven't considered before."

Drumpf looked stumped. He paused and thought about the Secretary's argument for a moment.

"You might be right about that, Jim. You might be right. And so I might listen to what you have to tell me today. I won't make any promises, but I might. But there's one thing that I want everyone here today to understand. The most important thing going into the summit next week is attitude. My attitude. Hell, even Kim's attitude. If he and I can create a good relationship, with a positive attitude, we can solve this Korea problem."

"No one here today doubts the importance of attitude, Mr. President," said the Secretary of State. "And I think, based on my meetings with him several weeks ago, that Kim Jong Un has the right attitude to work with you. I think there is a good chance that you and he will see eye-to-eye."

"And if that's possible, fruitful discussions are possible," added the Secretary of Defense. "But if his attitude isn't right, you'll need as much information as you can have to guide your discussions."

Martin had seen other people speak to the President this way, and it typically didn't go well. The President did not like being lectured to, and the Secretaries were almost there. 'Perhaps Drumpf takes it better coming from these two?'

Just then there was a knock at the door. Everyone looked up as the door opened.

Dennis Roddman, with numerous face piercings connected by chains, a bright purple three piece suit, and a fluorescent pink pashmina, strode into the room. "Ronald!"

"Mr. President," the Chief of Staff muttered under his breath, hoping that Roddman would act with some level of decorum.

"Dennis! My man!" The President jumped up and came around his desk to greet the former NBA star. "I'm so glad you could make it." The two shook hands and then the President turned to the rest of the group. "Would you believe this guy? Look at these chains! Look at this outfit!"

"Mr. President," Roddman greeted him. Perhaps he heard the Chief of Staff. "I know that these are important times. I'm here to help any way I can."

"Do you think you could come to Singapore with me?"

At least three people in the room began to protest the President's question, but it seemed that Roddman got the hint.

"I don't think that would be a good idea," Roddman said. "Well. I can be there. I can certainly visit Singapore, but I think your people might have other plans."

"We don't want Mr. Roddmann stealing the spotlight, sir," said the Secretary of State.

"You know, Mike. With just about anyone else, that comment might upset me. I mean, seriously. Who could steal the spotlight from me? But look at this guy!" Drumpf was smiling a massive smile and pointing to Roddman's piercings, chains, and outfit. Roddmann certainly could steal the spotlight.

"But you know that I'll be close by and ready to help in any way I can," Roddmann offered.

"Fantastic. That's fantastic!"

"Mr. President," the Chief of Staff interrupted. "Now that everyone is here, why don't we sit down and start our formal discussions?"

The President looked skeptical but turned from Roddmann and made his way back to his desk. He stepped behind it but then looked at Roddmann before sitting down.

"Dennis. You wouldn't believe these people. They think that I need to be more prepared for my meeting with Kim Jong Un. They think that they can tell me things that I don't already know."

"You know, Mr. President," Roddmann said matter-of-factly. "Even I've been helped by great coaches, great trainers, great agents. Even the best of us occasionally need to rely on other brilliant people."

Martin couldn't believe it. Was Roddmann going to convince the President to do something his senior advisors tried and failed to do for weeks?

"Wait," Drumpf replied. "So you're telling me that I should listen to these guys?"

"Would I steer you wrong?" Roddmann asked.

"You've never steered me wrong before."

Roddmann broke out into a huge fit of laughter. "Well, there was that one time in New York!"

Drumpf also cracked up. "Hey, Dennis! Hey. Let's not talk about that time in front of these guys. They might not understand ... the intricacies of that situation."

The President's response only caused Roddmann to laugh harder. "Intricacies? Ha! Some of those straps were intricate, that's for sure."

"That's what she said!" Drumpf laughed even louder.

Roddmann bent almost in half from his uncontrollable laughter.

A few of the other people in the room were laughing, although Martin was sure that none of them were in on the obviously-private joke. The Secretary of State had a tight smile on his face. The Secretary of Defense merely stood there stone-faced. The Chief of Staff was glancing at some papers in a folder.

After what seemed like several minutes, the President's laughter subsided. He finally sat down in his chair, which was the signal for everyone to sit. Martin, Watterhoot, and several other low-level personnel stood around the perimeter of the room.

"Dennis," the President began. "Before we go any further, I do have a question for you."

"What is it, Ronald?"

"Mr. President!" the Chief of Staff hissed through clenched teeth.

"Have you spoken to Kim recently?"

"Actually, I haven't," Roddmann said. "It's been awhile."

"Oh. That's too bad. Too bad."

"But I can reach out to him if you'd like me to."

"We don't think that will be necessary, Mr. Roddmann," the Secretary of State interjected. "We have several lines of communication open with Mr. Kim."

"I'm sure you do," Roddmann said. "I was just offering."

"We certainly appreciate the offer."

"Yeah," Drumpf agreed. "We appreciate it. I also appreciate you being willing to go to Singapore. It might be useful to have you there during our discussions."

"Anything for you, Ronald. Anything."

Martin thought the Chief of Staff was going to explode.

"You know that I gave him a copy of your *Art of the Deal*, don't you? I think it helped him to understand you. I really think it helped a lot."

"I'd heard that, Dennis," Drumpf said. "Thank you for that. And he read it?"

"He absolutely did."

"You know, some of my staff think that I should write a new book. Another 'Art of the . . .' " book. What do you think?"

"I'll be the first one to buy it. I always learn new things from reading your books."

"That's very kind, Dennis. Very kind."

Fifteen minutes later, the formal meeting still hadn't started. Finally, the Chief of Staff came over to Martin and whispered quietly to him, "Clear the rest of the morning. Wipe it."

That was Martin's signal to leave the Oval Office.

PATRIOTISM

"The higher-ups are freaking out," Amanda said.

"What? Why?" Martin asked.

"Drumpf released a statement and now everyone is trying to react to it."

"How is that unusual?"

"Because it's going to fall on us to try to fix it," she said.

"Us?" 'That doesn't sound good,' he thought.

"Oh, yeah. Tomorrow was going to be the Eagles visit," she said, referring to the Philadelphia Eagles visit to the White House. "Well, that's not the case anymore. The President cancelled it."

"What? Shit! I was hoping to get some autographs."

"You're an Eagles fan?"

"No. Jaguars," he said. "But it's not often you get a chance to meet professional athletes."

"Well, too bad. You can kiss that idea goodbye."

"Why'd he cancel it?"

"Why's he do anything?" Amanda asked

"So what did the statement say?"

"Here. Read it." Amanda spun the computer monitor his way for him to read it.

Martin read the statement. Not much jumped out at him as unusual, until he came across one number. "The one thousand fans planning to attend? That's not what we were told to expect last week. That's not what we've been planning for."

"Well, no one told the President that."

"So what does that mean for us?"

"It means that we get to play the role of fans," she said.

"Wait," he said. "What?"

"We're still going to hold a celebration tomorrow. They're calling it a 'Patriotism Event.' To ensure the crowd is big enough, we're all being told to attend. Check your email."

He reached for his phone; there was no way she was going to give up the computer. Sure enough. He had received an email, only in the last thirty minutes, directing his participation in the event. It was to start at 3:00 P.M. the next day.

"So what does a person do at a 'Patriotism Event'?"

"Formally, it's a 'Celebration of America.' But I guess we'll all find out." Amanda shrugged and pulled the computer monitor back to her.

"Wait a second," he said,

She looked up at him. "What?"

"I don't think any of the Eagles even kneeled during the year. Did any of them protest the American flag?"

"How would I know?" she asked. "Not a football fan."

"But isn't it strange that the President cancelled the event with the Eagles when none of the Eagles did anything that pissed him off?"

Amanda only shrugged. She'd already lost interest

•   •   •

The next afternoon was almost a perfect DC summer day. The sky was blue; the sun was shining. It was a fairly typical afternoon, except in one way: The humidity was low for an early June day. Thankfully. Martin was pleasantly surprised to not be sweating buckets within minutes of stepping into the afternoon heat.

His task, and that of several other junior staffers, was to direct traffic, i.e. assist the incoming crowd in moving to the audience area for the event. Martin had been stationed just inside the security perimeter and was instructed to cheer for the Eagles, despite the team not coming, as a large percentage of the crowd was expected to be Eagles fans.

His occasional "Go Eagles" or "Congratulations, Philadelphia" was only met with blank stares or outright confusion from the attendees. It didn't seem that there were any Eagles fans present. Martin didn't see a single one—no hats, no jerseys, nothing.

Once the crowd had gathered, Martin looked around. He saw a lot of staffers standing around. In fact, they seemed to make up a large portion of the crowd. He wandered over to Scott Bokor, standing close to him.

"Where are the one thousand Eagles fans?" Martin asked Scott.

"Where are *any* Eagles fans?" Scott replied.

"Surely, some of these people are fans," Martin commented.

"How many reacted to your half-hearted cheers for the team?"

"Not so many."

"Exactly."

At that moment, the United States Marine Band began to play.

"Here he comes," Martin said.

The President appeared and made his way to his position in front of the crowd as the Marine Band played behind him.

And then a voice said over the public-address system, "Ladies and gentlemen, please join us in singing our country's national anthem."

Martin began to sing the anthem. His parents had always insisted they sing along when they went to sporting events. When he was little, Martin enjoyed it. As a teenager, he thought it was corny. But as an adult, it seemed like the right thing to do. He watched Drumpf. 'Did he just stumble over the words?' Martin wondered. 'No, couldn't be. He must have just taken a breath.'

Drumpf then launched into his prepared remarks, short and to the point. Martin only barely paid attention; he was scanning the crowd around him, trying to see if Brianne had come out.

"…we proudly stand for our glorious nation under God," Drumpf was saying. "I want to thank you all for being here. This is a beautiful, big celebration. Actually, to be honest, it's even bigger than we had anticipated."

Martin glanced at Scott standing beside him and then looked around at the gathered crowd. It really wasn't that big. Then he looked closer—maybe he was missing something. He looked around once more and, upon further reflection, thought, 'No, this crowd is not that big.'

Then the voice over the public-address system spoke again, "Ladies and gentlemen, please join us in honoring our country by singing *God Bless America*."

The Army Chorus began to sing. Martin stood and watched the President again. This time, he was sure. Drumpf didn't know the words to *God Bless America*. It wasn't even close.

Martin wasn't sure what was worse—not singing or trying to sing and obviously not knowing the words.

"Do you think he—?" Martin began.

Scott cut him off. "No. Not at all."

And then a face caught Martin's eye. His heart skipped a beat. 'Could it be?'

"Hey, man," Martin said. "Hold on. I'll be back."

"Yeah, cool," Scott said as Martin walked away from him.

Martin walked up behind a girl, tapped her on the shoulder, and then stepped back an appropriate distance. She spun to face him.

He was right! It was Gabrielle.

"Excuse me," she began, before recognizing him and smiling. "Marty, right? Wow. How are you?"

"Yeah, hey, Gabrielle. I'm doing great. You?" She seemed happy to see him. Good sign! 'What was the name of that band?'

"Great. Really." And then her smile disappeared. "You know, I'm sorry, Marty. I meant to call you. But some things came up, and then too much time passed, and, you know how it is."

'Is she being sincere?' Martin couldn't read her. He wasn't sure how to continue. "Naw. I get it. It's only been four and a half months." 'Ouch,' he thought. 'That wasn't too creepy.'

A quick 'what-the-fuck' look flashed across her face, and then it disappeared. "Uh, okay. But I'd still be interested—"

"Are you an Eagles fan?" He didn't mean to cut her off. 'Shit.'

She laughed. "Actually, yes. Born and raised. I'm from Philly."

'Maybe I'm okay.' He stepped just slightly closer. "Philly? Wow. I didn't know. Hey, are you still playing cello for Deaf Monkey Wrench?"

She laughed and clapped her hands. "No, you have that wrong. It was Deaf Monkey Hammer, remember?"

'I'm in!' he thought. "Shit! That's right. How's it going?"

And then her demeanor changed.

'What happened?' he wondered. Then he realized that she was looking down at his chest—where the official White House badge was hanging around his neck.

"Wait. Do you— You work at the White House?" The disappointment was obvious in her voice and on her face.

'Shit, shit, shit. What do I say?' "Yeah. I do," was all he could muster.

"Did you work here back in January?"

"I did," he said.

"Oh. Well, that sucks."

He misunderstood her. "It's not actually all that bad. The hours aren't long, and the work isn't too taxing."

"No," she said. "It sucks that you work for that misogynistic pig."

"Oh, but—"

"Marty. You're a really nice guy," she said. "Really. But I don't want to hang out with someone who works for ... him."

"At all?" He couldn't hide the disappointment in his voice. And he felt his face pinch up—she wouldn't miss that.

"Don't get me wrong," she said. "I'm not some soulless bitch. I'd very much enjoy hanging out with you, if you didn't work for the administration. Maybe when your employment situation … changes."

"Seriously?" He was incredulous.

"Yes. Give me your phone."

He still didn't believe her.

"Give it to me, asshole."

He unlocked and handed her his phone. She typed in a number, saved a contact, and handed it back to him.

"Really?" he deadpanned. He wasn't going to fall for that nonsense.

"Try me," she said.

He called the contact she just entered. A phone rang close by.

She showed him that it was hers ringing and held it to her ear. "It's me, asshole."

They exchanged smiles.

"They eventually fire all of the good ones, right?" she asked.

"Those, and the really bad ones," he answered.

"So call me the day you get fired. And call me Gabby."

G7

A small group of the President's advisors was meeting with him to discuss the upcoming G7 Conference in Canada. The Treasury Secretary was briefing the President on the latest developments from his meetings with his counterparts from those nations. Martin was standing near the Oval exit, doing his best not to be seen by the others in the room.

"Mr. President," Munchkin said. "The statement was very clear; they are unhappy with our decision to impose tariffs on metals."

"Steve, fuck them!" the President almost shouted. "They can afford to be unhappy with our tariffs, because they've been screwing over the American people for thirty years! I was elected to fix these screw jobs, and I'm going to fix them."

"Absolutely, sir. I understand," Munchkin said. "Although it might be better not to say 'fuck them' to their faces when you meet with them next week in Canada."

"For fuck's sake! Who scheduled this event in Canada, anyway?" the President complained. "Justin is just trying to hog the limelight! Although he is a handsome man, a young, virile, handsome man..." Drumpf's voice trailed off and then returned with renewed rage, "But why does he have to be such a prick about things? He knows that Canada has been screwing America for a long time, a long, long time."

"Prime Minister Trudeau is very knowledgeable about the inner workings of the economic relationship between our two countries," Munchkin said. "He's made himself an expert in all facets of trade. And we're sure that the other G7 leaders are preparing to convince you to change your mind on the tariffs."

"They can try, if they want," the President said. "If they give me a hard time, I'll double or triple the tariffs. If 25% tariffs are good, then 50% or 75% tariffs would be even better!"

"Mr. President," the Chief of Staff said. "I'm sure that all of your advisors here today would strongly advise against tariffs at 50% or 75%. The 25% will be high enough."

Indignance erupted across Drumpf's face. He shrugged his shoulders violently. "Well, shit. Why am I even here? Steve, were you elected President? John, were you? If I want to raise the tariffs to 75%, I'll damn well do it."

"Sir, obviously, you could do that," the Treasury Secretary said. "It's certainly your prerogative as President. It's just that, beyond a certain point, the tariffs will hurt the American people more than they will hurt those other countries. The American people, even your fiercest supporters, might get upset."

The President eyed him dubiously.

"It's important that we keep the upcoming midterms in mind, as well, sir," the Chief of Staff added.

Drumpf nodded slowly. He looked from one man to the other and then began to scan the room.

Martin purposefully looked away; he was afraid that their eye contact might prompt the President to put him on the spot. When he hoped the President was done scanning, Martin looked back at him.

"Okay, I get it. Steve, I'll think about what you've said. Let's talk some more before the trip."

Both men were nodding. Various staffers were scribbling furiously in notebooks.

"Thank you, everyone," the President said. "That's it."

The various people in the Oval began packing up. The President picked up the few sheets of paper from his desk and began to tear them up. Martin's heart sank a little.

In minutes, the room had cleared. Martin standing near the door, Madeleine Watterhoot standing at the opposite side of the Oval, and the Chief of Staff were the only three left, aside from the President.

"The rest of your afternoon is free, sir," Watterhoot said.

"Thanks, Maddie."

Kellner turned to go and shot a glance at Martin, who took the hint and also moved to leave the Oval. "Good afternoon, Mr. President."

"Marty! Where're you off to?"

"Sir, Mr. Jermanski has some important tasking this afternoon," Kellner said. "Crucial work."

"What?" Drumpf shook his head. "Well, that 'tasking' can wait for a few minutes. Marty, let's chat."

"Sir, I don't—" Martin began.

"Sir, your time is too—" Kellner began.

"I'll just take a few minutes."

Kellner, who had been moving to leave, stopped and settled into his waiting stance.

"No, John. That'll be all. I know you're extremely busy."

Did Martin detect a hint of sarcasm in the President's voice?

"But, Mr. President—"

"I promise I won't take up too much of Marty's time."

"Yes, sir," Kellner said. He gave Martin a long stare.

Martin gulped involuntarily.

Kellner excused himself. Before the door was even shut, the President started.

"Marty. Being President is hard. This is the hardest that I've ever worked in my life. And I was already considered one of the hardest working men in real estate. I'm certainly the hardest working President in modern times."

The President's voice trailed off. Deep in thought, he absently raised an eyebrow. He took a long, slow, deep breath.

'Is he asleep?' Martin wondered. "Mr. President?"

Drumpf blinked and looked at Martin. "What's my golf schedule for the next week?"

"Well, sir. It just so happens that I asked that very question before coming to the Oval this afternoon. I have it right here…" Martin reached for his phone at the same time the President reached out his hand. "It's on my phone, sir."

"Shit, forget it. I don't want your phone. What's it say?"

"You play tomorrow, the next day, and then two days after that," Martin said.

"Okay. Good. But as I was saying, no modern President has worked as hard as I have. And I *have* to work that hard. I tried to surround myself with good people, competent people. And they're alright, I guess. Most are rich; you have to be brilliant, and hard-working to get rich. So they must be smart guys. Well, except for Jeff Sessoms. Marty, he's retarded."

Martin only nodded. He wasn't going to say a word about anyone during this conversation.

"He was a Senator. Not rich. Not very smart. And he should have told me that he was going to recuse himself from overseeing the Meiller investigation. The gall he has, to accept my nomination, and then step aside as the Meiller witch hunt continues its unlawful attack on me and on so many innocent people.

"Then there's Bull Dog," the President continued. "Also, not rich. But a Four Star Marine. Do you know what a Marine has to do to make it to Four Stars? Brilliant Marine, but sometimes I don't think he's strong enough. He's talked me out of military action so many times. Why is the former General talking me out of using his military? I don't get it. If he was as strong as everyone says is he, as strong as I thought he was when I selected him to be my SecDef, we would have done more … military … things! I'm worried he's weak, that he's making me look weak, worried that he's making our great country weak."

The President shook his head and took a deep breath.

"Marty. I just don't understand why I have a Chief of Staff. I mean, what's the point. What does he do for me that I couldn't do for myself? I've strongly considered getting rid of him, but I told you that already."

Martin began to feel decidedly uncomfortable. He hoped the President wouldn't press him on his thoughts regarding Kellner. With the others, Martin had no strong opinions, because he didn't work for them and didn't know them that well. With the Chief of Staff, on the other hand, Martin knew and liked him.

"Do you know that John has prevented people from coming to see me? He's prevented me from talking to people! No one should prevent the President from doing anything! I'm the fucking President! Do you think Vladimir Putin has people who tell him no? Do you know what he would do to someone who told him no?"

The President leaned back in his chair, shrugged, and then smiled. "Well, I don't really know, but I can guess. I know that it wouldn't go well. But why do I have a Chief of Staff?"

It took a moment for Martin to realize that the latest question was not rhetorical. The President was looking at him, actually waiting for an answer.

"Well, uh, sir." Martin looked around. 'What should I say?' he asked himself. 'What *can* I say?'

"Mr. President. You have a very large staff working for you, and … if you didn't have a Chief of Staff, all of those people would come directly to you with their problems, their complaints …" Martin started to feel better. 'I think I'm on to something,' he thought.

"The Oval would be packed, daily, with people coming to you for advice, for help with their problems, to ask you questions."

The President seemed pleased, but as Martin continued to speak, his face began to change.

"There would be so many people waiting to see you. It would seriously cut into your Executive Time. It might get so bad that you wouldn't be able to play as much golf as you need."

The President seemed taken aback.

"Your work days, already extremely long, longer than any other modern President, would only get longer. There'd be a line through the door and down the hall of people waiting to see you, to learn from you."

"Whoa, Marty. I get it," the President said. "I hadn't considered that. Maybe John does have a purpose. So you're saying I should keep him around?"

"Mr. President. It's not my place to tell you anything, but I think that would be best."

"Thanks. I think you might be right. So what do you think I should do about the G7?"

"Sir?" 'Oh, shit.'

"The G7 Conference next week. Whaddya think?"

"I think the Treasury Secretary knows what he's talking about."

The President considered that for a moment. "Steve is a really smart guy, really smart. He wouldn't be a part of my Cabinet if he weren't. Maybe his advice is decent. But let's face it. Have you seen his wife? And have you seen him? Well, of course, you have, but that's the power of money. There's no way in hell that she would've married him if it weren't for his wealth. He's a rich man. Not as rich as I am, but he's got a lot of money. And that money draws beautiful woman like few other things do."

Martin didn't respond.

"Okay. Thanks, Marty."

"Yes, sir." He glanced at the desk. The President had forgotten about the papers he started to rip. They were only quartered. Martin stepped toward the desk and reached out his hand. "Sir, may I?"

Drumpf was obviously preoccupied with something. He handed the papers to Martin without tearing them any further or saying anything.

Martin left the office.

BOOK INTERVIEW

"You really want to do this?" the Chief of Staff asked him.

They were standing outside the Oval Office. In a few minutes, Martin's first sit-down with the President to discuss *The Art of the Presidency* was scheduled to begin.

"Well, sir, I don't see me rising very fast around here. Maybe this is a way to make a name for myself."

"Or maybe it's a way to end your time in the White House." Kellner shook his head. "I'll be honest with you. I tried to talk the President out of this. At least, out of letting you be his ghost-writer. He overruled me. He insisted that it's a great idea."

"I don't understand, sir."

"You heard about the last person who wrote a book about this White House."

"Wolff? Yes, sir."

"I wasn't here when he was doing his reporting, but I talked to a lot of people who were. I question a lot about his process. But he wrote his book; it worked out well for him."

"I don't understand your point, sir."

"I just don't see how this is going to work out well for you," Kellner said.

"I appreciate your concern," Martin said. "But I'm okay with my chances."

The Chief of Staff shrugged. "Okay. Well, then good luck. You better get in there."

Martin knocked twice and entered the Oval Office.

"Marty! What are you here for this afternoon?"

Martin wasn't completely surprised by the question. The President almost never paid attention to his schedule. Sometimes, he seemed to actively fight it. "Sir, it's our first meeting to discuss *The Art of the Presidency*. I was hoping to get some initial ideas from you and then start working."

"The book, Mr. President," Watterhoot added. "Mr. Jermanski is here to talk about the book."

'She is *always* here,' Martin thought.

"Are you on my schedule?" Drumpf opened a folder on his desk and pulled from it a single sheet of paper. He looked it over. "Mmm. It says you are." He slid the paper back into the folder and looked up at Watterhoot. She nodded. "Look, Marty. It's been a long day today. I'm not sure I'm up for this right now."

Martin wasn't necessarily surprised by this, but he was hurt nonetheless. It wasn't even 4:30 yet. "We can reschedule, sir."

"I'll tell you what. Let's talk for a few minutes; we'll see how it goes. Pull up a chair."

Drumpf got up from his desk and walked to an arm chair. Martin moved to the couch and pulled out a pen and notebook.

"Pen and notebook, eh? That's good," Drumpf said. "So many people around here just type on their little … devices. I prefer the good old pen and paper."

"Thanks, sir. Me, too," Martin said and took a second to gird himself. "But let's talk about the book a bit. I'd like to hear your thoughts on what is most important about your time in office. What have you learned or what new advice can you give your readers?"

"Learned? I haven't learned anything. Nothing has surprised me. Well, except for the level of incompetence throughout the government. It's actually worse than I thought! Nothing gets done around here unless I do it myself. How did this place function before I got here?"

Martin almost interjected but realized that the President was just warming up.

"Actually, I'll tell you how. It didn't. Most of the people who work for the government can't do their jobs. And most of the ones that can, they're actually doing other things instead. The Deep State is alive and well, and it's working against me."

The President's voice rose. "If those people, who were obviously brainwashed by the Democrats, the Hillary-ites, the United Nations types, if they would just do their job instead of attack me, or stand in the way, the government would function like a well-oiled machine."

Martin realized that line of questioning wasn't going to yield anything interesting or new. He tried a different angle. "What is the art of the presidency?"

"Marty. You're the author. You're supposed to tell me what the art of the presidency is."

Try again. Same question, slightly different words. "What is the Drumpf art of the presidency? What does The Ronald think of the presidency?"

"In my case, it's hard work. Very, very hard work. It's understanding what needs to be done and then doing it." Drumpf looked down at his feet. He wasn't in the mood for this conversation.

And Martin could sense that. But he had nothing; he thought that he could squeeze out a page or two based on their conversation. He hoped.

The President took a deep breath. "That's all for today, Marty. It's been a long day, a very productive day. It's time for me to watch some Fox. I can always count on them to keep me informed." Drumpf stood up, which was Martin's signal to do the same.

"I'll try to get on your schedule a little earlier in the day next time, sir. These discussions can be grueling so late in the day."

"That's great, Marty. Great," he said as he walked to his desk. "Before we talk about the book again, I'd like to read what you've written. That will give me an idea of where we're at and where we're going."

Martin wasn't sure what to say. There wouldn't be much for the President to read. Of course, that might be a good thing—everyone knew that the President didn't like to read much anyway.

"Yes, sir." He wasn't sure what else to say, and then, "Is there anything you need before I go, sir?"

"No. But, Marty, try to be a little better prepared before we sit down next time. A professional author would have done a better job today."

"Yes, sir." 'What the hell?' Martin thought. As the thought crossed his mind, he turned from the President to walk to the door. He hoped that the President didn't notice the look on his face before he turned.

The walk back to his office seemed longer than normal. Martin wasn't sure what to think about the meeting.

Drumpf spent a grand total of seven minutes with him, out of a scheduled forty-five. He didn't offer any thoughts, no keen insights. It was just the same old schtick.

What had Martin gotten himself into? And then he thought back to what he had read about Tony Schwartzman. He admitted to himself that a small part of him had hoped that Schwartzman was just being bitter, that Drumpf was a perfectly fine subject to write with and that Schwartzman was just after some free publicity when granting those recent interviews.

Perhaps *none* of that was true. Perhaps Schwartzman had been completely truthful in those interviews. Martin then realized that this whole idea might have been a big mistake. Maybe Kellner had been right to warn Martin about the project.

"Why did the President's schedule include a one-on-one meeting with you?!"

It was never a normal greeting with Amanda. It was either an attack of some kind or nothing at all. There was no in between.

"What do you mean?" Martin asked.

"Don't bullshit me," she said. "Everyone saw the item on the President's schedule. Executive Time. POTUS, Jermanski."

Martin had to think fast. He checked the time. 4:42. "He wanted to ask about my dad down at Mer-a-Lago. He knows that my dad and I are close."

The unexpected answer seemed to confuse her. She eyed him warily.

"Look what time it is," he continued. "I was in the office for eight minutes. What do you possibly think we could have talked about in eight minutes?" A little bit of truth makes every lie easier.

The logic—faulty or not—worked on Amanda.

But she wasn't finished. "That's a stupid thing to put on the President's schedule. Why list it at all?"

"Why does anything appear on the schedule?" he responded. "We all know how much that document is ignored."

She seemed to buy it. He started to relax.

But the thought stuck in his head: *A little bit of truth makes every lie easier.* 'Is that part of *The Art of the Presidency*? It just might be.' Then he realized that it was probably a truth for every President. Truth and fiction seemed to be slightly different here than anywhere else in Martin's experience.

TWITTER NUMBERS

Monday morning, June 11th found Martin reporting to his office in the White House. He was disappointed. He was still stinging from the higher-up's decision to exclude him from the Singapore trip. He had never been to Southeast Asia and had been looking forward to it.

As was typical when the President was on travel, many of the staffers had little to do. Martin had been told that, in other administrations, the Chief Executive's absence made life more difficult for the staffers. They were required to finish various tasks that couldn't be completed when the President was in town.

That rule didn't seem to apply in the Drumpf administration. Boredom was the order of the day until, of course, some number of them were tasked with assisting the higher-ups respond to the random tweet or bizarro press conference comment. The crises always came. Eventually.

And so everyone was waiting, including Martin and Amanda, sitting in their office. She was on the computer, surfing porn sites. Thankfully, she was wearing ear buds. He was on his iPhone, surfing other random sites.

His phone beeped with an incoming email. Her email, minimized on her desktop, also chimed. They opened the email together.

It was an All-Staff announcement. Amanda said "Fuck it" and went back to watching beautiful people doing just that.

Martin, more paranoid, read the email to its conclusion. "We have a meeting over on the first floor of the Eisenhower. There's a list of twenty-five names. You're on it."

"You'll sign in for me, right?" She asked without looking up from the nubile bodies doing things to each other.

"Uh, no."

"Come on, bitch."

"Fine." It was easier to not fight. He'd sign the attendance sheet for her. But he wouldn't do anything beyond that.

·   ·   ·

Martin entered the large conference room a few minutes before the meeting was scheduled to commence. Almost twenty staffers, most young but a few older, stood around the room, waiting for the meeting to start.

"Jermanski," one of the newer staffers called out. "Any idea what this is about?"

"Nope," Martin responded. "I just scanned most of the major news sites. I didn't see anything that would require work."

"I have more important things to do than attend this meeting," said an older man to Martin, as if Martin was the one who called the meeting.

Martin shrugged. He only vaguely recognized the man who made the statement. "You are?"

The man harrumphed and turned his back on Martin.

A moment later, one of the senior personnel in the Communications Office entered the room. She was no Hope Hills, that's for sure. Tidy and businesslike, the woman wore a plaid business suit, her hair done up in a bun. She moved to the end of the conference table, put down a pile of folders, and then opened the top one.

"Ladies and gentlemen. Please find your name and sign next to it. Could you pass this around?" She handed a piece of paper to the staffer closest to her and then continued, "As you are all aware, the President left Canada and is now in Singapore. The official summit will commence this evening, our time. We need to ensure a full communications offensive heading into this important time. This summit may be the most important event in the President's first two years in office."

Martin looked around. The faces of those present were typical of a group of people who didn't want to be present, who were only half paying attention to the speaker, and who couldn't wait to get back to their regularly scheduled afternoons. It was, he realized, a typical staff meeting.

"This communications offensive is extremely important. As such, our office recently conducted a review of the President's Twitter followers. We have determined that the twenty five of you are not currently Twitter followers of President Drumpf. That needs to change, today."

Several hands shot in the air.

"What does that even mean?"

The speaker raised an eyebrow. "It means that you'll become a follower of the President before leaving the meeting this afternoon."

Several more hands shot in the air.

"But I'm not on Twitter at all."

Her eyebrow raised even further. "Time to get on."

"What if we choose not to?"

Her eyebrow raised so high that it seemed to disfigure her entire face. "You'll be terminated. Friday'll be your last day."

Several hands dropped.

"Before I answer any more questions, let me explain a bit more. I have two forms here. You will complete and sign one of the two before you leave the conference room. Oh, and please tell anyone who signed-in but is not actually present that they will be required to report to my office no later than five this afternoon to complete one of the forms. If they do not, they will be terminated, also as of this Friday."

Several more hands dropped.

"Yes?" she asked a guy whose hand was one of the few still raised.

"What are the two forms?"

"Good question. The first form is a simple sheet that includes your name, directorate, office and phone number, and your Twitter handle. Obviously, for those of you who don't have a Twitter account, you can create it now before completing the form."

"Once you complete the form, someone from my office will follow you on Twitter to verify that you're following the President. And, again, failure to do so will result in your termination."

"What is the second form?" a staffer called out from the far end of the conference room. He didn't even bother to wait to be called on.

"The second form is slightly less pleasant. Effectively, it is a resignation letter, stating that you intend to resign on Friday and that you have fully enjoyed your time working in the Administration. Also, that you wish the President every success in the future." She smiled a huge grin. And it actually seemed sincere.

A hand went up and then slowly went back down.

"I'll pass the Twitter form out. Can you please pass this one around?" She handed it to the closest staffer to her left. "And, for those less inclined to join Twitter, this second form. Please?" She handed the second form to the closest staffer on her right. "If anyone wants to talk to me privately, I'll be sitting here until I have twenty-five forms."

"There're only twenty-three of us present."

"Like I said, please inform those not present of the deadline for this afternoon." With that, she sat down and looked around.

A young lady approached the speaker. "Can I speak to you in private?"

"Of course. Go ahead."

The young woman looked around. "This really isn't in private."

"Well, it'll have to do, won't it?"

"Um. Okay." The young lady pulled a chair closer to the communications staffer and sat down next to her.

Martin took a few steps closer, so that he could hear.

The young lady leaned close and spoke almost in a whisper. "See, I'm not really a fan of the President. I'm working while I wait for my next opportunity. If I follow him on Twitter, several of my close family and friends will get the wrong idea."

"The wrong idea?"

'Uh-oh,' Martin thought. 'This is not going to go how she hopes it will.'

"Yes." She nervously looked around to see if anyone was listening. Her cheeks flushed slightly.

Martin realized that she was probably feeling slightly embarrassed. What she failed to understand, that Martin did, was that she should have been looking for allies to join her in the discussion. The communications staffer that she was talking to was not on her side.

"See, most of my family are strong anti-Drumpfers. They think I am working in the Administration merely to learn as much about his corruption as possible."

'Why would she say such a thing?!' Martin wondered. 'Especially to the communications staffer. The girl was naïve or stupid, or both.'

"Well, I completely understand," the staffer replied in a firm, businesslike voice. "I think the best thing to do going forward is to complete this form." She handed the girl a form.

"Oh, okay." The girl said, not quite understanding what was about to happen to her. She looked down at the form. "Wait. I don't understand."

'She doesn't understand,' Martin thought, 'but she's about to.'

"I just need you to fill out this form."

"But, I don't want to quit. I don't have anything else—"

"I'm sure you'll figure something out," the communications staffer interrupted her and said smugly. "Perhaps your family or friends will have some suggestions for your next employment."

The young girl started to plead, and then she started to cry.

"Now, now, dear. This is best, for all of us. If you want to think about it, you can. But I'll need one of the forms to be complete and on my desk by five this afternoon. I recommend that you complete this one."

Martin glanced around. Most of the people in the room seemed to pity the young girl. Others had nothing but contempt on their face. Some were trying their best to ignore the situation at the head of the table; their faces were buried in forms or their phones. Martin grabbed a copy of the Twitter form; it was time to sign up for Twitter.

Martin Jermanski. @MJermanski. Now to follow the President: @realRonaldDrum1.

'Who screwed up *that* Twitter handle?' Martin wondered. 'They couldn't get @realRonaldDrumpf?'

Martin had avoided Twitter since January when it was suggested that he sign up. He created an account on his phone, and then completed the staffer's form with the appropriate information.

Martin looked up from the form to see that the young girl was nowhere to be found. She must have left while he was signing up and then completing the form. He walked the paper up to the communications staffer and placed it on the table in front of her.

"Thank you!" she exclaimed. She was surprisingly upbeat after causing the girl to cry.

"Sure," Martin responded and then left the conference room.

·   ·   ·

"Well, did you sign the attendance sheet for me?" Amanda asked him the question before he even entered their cramped office. He wasn't even sure how she saw him before asking.

"No; there wasn't one."

"What? No attendance tracker? They're getting stupid."

"No. Actually, we each were given the choice to fill out one form or another. You had to be there to complete it in person." Martin went on to describe the meeting, including what she needed to do that afternoon.

Amanda protested. Then argued with him, as if the meeting was his doing. Then she cursed him out, which wasn't unusual. He just shrugged.

"Why didn't you grab me a form?"

"I wasn't sure which form you wanted."

"Fuck!"

"Sorry. You're gonna have to head up there yourself."

"What about you?"

"I'm done," he said. "I'm not going back there."

Amanda cursed him out again. He didn't budge. Finally, she stood and stormed out. To Martin, it actually felt nice.

Martin pulled the monitor around, glanced at the image of nude bodies intertwined with each other, and then closed the web browser. It was then that he noticed that she was surfing porn on his login. "Bitch," he muttered.

SPACE FORCE TROOPERS

"It might be his 'Mission Accomplished' moment."

"His what?" Martin asked. He was having lunch with Nora Powell, an expert both in International Relations and National Security Affairs in the Drumpf administration. In her mid-thirties, she was short, just over five feet tall, and had her dirty blonde hair pulled back into a small pony tail. Martin had asked around for the name of someone to explain to him what had just happened in Singapore during Drumpf's summit with Kim Jong Un. Powell came highly recommended.

"His 'Mission Accomplished' moment," she said. "Like George W. Bush."

"Not familiar," Martin said.

"What? Really?" She blinked—something, Martin noticed, she did when something surprised her. "Okay, so shortly after the invasion of Iraq in 2003, after our forces rolled through the country and toppled Saddam Hussein, President Bush landed on an aircraft carrier and, in front of a gigantic banner that read 'Mission Accomplished,' gave a speech saying just that."

Martin still wasn't following. "And?" he asked.

"Well, we were in Iraq for another decade, and the mission was anything but accomplished. It was a bit of premature ejaculation."

"Got it," Martin said. "You're saying that Drumpf's touting the summit but not much happened."

"Frankly, all of about *nothing* happened, okay? The joint statement that they signed was less definitive than most of the previous statements signed by the two countries—the same statements that the President said were proof that the U.S. had been played by North Korea over and over."

"But it was still a good thing, right?" Martin asked. "I mean, they sat down and talked. Has that ever happened?"

"Martin, listen. They talked, Drumpf saluted one of their generals, lots of photos were taken. Who wins from that?"

Martin wasn't stupid. He could tell that the answer to the question was obviously Kim Jong Un. He just didn't exactly know why.

"If *nothing else* happens, who wins from a picture of them shaking hands?"

"K.J.U.?" Martin offered.

"Yes! Because he can show his people that picture as proof that he, their great and exalted and probably insane leader, was able to sit down, as equals, with the most powerful man on the planet. With their enemy, an enemy who is on camera saying good things about their leader. The PR is absolutely priceless."

"So what if he gets a little positive PR," Martin said. "Is that such a bad thing?"

"How much do you know about K.J.U.?"

"Not much, really," he said.

Nora looked at him with a raised eyebrow.

"Okay, nothing."

"North Korea is a police-state," she started, and then in a rapid-fire voice, "A large percentage of its population, including women and children, live in concentration camps. Most of the population, except for well-placed elites, live in poverty. K.J.U. has killed members of his own regime to maintain his grip on power. In the past, they have used foreign, humanitarian aid to beef up their military while their people starved."

She paused and reached into her purse for her phone. "Let me show you something." She typed for a few seconds, and then showed him a picture. "Have you ever seen this?"

It was a picture of the Earth from space at night. The outlines of the continents were clearly visible due to the splotches of light where cities were located. "Yeah," he said. "I've seen several like this. I grew up in Florida; I love NASA."

"Okay, how about this?"

It was another picture, more of the same.

"Okay." He didn't recognize the outlines of light, so he wasn't sure of the location the picture showed.

"So this is Japan," she said, pointing to the picture. "This is South Korea. China. Russia."

"Okay," he said.

"Look at that." She pointed to a big dark area surrounded by bright lights all around.

"Yeah."

"That's North Korea."

"Oh," he said.

"In terms of number of active personnel, they have the second largest military in the world. And yet, as a nation, they are too poor to light their country at night."

"That doesn't sound so…" Martin trailed off. The horrors of North Korea were starting to sink in. He looked up at Nora, who raised a questioning eyebrow at him. "I think I get it," he said.

·   ·   ·

An hour later, Martin was back in the White House heading toward his office. His plan was to stop in, see if Amanda had anything of importance, and then swing by the Oval to see if there was any garbage to remove. As it was getting late in the afternoon, he thought there was a good chance the Oval would be empty.

He silently stepped to the door of their office. Amanda was sitting at her computer, staring intently at her screen and typing.

He watched her for a moment and considered doing something to startle her; he decided it was better not to. He walked into the office.

She looked up. "Hey, bitch. How'd your lunch with N.P. go?"

"What?" he asked as he pulled out his chair to sit down. "Are you on an initials-only basis with her now?"

His question confused her, and she was starting to get angry. "What are you talking about?"

"You know; you call her N.P. She calls you A.C. Initials only."

"Oh, fuck off, Jermanski."

"I'm on it," he said. "Anything going on?" He pushed his chair back in; he didn't think he was going to be sitting down after all.

"Does it look like anything's going on?"

He shook his head. "You going to make the afternoon garbage can run?"

"Shit. Me? I haven't done an afternoon run in a few months. That's why I have you. Now get on it."

Martin flashed her a quick smile and then left the office.

"What the hell was that for?" she called. He didn't bother to answer her question.

Martin saw that Jeremiah, so-named due to his inhumanly low voice, was on duty outside of the Oval. Martin approached and smiled at him.

"Quite a gathering in there," Jeremiah said.

"Oh?"

"I believe they're discussing Mogul's trip. Last time the door opened, it sounded pretty heated."

"Think it's safe to go in?" Martin asked.

"For you? It's a toss-up." Then Jeremiah knocked twice on the door and opened it wide, revealing to everyone in the room Martin standing in the doorway.

Through the open door, Martin saw the President, the Secretary of Defense, Mike Pompeii, the newly-confirmed Secretary of State, the Chief of Staff, and a handful of high-level staffers. He said a quick "Thanks" under his breath to Jeremiah and then stepped through the door.

"My pleasure," Jeremiah said quietly as he pulled the door shut.

The mood in the room was tense and several of the people frowned at him. But not the President.

"Marty! Come in. You're probably here to grab my papers, but you may as well stay awhile."

"Yes, sir," he replied.

"Mr. President—" the Chief of Staff began.

"John," the President said. "I already know what you're going to say. Marty can stay, okay?"

"Yes, sir," the Chief of Staff said to the President and then turned to Martin, "Mr. Jermanski." Kellner's eyes sent the very clear message that Martin was to empty the garbage can and then stay out of the conversation.

Martin merely nodded and moved to get the garbage can.

"Sir," Secretary Matthews picked up, apparently where he was interrupted by Martin's entrance. "There are a variety of problems with immediately cancelling all wargames with South Korea."

Martin bent to retrieve the can; there was a sizable pile of papers at its bottom.

"SecDef is right, Mr. President," Secretary Pompeii added. "I think we should—"

"Mike!" the President cut him off. "You were the one who told me that K.J.U. seemed to be worthy of consideration."

Martin stood up and began to back away from the President's desk.

"Oh, hold on, Marty." The President waved him closer.

Martin stepped up to the desk. Drumpf pulled a lighter from his pocket. He flipped it open and ignited it, and then nodded his head, indicating to Martin to bring the garbage can closer.

"Sir?" Martin asked.

"Sir, I—" Secretary Pompeii began.

"I considered him," the President said. "And decided to extend the offer. Martin, closer."

Martin stepped closer to the President, who reached into the garbage can with his lighter and set the pile of papers on fire. Martin gulped and stared at the President in horror.

The President only smiled, hugely, in return.

Martin realized that everyone in the room had stopped talking and was staring at him and the garbage can of burning Presidential papers. 'God, the DRT,' he thought to himself. He turned and almost sprinted away from the desk. There! He spotted a glass of what he hoped was water on the coffee table. He bee-lined for it and dumped it into the can. Wet papers are shitty, but they are infinitely better than burned papers.

"Oh, hell," the President said.

Martin looked up to see the disappointment on Drumpf's face. Everyone else was wearing a blank expression, except for the Chief of Staff, who actually appeared impressed.

"Mr. President," Matthews said, seemingly trying to jumpstart the conversation. "We can support you better if you keep us in the loop on your decisions. I would have walked you through the pros and cons of wargames with South Korea."

"Bull Dog, Mike, everyone, listen," the President began. "I don't understand what's going on. I had a great summit with Kim Jung Un. We had a good conversation; I got to know him better; there were some beautiful photos. It was a success. Or so I thought, until all of you started discussing it with me. I hadn't even landed back here in Washington, and several of you were trying to tell me about … issues. The press, biased, crooked, and treasonous as they are, are raking me through the coals. There are even Republicans, Republicans (!), who are saying that the summit was a failure. I'll tell you what—are we talking about the same summit? Because I'm seeing a very different summit than you're seeing."

Martin moved to stand at the wall near the exit. He put the garbage can on the ground beside him. While he was worried about the burned and soaking papers that it held, he didn't want to step out of the meeting. After all, the President had invited him to listen in.

"Mr. President," Secretary Matthews said, "there were successes to be sure, however—"

"Bull Dog! I'm glad you reminded me. There was one very important success that I forgot to mention to any of you, yet. I promised Kim Jong Un that I'd sign an agreement to end the Korean War."

"What?" Pompeii blurted.

"Jesus Christ," Matthews slipped.

"Fucking shit," the Chief of Staff muttered.

'Holy shit,' Martin thought.

"Mr. President," Pompeii said. "That was an extremely unwise promise to make."

The President looked around in shock. "What are you people talking about? We're going to end the Korean War! We've been at war since the fifties, and now I'm going to end it. This is a great victory for me. And for America!"

All three men were shaking their heads.

"We're talking peace on the Korean Peninsula," the President continued. "Do you know how much money we're going to save? We'll bring all those troops home. The South Koreans will finally have to stop freeloading on our generosity."

"Sir," Matthews said. "We need that foothold in Northeast Asia. It serves as a counterweight to the Chinese, to the Russians."

"Having American troops in the region is good for stability; it's good for the world," Pompeii said. "And we're not sure of Kim Jong Un's willingness to comply with our wishes. He's a long way from giving up his nukes."

"You're the Secretary of State, Mike. What do you know about my troops in Korea?"

"Sir," said Matthews, "Mike is right. Those troops, your troops, stabilize the entire region."

"The little Rocketman was really excited when I offered to end the war," the President said. "I think he's willing to give up the nukes. He told me so. And I believe him. He and I are going to be good friends."

The President sat there looking up at the others. Finally, he shook his head and said, "I tell the American people all the time. I tell them that I have the best Cabinet in history. In history! Sometimes, when you guys are talking to me, I wonder if that's actually true."

"Mr. President, we're honored to serve on your Cabinet," the Secretary of State began.

Martin couldn't imagine Matthews or Kellner saying such a thing.

"And we want nothing but the greatest success for your administration and our great nation," Pompeii continued. "But we have to approach North Korea with an appropriate level of caution. We need to have our eyes fully open in all of our dealings with them."

Drumpf nodded. He didn't seem convinced. "I still think that the Summit was a success. Don't care what you guys tell me, don't care what the press is saying, don't care what Congress is saying. It was a success. I bet if Dennis was here, he'd tell me it was a success."

"We're sure he would, sir," Kellner said.

"Mr. President, this might be a good time to talk about the upcoming Conference with President Putin," Matthews said.

"There are doubts about the optics of you meeting with President Putin," Pompeii said.

"Optics? What optics?" The President's voice was rising. "The optics are this: President Putin is a great leader for the Russian people. I am a great leader for the American people. The world'd be safer if our two nations were better friends. The world'll become safer when he and I become better friends."

"Sir— Kellner began.

The President exploded. "Don't start with me about Meiller and his 'investigation'. Don't get me started on Sessoms and his spineless failure to stop that witch hunt. There was no collusion!" Drumpf took a deep breath, flashing a fierce frown at his advisors.

"You're going to tell me that we need to get tough on Russia, tough on Putin. I get it. I'm ready to do that. Do you know what he told me when we spoke last year?" He looked around at each of the men. "Of course, you don't. The only people there were Tilleson and me. And he flaked out, so now he's back in retirement. I should have never chosen him to be my Secretary of State. Poor decision. I was getting bad advice at the time."

"But do you know what Putin told me? Did you know that they established the Russian Space Forces back in 2015? Actually, they reestablished them, but still. So today Russia has a Space Force, and the United States does not. You wanna get tough on Russia? Let's create a space force. Show them that if they can do it, we can do it bigger and better!"

SecDef opened his mouth to respond, but the President cut him off.

"He was very proud of those Space Forces. Very proud. He flashed his shit-eating grin at me and then poked fun of me, of America. 'How can a super power consider itself super if it doesn't have a Space Force?' he asked me. Then he laughed at me. He laughed at me!"

All three advisors to the President began to shake their heads.

"Sir, we don't need a Space Force," Matthews said. "During this time of fiscal constraint, it doesn't make sense."

"Doesn't make sense?" the President sneered. "If Russia has a Space Force, America needs a Space Force. We can't allow them to possess a capability that we, ourselves, don't have. We'll look weak to Russia, and to the world!"

"Putin was baiting you, sir," Pompeii said.

"Baiting me? For fuck's sake, Mike. That's bullshit! No one baits The Ronald. The Ronald baits them."

"Sir," Kellner spoke in a calming voice. "Everything that their Space Forces are organized to do, our Air Force already does. There is no need for the Pentagon to establish a separate Space Force."

Drumpf glared at Kellner and then turned to Matthews.

The Secretary of Defense nodded firmly.

The President growled.

"Each of the Armed Services has components that operate in or deal with space," Matthews said. "And those components operate jointly, as one team, to accomplish our nation's military needs. The costs of reorganizing the Pentagon, to create a separate Space Force, far outweigh the need, or utility of doing so. We can, if you desire, examine ways to better fund those space components. We can strengthen our space capabilities without creating a Space Force."

It was obvious to Martin that Drumpf stopped listening shortly after the SecDef started speaking.

"I hear what you're saying, Bull Dog, I do. I just think it would send a message to the world that we are serious about outer space." The President seemed tired of the conversation.

"All three of us are in agreement that the United States, at this time, does not need a Space Force," Kellner said.

"You three might be in agreement, but ..." The President was looking around, seemingly trying to find an argument to convince his advisors. Then his eyes settled on Martin.

Kellner spun to see what the President was looking at, spotted Martin standing there, and immediately frowned. "No, sir, Mr. President—"

"Marty!" the President called.

The Secretary of Defense realized what was about to happen. "Mr. President, Martin is a fine, young staffer—" he began.

"What do you think of a Space Force?" Drumpf asked.

"—but he isn't an expert on defense issues," Matthews finished.

"I want to hear your thoughts," Drumpf said.

Martin cleared his throat. "Sir, I'm not an expert on these issues."

"Don't be humble, Marty. I know your expertise. I just want to hear your opinion." The President smiled warmly at him.

Martin concentrated on the President's smile; he could tell that the three other men were glaring at him but tried to ignore it. He racked his brain. He enjoyed science fiction; he had read and enjoyed *Starship Troopers*, *Ender's Game*, *The Forever War*—all books that dealt with space warfare. It seemed to him that if Russia had a Space Force, then the United States should as well.

Martin also knew a little about Ronald Reagan's Star Wars program, and the fact that the Berlin Wall came down and the Soviet Union fell apart a few years after Reagan started that program.

"Uh—"

"Come on, Marty," the President enthusiastically prompted.

"Sir, Ronald Reagan created the Star Wars program, and the Soviet Union fell apart a few years later. If we need to be tough on Russia, we should create a Space Force."

The President's smile only grew larger. He slapped his desk with both hands. "It's settled! The United States is going to create a Space Force."

The three advisors to the President stood stone-faced before him. He smiled up at them.

"We'll make it official in the next few days. John, make the arrangements for a press conference. Bull Dog, get with the others and get me a draft letter."

FAMILY SEPARATION

"I'm getting destroyed!" Drumpf thundered. "This is bullshit, it's fucking bullshit! This policy is costing us."

"Mr. President, the policy is doing exactly what we want it to do," Steve Mills said, trying to calm Drumpf. "It is highlighting the failure of our Congress to devise an effective immigration policy for the nation."

"Steve. I understand that," the President said and then raised his voice. "But the biased, fake-news, liberal press doesn't seem to get that. They're actually blaming me, me(!), for the problems at the border."

"Sir—" Mills tried to interject, but the President was growing more agitated.

"They are personally blaming me for those little kids being separated from their parents, from their mommies. Have you seen those videos? Did you hear the audio? Little kids screaming for their mommies. It's horrible!" The President almost sounded sad, and desperate.

Mills didn't seem phased. "Mr. President. We knew that this was going to happen. We knew it was going to cause a sensation in the press, and not the good kind. We wanted this to highlight the broken system." He was calmly trying to talk the President down.

"You're one of my top guys, Steve," Drumpf said. "One of my top guys! But I didn't want this. I didn't think it would get to this point."

"Mr. President," Mills tried again, speaking calmly and firmly. "This is putting real pressure on the Democrats and Congress to fix immigration. And they will; they're gonna have to."

"Mr. President," Kelly Conville interrupted, also in a calm voice. "It might be time to try a different tack, time to move in a different direction. We might need to rethink this."

"Oh, fuck you, Kelly!" Mills said. "You were completely on board with this when we rolled it out."

"I never said that I wasn't," Conville shot back angrily. "But it might be time to … to adjust."

The President was sitting back, watching his two aides discuss the issue.

"No, this isn't the time to 'adjust,'" Mills said, mocking Conville. "What the fuck does that even mean?" Then he turned back to the President, "We need to stick to our guns. Need to stay strong. We need to continue to hammer Congress. This is moving in our direction."

Drumpf shook his head. More so than Martin had ever seen, Drumpf actually seemed distressed.

"You say keep it," Drumpf said pointing at Mills. "You say adjust," he said pointing at Conville. "I don't like how it's playing in the press. They're not listening to us."

"Mr. President." Andrew Breiburg spoke up. "I think they're both right, or they both *were* right."

"What the fuck does that mean?" Drumpf shot back.

"Everything we do for the next few months has to take into account the midterms. Steve's policy is the right one; it was the right one. But it doesn't take into account the midterms," said Breiburg. The President was listening.

"If this was six months ago or last fall, we could have outlasted the media's fake outrage; we could have outlasted Congress," Breiburg continued. "But because the midterms are getting close, the timing is working against us. We need a win on this one, and, right now, we're losing."

"Fuck that!" Mills said. "Precisely because the midterms are getting close is the reason to stick to our guns. Sir, your base, the people that are going to vote for your Republicans this fall, they don't care about Mexican kids being separated from their parents. They want them all sent back!"

"Mr. President," said Breiburg, speaking in the calm voice that Mills had abandoned. "You know that I supported this policy when we instituted it. I agreed with Steve then. I still agree that the policy is sound, but the timing is killing us. We shouldn't be worried about your base; they'll always stay strong. But some of your voters aren't strong supporters. We can't risk losing them. The Republicans can't risk losing them this fall."

The President shook his head. He seemed to be in pain. Finally he looked up and scanned the faces of the others in the room.

"Marty. What do you think?"

"Jermanski?" Mills raged. "Seriously? Mr. President, you're going to ask one of the junior staffers?"

Martin was as surprised as anyone. He and the President had many talks outside of formal meetings, but, with the single exception of the discussion about the Space Force earlier that week, Drumpf had never asked his opinion during one.

"Steve, calm down. Marty has proven himself. I trust his opinion."

"Proven himself? Mr. President," Mills protested again. "There's a reason he's only a junior staffer. There are reasons he hasn't been accepted into any more important positions."

Martin didn't think Mills even knew who he was. What did *he* know about Martin? And what did he mean when he said 'there's a reason he's only a junior staffer'?

Drumpf shrugged and seemed to weigh Mills' words in his mind. Then he looked at Martin, "Marty, what do you think?"

Martin's stomach did a back flip. He'd never been put on the spot like this before—not in front of this many principals and other staffers. He gulped; then he hoped that it didn't sound as loud to the others as it did to him.

"Well, Mr. President." Martin didn't know much about the issue. He knew that kids were being separated from their parents at the border. He had heard that a lot of people were up in arms about the policy. He had seen a video clip on his phone that supposedly showed one of the 'camps' were those kids were being held. It didn't look good. "It doesn't look good. Aren't there other ways to stop people from crossing the border?"

"No," Mills stated emphatically. "All the other ways have been tried. They all failed."

"Well, maybe so," Martin responded and then turned to the President. "But it doesn't make you look good. I don't like, and I don't think the American people like, the sight or the feeling of families being separated. It makes you look like a monster. People need to know you're not a monster."

"But—" Mills began to protest, then the President cut him off.

"Steve. I know what you think. I know what Kelly thinks. Now I know what Marty thinks."

"Who cares what—" Mills started to ask.

He was again cut off by the President. "I did. I do." And then to Martin, "Thanks, Marty." Drumpf took a deep breath. "Okay, everybody. I've thought long and hard about this. I've made up my mind. Steve, I know that you care deeply about this issue, this policy. I understand that there are others who feel differently. I love the policy. I think it's a great idea; I really do. But we're going to change it."

Mills shook his head in disappointment. Martin was excited—did he actually help persuade the President to change the policy?

"I want an Executive Order ready for signing tomorrow. Work out the details; get back to me this afternoon with the draft. Keep it short. You know I don't like long documents. Can't stand 'em." The President paused and looked around with eyebrows raised. No one else said anything. "Good work, everyone. Get back to work."

The Oval Office began to clear. Martin made his way toward the door. Just as he reached it, Steve Mills called out to him.

"Hey, Jermanski! Wait for a second outside."

Martin nodded and then let himself out. Mills had never spoken to him beyond the typical 'do-this-do-that' conversations that junior staffers are typically subjected to. He waited.

In a few moments, Mills emerged from the Oval Office and walked straight up to Martin. "I don't know who you think you are, and I don't know what you've done to gain the President's trust." He took a step closer and poked Martin in the chest. "Watch yourself. Don't get in my way again. Understand?"

Martin found himself taking a step backward. It was the most overtly confrontational anyone had been toward him since his coming to the White House. Except for Amanda, but she was her own thing. "Yeah. Sure. I understand."

.   .   .

The next morning, Martin stopped in the Oval Office to check for any papers that needed disposing of. The office was empty when he passed through; the pile of papers was small that day. As he was leaving the office, he heard the other door open.

The President entered the office, talking to the Vice President. Drumpf saw Martin as he was in the process of pulling the door shut on his way out.

"Marty!"

Martin stopped, reopened the door, and stepped back into the Oval.

"Marty. I'm signing that Executive Order later today. I want you to be in the Oval Office for the signing."

Marty had been in the Oval Office for various official functions, typically as a runner or assisting more senior staffers, but this was different. "Thank you, sir. I'll be there."

About twenty minutes prior to the appointed time, Martin made his way to the Oval Office. The press was already starting to file in, photographers, cameramen, various journalists. He recognized all of them by face, most by name. It was strange to come to the Oval Office and not have to herd the press in or out. He took a place by the wall, off to the right of the President's desk.

About five minutes prior to the appointed time, Drumpf entered the office with Spence and Kristen Nelson, the Secretary of Homeland Security. They were chatting together. Drumpf took his seat behind his desk; the two others took spots just behind and to either side of him.

Finally, it was time. After receiving the signal from an aide and a cameraman, the President began speaking, "Well, thank you very much. We're signing an executive order I consider to be a very important executive order. It's about keeping families together while at the same time making sure that we have a very powerful, very strong border."

Martin looked around the Oval Office. The crowd of reporters was larger than normal. Apparently, this family separation issue was a big deal.

"… the families together," the President continued. "I didn't like the sight or the feeling of families being separated. It's a problem …"

Isn't that what Martin had said the day before? He was almost sure that it was. But he quickly got over his excitement and scanned the room. Every Oval Office function was the same – Secret Service, staffers, press of all varieties (except maybe CNN), and always the strap-hangers. The strap-hangers were those people that had nothing to do with the event whatsoever, at least as far as Martin could tell, but always found a reason to be in the Oval Office. His mind began to wander, and then the President finished.

Mike Spence started to speak. The President looked right at Martin. They made eye contact. At least, Martin thought that they did. The President continued to look around. And then he flashed Martin another look. Their eyes locked and the President gave him a knowing smirk. Martin was sure of it. For whatever reason, that little smirk made Martin's day.

Martin's good mood lasted through the end of the ceremony and all of twenty minutes past that. He returned to his office and was immediately attacked by Amanda.

"Word on the street is that you—you! of all people—convinced the President to sign the Executive Order today. The fuck,
Jermanski!" Amanda yelled, as soon as he appeared in the doorway
to their office.

He couldn't help but smile, which only further pissed Amanda
off. "Who do you think you are?" she thundered.

"Keep your voice down," he protested. "You know that's just a
rumor started by the others." He wasn't sure he wanted Amanda to
know that it was, in fact, him that had convinced Drumpf to adjust
the policy. He wasn't even sure why, but he felt that a target would be
placed on his back if the other staffers learned of his apparent pull
with the President.

Amanda obviously didn't want to believe it; she quickly accepted his denial. "For fuck's sake! I didn't think so," she said. "Who
comes up with this shit?" She started to smile and then she peered at
him through narrowed eyes. "But you were at the meeting yesterday,
right? When Drumpf changed his tune?"

"Yeah, I was there. But it wasn't me. It was Conville and
Breiburg. They were able to convince him." Martin hoped that there
was enough truth in the lie to make it stick. He really didn't need
the hassle.

"Okay, well, that makes more sense," Amanda said. She seemed
satisfied.

And then the phone rang.

As usual, Amanda's hand was quicker than his. "Yeah?" she
asked. "Yeah, he's here. Can I ask—" She frowned and then her face
grew red. "Who the—?" She listened for a moment longer. "Fuck
you," she said and then hurled the handset at Martin.

He snagged the cord out of the air, causing the handset to spin
around his hand like a yo-yo. It almost hit him in the face, but then
he plucked it from the air with his other hand. "Shit!" to Amanda,
and then into the phone, "Jermanski."

"She's a feisty one, your office-mate. You know that?" It was
Steve Banyan, sounding impressed.

"She's a winner," Martin responded. He couldn't imagine what Banyan could have said to her to cause her to throw the phone at him. He quickly decided he really didn't want to know.

"You fuck her yet?" Banyan asked and then his tone abruptly shifted. "What the fuck is the President doing?"

"What do you mean?" Martin asked.

"The family separation policy," Banyan said. "I just watched the ceremony live. What's he doing?"

"He changed his mind," Martin replied.

"No shit, Sherlock. Why?" Banyan's agitation grew. "Who changed his mind? Where's Mills?"

"Mills was in the room," Martin said, and then regretted it.

"In the room?" Banyan asked. And then accusatorially, "You were in the room, weren't you?"

'Shit,' Martin thought as he looked at Amanda. She was paying close attention to the conversation and had a strange look on her face.

"When was the decision made?" Banyan asked. "Why didn't you tell me about it?"

"The decision was made after we last spoke," Martin said. "It was made yesterday."

"Yesterday?" Banyan said. "Shit. That was fast."

He was silent for a moment; Martin waited.

"But you're still not helping me. Who convinced the President? Why did he change his mind?"

In hindsight, Martin's next words proved to him that he wasn't very smart. But in the moment, he took extreme joy in telling Banyan, "I did. It was me who convinced him!"

"Fuck!" Amanda shouted. "I knew it, you asshole."

And simultaneously, Banyan said, "Are you fucking kidding me? Asshole!"

"What?!" Martin asked, to both of them. "Why'm I an asshole?" It should have been obvious to him why Amanda would think that, but for Banyan, it was less so.

"You just told me you didn't," Amanda said. "You fucking liar."

"You're supposed to be the wallflower on the inside," Banyan said. "Not the puppet master on the inside."

Martin was trying to comprehend both comments and simultaneously think of responses to both. He was too slow.

"Why the fuck is he listening to you?" Amanda asked.

"How long have you been working him?" Banyan asked. "And where did you learn 'to work' anyone?"

Martin couldn't do it. He didn't even try.

"They're not going to believe this shit," Amanda said.

"I don't believe this shit," Banyan said.

Amanda jumped up from her chair. "This takes the cake! People need to know." She disappeared down the hall.

"This changes everything," Banyan said.

Martin couldn't tell if Banyan was talking to him or to himself. He didn't get a chance to ask.

"I might have underestimated you, Jermanski," Banyan said. "I gotta run." And he hung up.

Martin was left alone in his office, trying to figure out what had just happened.

·   ·   ·

It had been a couple of weeks since Martin had last called his parents. He figured the day's events were worthy of a phone call.

"Bill, get on the phone! Martin has some news for us!" Martin heard his mom call to his dad, and then to Martin, "He'll be right on."

"Thanks, mom. I just had some news that I thought you'd both like to hear."

"You know we like to hear about everything that's happening up there. But your dad's been really busy, okay? Don't mind him if he's a little short."

"Of course, mom. I know dad's working hard."

"Hello?" his dad asked.

"Hey, dad."

"Marty. How're you?"

"Good, dad. Just had something to share. I thought you might be interested."

"Sure," his dad said. "Shoot."

"Well," Martin said. "I'm sure you've both been paying attention to the immigration situation. And you might've even seen that this morning the President changed his policy."

"Yeah," his dad said. "The press conference was on at the Club. We watched a bit of it."

"It wasn't a good policy," his mom said, sounding distressed. "It just wasn't. It was dreadful what was happening to those poor families."

"I'm sure Mr. Drumpf knows what he's doing," his dad interrupted. "The President has lots of very smart people working for him, and he's extremely intelligent himself. Immigration is important, and he'll take care of it."

"But, Bill. Those families!"

"And the President will do right for those families. He's not a monster. He's not nearly as bad as the *liberals* say he is."

"That's the news I wanted to tell you!" Martin said.

"What?" his parents asked simultaneously.

"I helped convince the President to change the policy."

"Oh, Martin!" his mom said while his dad burst into laughter.

His dad's laughter continued for a few seconds before his mom said, "Bill. Stop it!"

"I'm sorry," his dad said. "But you?"

"Dad, that's what I'm saying! I helped him make the decision to change the policy."

"Marty. Come on," his dad said. "I get it that you're writing the book. That makes sense—you're a writer; you always have been. But helping the President make important decisions? You?"

"Dad, listen. Wasn't it you, on the phone a few weeks ago, who told me the President 'goes with his gut' and 'picks people he trusts'? He trusts me!"

His dad laughed again.

"Bill," his mom said in her 'you-behave' tone.

"Marty, listen," his dad said. "If you tell me the President trusts you, I believe you. He must trust you, if he's letting you write his book. Just don't let your head swell too much. Okay?"

"Sure, dad."

"I love you, son."

"Love you, too, dad," Martin said.

His dad hung up

"Don't worry, Martin. Your dad believes you. He's so proud of you."

"I'm sure he's proud of me, mom," Martin said. "As far as believing me? That's okay."

"He is proud of you. And we both love you very much."

"I know. I love you, too. Good night, mom."

PROGRESS REPORT

It had been almost two weeks since Martin's first sit down with the President to discuss *The Art of the Presidency*. That first meeting had left him dejected, so he promised himself that he'd do better during the second.

He realized that he had to actually give something to the President to read before the next sit down. He spent the better part of a week Googling Drumpf, others' thoughts on Drumpf, and analyses of his Presidential style. He treated it as a college writing assignment: "Examine the words, tweets, and pronouncements of President Drumpf, and, in no more than 2750 words, write your version of his style and philosophy for governing the United States."

By forcing himself into that student mindset, Martin immediately felt more able to accomplish the task. Over three evenings at his apartment, he wrote, edited, and polished 2700 words. At the top, he gave it the title, 'The Art of the Presidency.' He printed the document and ensured that it was inserted into the President's daily folder.

That had been several days ago—to give the President time to read it. The moment of truth was now upon him. He knew that what he wrote wasn't a whole book, or even a significant portion of one, but if the President liked it, he felt that it would give him the confidence to push on.

He stood waiting outside the Oval Office. Jake was on duty. Martin had heard that he had been Army Special Forces before leaving the military and joining the Secret Service. Martin didn't know what to think about that, but he did know that Jake seemed to have too much gray hair for someone as young as he otherwise appeared.

"How are you today?"

"Fine, Marty. You?"

"A little nervous."

"You wrote something for him to read, right?" Jake asked.

"Yeah. I'm hoping he liked it."

"I'm sure it'll be fine. He likes you, you know."

"I think he does, but I don't know if he likes my writing."

Jake squinted slightly and then knocked twice on the Oval Office door. "You're up."

Martin opened the door and then stepped in. The President was sitting at his desk, talking on his phone. Madeleine Watterhoot was standing just on the other side of Drumpf. She nodded at Martin when he entered.

'Shit,' Martin thought. 'She knows about the book?'

"Would you believe that?" the President asked. "Total bullshit, I know." He nodded and listened intently.

Martin approached the desk. He moved to within ten feet of the President and then waited.

"What the fuck are you going to do? Don't I know it." The President slowly spun in his chair. He finally noticed Martin. "My next appointment just walked in, I have to let you go. Thank you, thank you. You, too."

The President hung up and then smiled at Martin. "Marty. Sit down. Here to talk about the book, right?"

"Yes, sir." He spun the armchair closest to the President's desk so that it faced him and took a seat.

"Marty. This is a huge improvement over last time; it really is. But this isn't a book. This is barely an article. In a kid's magazine."

Drumpf shrugged, trying to find words as he looked down at the few sheet of papers in front of him. It was Martin's initial draft. "There's definitely some Drumpf wisdom in there, which is good, but there's not much else."

"I understand, sir," Martin replied.

"Let me tell you something, Marty," Drumpf said. "When I sat down to write *The Art of the Deal*, I had a lot more time on my hands. I was able to do a lot of the actual writing, able to tell a lot of good stories. And I had a proven author working with me. Now, everything is different. I'm President, for God's sake. I'm running the entire world—which is a big deal. I'm extremely busy. You and I both know that running the U.S. government is taking all of my time."

Drumpf paused. A stray thought seemed to have popped into his head. He reached for his folder and pulled out his schedule. "Marty. Is my schedule for tomorrow written yet?"

"Yes, Mr. President—" Watterhoot said.

"Maddie," the President said, spinning to look up at her. "I know you know my schedule. You always do. I'm just curious to know if Marty knows it." He spun back around to face Martin.

"I believe so, sir. But you probably haven't been given a copy of it yet."

Drumpf seemed disappointed. "Oh. Shit. Well, do you know when my scheduled tee time is tomorrow?"

"Yes, sir. I believe it's 8:30," Martin said.

"Right. Okay. That's good. So what was I saying?"

"You were talking about how busy you are," Martin said.

"Yeah," Drumpf replied, obviously trying to remember the conversation.

"And how that impacts writing the book," Martin added.

"Right! On top of all that, you're not a proven author. You're still a kid. So the pressure's on you. It's a big challenge and a big deal. But I'm sure you can handle the pressure. You just need to do a lot more writing."

"Yes, sir. I completely understand," Martin said.

"So, more writing for next time, okay?" Drumpf asked.

"Absolutely, sir," Martin replied.

The two sat and stared at each other for a long moment. Martin finally got the hint that the conversation was over. He stood up awkwardly.

"Have a good afternoon, sir," he said.

"You, too, Marty."

Martin turned to go and then turned back. "Do you want me to take that for you, sir?" He was referring to the draft manuscript on the President's desk.

The President looked down. "No, that's okay, Marty. I might read through it again."

'He's not gonna read through it again,' Martin thought. He glanced down in the President's garbage can. No papers for pick up. Someone must have gotten them earlier that day.

Martin left the Oval Office with no clue how he was supposed to turn this 'kid's article' into a book. 'Shit.' He walked back to his office.

He hoped that Amanda would be gone for the day by the time he reached their office. He was not in the mood to deal with her. He had to think about the book.

"Hey, bitch!"

It figured. She probably waited around just to give him shit.

"Hey, Amanda." It was easier just to be neutral toward her.

"What the hell were you doing with the President?" she asked.

"What do you mean?" He doubted that feigning ignorance would work, but he had to try.

"Come on," she said. "The schedule may only say 'Executive Time,' but I know you were in the Oval Office for the last twenty minutes."

Martin had nothing. He didn't know what to say. And didn't have the energy to argue. 'It was more like ten minutes,' he thought but didn't voice it.

"What were you doing there?" she insisted.

An idea! "We were doing a comprehensive review of all of the White House staffers," Martin said. "You know he values my opinion. We finished with you."

He got her! 'She doesn't know what to say,' he thought gleefully. She sputtered for a moment as he sat down.

"He was very interested in your interpersonal skills, particularly your tendency to refer to all of your coworkers as 'bitch.' He said that he understood the fun of it but questioned if that behavior was appropriate in the White House." Martin had to lay it on thick; he was having fun.

"You didn't," she muttered. "He didn't." It was clear to Martin she didn't know whether or not to believe him.

Trying to completely ignore Amanda, Martin pulled the monitor around to face him and dragged the keyboard across the desk. She had already logged off for the day. He began to log in.

Martin fought to keep the smile off his face. And then he remembered his meeting with Drumpf. 'Shit. How am I going to write enough material for *The Art of the Presidency*?'

"Does he really know that I call people 'bitch'?"

"What? Oh. Yeah, he was the one who brought it up," Martin said. "He must know about it." Then it hit him. His journal! He'd written hundreds of pages in his journal since arriving in DC back in January. What if he wrote a behind-the-scenes book from the perspective of a White House staffer? He wasn't sure how that would be *The Art of the Presidency*, but he could figure something out.

Martin was excited; it just might work. He glanced at Amanda. She was visibly squirming in her seat. It was so good.

But the question remained: Would the President go for a junior staffer book? Martin wasn't sure. How could he spin it so that Drumpf would? He had no idea. But he hoped that something would come to him while he typed his handwritten journal. It was going to be a lot of typing, and it was going to suck.

The phone rang.

Amanda's hand was quicker than his.

"Chung. Yes. Yes, sir," she said and then listened for a moment. "Got it. Yes, sir." She hung up the phone. "Chief of Staff. Wants to see you."

"Shit," he muttered. Martin was hoping to get home and start typing.

"What did you do this time?" she asked.

As if he had ever done anything.

He stood up. He gathered a notebook, pen, and opened then shut his drawer. Stalling, trying to think of something to say.

"Well," Martin said. "He did overhear some of my conversation with the President. Maybe he wants to talk about your interpersonal skills." He stepped out of the office before his smile could betray the lie. It was so good.

·   ·   ·

"The President mentioned to me your little project and how it's going," Kellner said. "Doesn't sound like it's going too well."

Martin wasn't sure how to respond. He knew that Kellner was against the book. What did he want Martin to say?

"I tried to talk him out of it again," the Chief of Staff said. "He wouldn't listen."

Martin didn't want to express his doubts to Kellner. His personal doubts on top of Kellner's would just drive Kellner to shut it down more forcefully. But, aside from the President, there wasn't anyone else who he felt he could talk to.

"The President hasn't given me much to work with," Martin said, "I don't think I could come up with enough material for a book if I tried."

Kellner listened, smirked slightly, but said nothing.

"I do have one idea, but I'm not sure if he would go for it."

"Oh?" Kellner asked. "What's your idea?"

Martin hesitated.

"Come on, Jermanski. You know I'm going to read it regardless. Better for you to tell me now."

"Well. Since I got to DC, I've been keeping a journal," Martin said.

"A diary," Kellner interrupted.

"Yes. Diary," he said. "Anyway, I thought that maybe I could write the book from my perspective as a staffer and show what I've learned from the President. Explain how he works. Elaborate on his Presidential ... ness."

"His 'Presidentialness'?" Kellner frowned, obviously not impressed with the word. His frown deepened; he didn't seem to like the idea, either.

Kellner paused, and then he surprised Martin. His frown disappeared. "I think it's a good idea. I think you should run with it."

"Huh?" He stammered and then stopped trying to talk.

"I'm going to cut down on your official responsibilities," Kellner continued. "This will become your number one priority. I'm not going to eliminate everything, but I'll arrange it so that your workload drops."

"Sir?" Martin still had no response.

"That'll be all, Martin. Thank you for getting here so quickly."

POLITICO

"Did you hear?"

"Hear what?" Martin asked.

"The article dropped today."

"Dropped?" Martin asked.

"The article came out today."

"What article?" Martin asked.

"Seriously?" said Scott Bokor. "The Politico article."

The two were eating lunch a block and a half from the White House. The sandwiches were good; the bright, sunny day was better.

"Oh, yeah." Martin hadn't thought much about the interview since it happened. But he was curious now. He reached for his phone.

"I already read it," said Scott, and then stopped talking.

Typing keywords into his phone to find the article, Martin was getting annoyed. Scott was being a tool. "Well?" he asked, trying and failing to keep the annoyance out of his voice.

"Shit. You're gonna just have to read it."

Martin thought he found it. "Young Drumpfies Hit DC? Politico.com?"

"That's it," Scott answered.

Dan Lippman and Ben Schreckinger. The authors. Martin remembered them.

"Drumpfie?" Martin asked.

"Yeah," Scott said. "We're all Drumpfies. Shit. Your dad has worked for him for a long time, right? You've been a Drumpfie longer than most of us."

"Yeah," Martin said. "Whatever. It's just a horrible word." Then he started to read. "Do you know this Matt Mowers dude?"

"Who?"

"Matt Mowers," Martin said. "He's mentioned in literally the very first sentence of the article."

"Uh, no," Scott said. "Never heard of him. Is he in the White House?"

Martin read further. "No, apparently, he's a State guy."

"State?" Scott asked. "I don't know anyone over there. At least, I don't think so."

"I still don't know why anyone would care about this," Martin said.

"There are people who will care about just about anything."

Martin read the article in silence. It was interesting to read something about him, despite the fact that it wasn't specifically about him. It was close enough, he reasoned.

"Shit," Martin said.

"What is it?"

"They 'outed' Rebellion," Martin said. "Do you think that's gonna be a problem?"

"Rebellion?" Scott asked. "The bar? No. That's not going to be a problem. At least not for us." He laughed at his own joke.

Martin shook his head. They could always find another bar to hang out at. Could Rebellion survive being outed as a Drumpf-friendly bar?

Martin finished the article. It certainly wasn't Earth-shattering. He found no great revelations. And people were excited for this? He didn't understand the excitement before and, after reading the article, still didn't understand it.

"What'd you think?" Scott asked.

"About the article? Meh," Martin said. "Pretty cool to read something about us, I guess."

"Bullshit," Scott said. "You're all about that article. You dig that shit."

"I said it's pretty cool. What do you want from me?"

"Well, it's better than *Fire and Fury*, or whatever the next book is going to be."

"Next book?" Martin was concerned. Had word of *The Art of the Presidency* leaked? "What do you mean?"

"You know there're going to be more books like that," Scott said. "Every Presidency has their scandals and the books that talk about them."

"We seem to be having more than our fair share of scandals."

"Product of the times," Scott said. "The press always beats up the administration."

"Seems to me we're getting the shit kicked out of us," Martin said.

"Standard, man. Nothing different."

Martin shrugged. It didn't feel normal to him, but he had to admit he never really paid much attention before living in it. Maybe it *was* normal. "Do you know of any other books being written?"

"There are rumors that Bob Woodward is writing a book. He's apparently been interviewing people."

"Who?" Martin asked.

"Bob Woodward. Big time journalist," Scott said. "He's worked at the Post a lot longer than you or I have been alive."

"The Post?"

"Washington Post?" Scott asked. "The newspaper?"

"Oh." Martin felt like he probably should have known that.

"Seriously? How long have you lived in this town?"

"A little over five months."

"That's it?"

"Yeah," Martin said.

"Wow. I thought you had worked in the White House a lot longer before I met you."

"Why's that?"

"Because of how tight you are with the Prez," Scott said.

"What do you mean by that?"

"Seriously. You are completely fucking clueless. I guess the shit's all true."

Martin was starting to get pissed. "What are you talking about?"

"You have no idea what other staffers say about you, do you? Do you realize how jealous Amanda Chung is?"

Martin felt himself getting angrier. "Dude, seriously. What the fuck are you talking about?"

"You're the kid staffer who doesn't know much but seems to have the President's ear. Chung talks about you all the time; how the President listens to you, takes your advice, even seeks your opinion. Mills was ranting about you. Some of the other higher-ups were, too."

"Fuck!" Martin stood up. He pulled a twenty from his wallet, dropped it on the table, and said, "I'm out. I gotta get back to the office."

"That's cool, man," Scott said. "But seriously, just calm down."

Martin left the restaurant. It was only a fifteen minute walk back to the White House. It took that entire fifteen minutes to calm down.

'The kid staffer who doesn't know much.' It *was* true. To his knowledge, he was the youngest person working in the White House. And although he had learned a lot during his time in Washington, he came to the job with almost no knowledge whatsoever of politics, the Presidency, or Washington, DC. Maybe he shouldn't have gotten so angry.

Best of all, the President *did* listen to him. He had bragged about it to his parents.

'I guess it's all true. And Amanda's jealous of me,' Martin thought. He smiled. 'That's fantastic.'

A few minutes later, Martin reached his office. Amanda wasn't back from lunch yet. Maybe she wasn't coming back today. Not much point in doing so on a Friday afternoon.

Martin logged onto the computer and did a quick scan of his email. Nothing important. 'Probably a good time to do the rounds,' Martin thought. Unlike Amanda, who could sit in the office and stare at her computer for hours, Martin had to get up and walk when there wasn't much to do.

He wandered through the West Wing, past the Cabinet Room, past the Oval Office. A few people were around, but the White House seemed quiet to Martin. Or maybe he was just imagining it. He wandered past the Chief of Staff's office.

"Martin," Kellner called as he walked past.

"Sir?"

"You busy?"

"No, sir."

"Come in for a moment," Kellner said.

"I've been thinking about *The Art of the Presidency*. I know that I told you the other day that I was going to shield you from work, to give you time to work on the book."

"Yes, sir."

"I'm going to go one further," Kellner said. "I want you to take the next week off. Completely. I want you to work from home and make as much progress on the book as you can. Come in a week from today to give me an update."

The idea of spending a week at home to work on the book actually excited Martin, although he knew the entire week would be spent typing his journal onto his laptop. It was work that needed to be done, before he could go any further. But then a thought occurred to him. 'There has to be a catch. What's the catch?'

"You look like you have a question," Kellner said. "What is it?"

'How'd he do that?' "Sir, I know that I explained my idea to you the other day, but I haven't briefed the President on it," Martin said. "I don't know if he's gonna like it or not."

"Leave that to me. I'll brief the President. I think he'll actually like the idea."

"Okay. Thanks, sir."

"That's all, Martin. Have a good afternoon and have a good weekend."

Martin got up to leave. He hadn't taken a week off from the White House since he started back in January. He was excited by the prospect. He left Kellner's office to continue his wanderings of the West Wing.

.   .   .

Later that afternoon, Martin passed the Chief of Staff's office a second time. As he approached the office, he saw that the door hung partially open; Kellner was inside talking to someone. Martin heard Kellner mention his name just as he was walking past.

Martin glanced in to see that Kellner was on the phone; he stopped just beyond the doorway and listened.

"Listen, Jermanski's a good kid," Kellner said. "He is."

Martin smiled. 'The Chief of Staff thinks I'm a good kid,' he thought.

"I just need to keep him away from the President," Kellner continued. "You know how the boss can get once he decides he trusts someone. Yeah, last week's Space Force debacle is proof of that."

Kellner paused. He was listening to whoever was on the other end of the line.

"Yes, of course."

Martin heard Kellner take a deep breath.

"I just need to minimize Jermanski's ability to suggest something to the boss that he'll latch onto. A few days ago, I assigned him a big project. And today, I gave him time to devote to it. I think it'll probably eat up most of the rest of the summer."

'What the hell?' Martin thought.

A pause. "He's going to author a book for the President."

Another pause. "What? That he'll finish it? I don't know, but I'm hoping to kill it between now and the time the President gives it the final okay."

A long pause. Martin could hear Kellner fidgeting with something at his desk.

"No. We don't need or want another *Fire and Fury*. That's not going to happen. I'll get it turned off. Yes. Okay. Thanks."

Martin heard Kellner hang up his phone and walked quickly away from the open door.

'Shit!' Martin was upset. 'Who was Kellner talking to?'

Martin considered walking back to Kellner's office and confronting him about what he had heard. He stood in the hallway, down the hall and around the corner from Kellner's office, for several minutes considering his options. In the end, he couldn't muster the courage. Upset, he continued on his way.

SECRET RENDEZVOUS

Martin had returned to his office, feeling upset and alone. Thankfully, Amanda must have actually left for the day. He would have had a hard time putting up with her after listening to Kellner on the phone.

He logged into his computer but wasn't sure why. He certainly wasn't in the mood to do anything work-related.

He kept turning over in his mind Kellner's phone conversation. Who was Kellner talking to? Was Kellner on his side or not? Should he write *The Art of the Presidency* or not? And just as important: If he wrote *The Art of the Presidency* the way he wanted to, would the President like it?

There was only one way to find out.

A few clicks on his keyboard called up the President's daily schedule. Martin checked the time. The President was leaving for 8th and I in a couple of hours. He *might* still be in the Oval, but more than likely was back in the Residence.

If Martin went past the Oval and the President was still there, there was a good chance that Kellner was there as well. He did not want to run into the Chief of Staff.

If he waited another thirty minutes or so, he was sure that the President would be back in the Residence. He decided to wait.

Thirty minutes later, Martin stood up and walked to the single filing cabinet in their office. He opened the third drawer and pulled from it a brand new, fully-functioning television remote control.

He took a deep breath, stared at the remote control for a moment, and then left the office. He made his way quickly to the Residence.

Squint was the first Secret Service Agent he met. When he wasn't wearing his sunglasses, he seemed to squint at everyone and everything. "Working late on a Friday, aren't you, Marty?"

"Uh, yeah. The President needed a new remote control for his television."

"Really?" Squint asked. "I hadn't heard that."

"No. Well, his is working properly, but apparently we were a little slow to get him a new one last time. He told me today he just wants to keep two in the Residence so he doesn't have to rely on us."

Squint looked at him. His expression was unreadable through his sunglasses.

"It's not like his phone, where the Comms Agency requires we maintain one-to-one accountability. These things are a dime a dozen."

Squint smiled. "The Agency can be strict with their security. Gotta love 'em for that."

Martin walked past. 'That was a close one.'

He was relieved to see that Phil was the Agent standing at the President's door.

Phil turned to watch Martin approach from down the hallway. "Squint told me you were coming."

'So they *do* know our nicknames for them!' Martin thought.

"What?" Phil asked. "You didn't think we know your names for us?"

"Is he in?" Martin asked.

"Yeah; I think he's watching the news," Phil said.

"You think?"

Phil knocked twice and opened the door.

Martin stepped into the room.

The President was sitting on his couch, talking on the phone, and watching his two massive televisions. He looked up when Martin stepped into the room.

"I know!" the President said into the phone. "Do you believe that shit? But listen, listen, I need to go."

The President laughed.

"No, seriously. Someone just stepped in; I need to talk to him. Who? One of my aides, working on a top secret project. It's going to push us over the top for the midterms. It's gonna be huge."

The President laughed again, louder this time.

"Shawn! I love you, you know I do! We'll talk soon! Okay. Goodbye."

The President hung up his phone and chuckled to himself. Once the chuckling died away, he turned to Martin. "Marty. They told me you were stopping in. You didn't come just to bring me an extra remote, did you?"

"Actually, no, sir."

"Okay. Then what is it?" He turned down the volumes on both televisions.

"It has to do with *The Art of the Presidency.*"

"Okay. Wow. You're persistent, I see. You weren't satisfied with our discussions in the Oval, so you've followed me back to the Residence. It's one of the reasons I like you so much. And it's why I had no problem telling Kelly that I made the right decision in choosing you to write the book."

"She brought me one of her stupid lists, a list of possible authors. I told her, no. No! You're going to write it. She tried to talk me out of it. John also tried to talk me out of it. But the fact that you're here right now proves I made the right choice."

"But I gotta tell you, Marty. I was nervous after our first meeting. I'm feeling better after the second, but I was questioning the decision after the first."

"I understand, sir. It's a great honor for me, to write your— to help you write your book. I had a few ideas and wanted to bounce them off you before next week."

"John told me he's given you the week off to get writing."

"Yes, sir. I have a lot to do, but I think that will help a lot."

"Listen," the President said. "Melanya and I are going to watch the Marines at 8th and I. We can't talk for too long, because I'll need to get ready to leave."

"Completely understand, sir. I'll be quick."

"Okay. So what's the idea?"

Martin was nervous when he first thought of coming to the Residence earlier that afternoon. But once he made the decision to do so, his nerves disappeared. The President's question brought them back with a vengeance. 'There's no way The Ronald is going to go for a book that's more about a junior staffer than it is about him!'

Martin took a deep breath. And then a second. He looked at the President who was staring intently back at him.

Drumpf raised an eyebrow.

Martin cleared his throat. "*The Art of the Presidency* has to be a different book from all your others. Because you're different from who you were when you wrote those others. Before, you were the most powerful real estate mogul in New York City; now you are the most powerful man in the world."

Initially, Drumpf appeared skeptical, but the 'most-powerful-man' flattery seemed to be working.

"Everybody understands that you're the hardest working President in modern history, so it would be impossible for you to devote the time and energy to writing this book that you devoted to writing your previous books."

Drumpf bobbed his head in agreement, although Martin knew the difficult part was coming up.

"And if the *Art of the Presidency* contains the same stories about your brilliance as the leader of the free world as Fox news already tells, as Shawn already explains, as you have spoken about time and again, it won't have the impact that it should. It might fail to push us over the top for the midterms."

Drumpf shook his head and frowned.

"Because of all of those things, *The Art of the Presidency* needs to be a different book."

Drumpf threw up his hands. "Wait, Marty, wait! I get it. That's a pretty good sales pitch. And you're talking to the best salesman in the United States. No one does sales like Drumpf does sales. But, like every good salesman, you need to know when to sink the hook. Play it too long, and you're going to lose your customer. Get to it."

"Sir, *The Art of the Presidency* is going to be about your leadership, your influence, your ability to cut through Washington's red tape, told from the perspective of a junior staffer who's learning by observing your brilliance."

Martin stopped talking; Drumpf obviously expected words to continue coming from his mouth. After several seconds, the President cocked his head to one side and narrowed his eyes.

"Wait. What?" The President appeared confused.

"The book will be about the 'meteoric rise' of a young staffer in your White House, who learns the Drumpf way of running the country directly by watching you."

"Young staffer? I don't want to write about a young staffer. I want to write about … Which young staffer?"

"Me."

"Oh."

That took the President by surprise. Martin felt the intense need to keep talking; silence was the enemy.

"Unlike your other books, this one'll be all about you, but from someone else's perspective. It will be from my perspective, looking up and admiring you and your Presidency."

"I'm not sure I like the sound of this," the President said. "What about the stuff you had me read last week—your short article?"

"Well, sir. I think it could be expanded a bit, but it would be the very last chapter of the book. The grand finale. Where all of your wisdom is distilled into a short digestible package."

"So the book would appear to be about you, but it'd actually be about me and the Presidency? And it would end with my Presidential wisdom, condensed?"

"Yes and yes, sir."

"It could be a self-help book for all the blue collar workers out there struggling to rise up," the President said. "You're blue collar, aren't you, Marty?"

"Are you still blue collar once you've graduated from college?" Martin asked.

"Was it an Ivy League school?"

"No."

"Then it probably counts as blue collar," Drumpf said, but he didn't seem sure.

"Even better!" Martin said. "It could be a guide book for your political protégés trying to succeed in politics. For those Drump-fies who aspire to one day run for President and continue the work you've done, build upon the great legacy that you'll leave behind."

"Now you're talking, Marty," Drumpf nodded. "I was skeptical at first, but the more I hear, the more I like where I'm taking this."

Martin was relieved. He seemed to have convinced the President. But he was fearful of Drumpf changing his mind. He was reluctant to open his mouth again.

"This is great, Marty. Really great."

"If that's how you feel, Mr. President, I'll start writing it as soon as I get home this evening. I'll be typing before you sit down at 8th and I."

"Brilliant! Good luck, Marty. Can't wait to read it!"

THE WRITING GAME

Martin took the entire last week of June off from the White House. He spent every day working on the manuscript for *The Art of the Presidency*. It was more tedious than he expected, and he found his journal writing to be dreadful.

Between straight transcription and re-writing and editing as he went, he was barely half of the way through his journal by that Friday morning. He needed a break. So he popped into the White House.

"What the hell, bitch?" Amanda was obviously glad to see him. "I come in Monday morning to find an email from the Chief of Staff saying that he gave you the week off? What's that about? Who do you think you are? And get this—I pick up papers from the Oval, and the President didn't even remember my name. How's that for some bullshit?"

She was on a roll. Martin didn't think he'd be able to get a word in, so he didn't try.

"The next day, I'm back in the Oval Office, and the President—who remembered my name that time—asked me where you were. Why is the President asking about you? You're just some piss-ant junior staffer. You're junior to me! When you started making regular Oval runs to pick up papers, did he ever ask about me? Huh?"

'The rage is strong in this one,' Martin thought to himself. He tried his best not to smile. He was worried that if he opened his mouth to speak, his lips would automatically bend that way. So he sat there silently, just looking at her.

"When you delivered remote controls to him, did he ever ask about me? So why the hell is he asking about you?"

There was no way he was going to open his mouth.

"Gone for a week, and now you don't even speak to me? Hello! I'm talking to you, jackwad."

He wasn't going to try to get to the computer. He was afraid of approaching any closer than the several feet their two desks forced between them. He cleared his throat; he had to steel himself to speak.

"Is there anything going on?"

"'Is there anything going on?' It's about time you say something. No! There's nothing going on. They're flying to his golf course in New Jersey this afternoon. It's been pretty quiet. Well, as quiet as it can be in this White House. All sorts of the normal hair on fire, but none of it reaching down to us."

"Anything I need to be aware of?"

"I'd tell you if there was, wouldn't I?" she asked. And then she cracked up. "Well, I probably wouldn't. You've been checking your emails, though, haven't you?"

"Only those from you."

She threw a middle finger in his direction.

'So predictable,' he thought.

"Well, if there's that much excitement around here, maybe I'll just take off," he said.

"Screw that," she said. "I've been here all week. I'm taking off. You can hold down the fort."

He shrugged. "That's fine. Have a good weekend."

She didn't know how to take his pleasant attitude. She threw two middle fingers at him as she left for the day.

He pulled the computer around to him and logged in. He actually hadn't spent too much time looking at his official email during the week. He only scanned his Inbox for emails from the Chief of Staff. There hadn't been any, so he didn't read any emails.

He scrolled up and down through the Inbox and was able to delete half of the emails without even opening them. It seemed like a typical week's worth of email.

Amanda had alluded to 'all sorts of hair on fire.' Martin wondered, if he had been around, would the President have asked him his opinion on any of it? Then he decided to find out.

By the time he reached the Oval Office, there was no Secret Service Agent present; the President was gone. 'How about the Residence?' he thought. And then decided against it; he had used his one idea to see the President in the Residence last week. 'South Lawn?' He could catch the President before he boarded his helicopter. Again, he decided against it.

From Amanda's story, it had sounded as if the President needed to talk to Martin. He felt that he owed it to the President to seek him out. He checked his watch; it would be another two hours before the First Family left via the South Lawn. He'd go back to his office to kill some time and then position himself on the South Lawn where the President was sure to see him. If the President had any concerns, he'd stop Martin on the spot.

"Jermanski."

Martin spun around to see the Chief of Staff approaching him. The frown on his face was intense.

"Afternoon, sir," Martin said.

"Shall we have this talk here in front of the Oval or in my office?" Kellner sounded pissed.

'Shit!' "Here? Sir?"

"Then here it is." Kellner drew closer and then lowered his voice. "What's the status of the book?"

'Huh?' "Sir?"

"You've had the last week to work on it. How's it coming?"

"Ah. Okay. There's still a lot to do."

The Chief of Staff seemed disappointed. "I thought a week would give you enough time. The President is anxious ... "

"He's anxious, sir?"

"He's anxious to read your full draft. When do you think you can have it complete?"

"Complete?" Martin did not expect his first conversation with the Chief of Staff after visiting the President in the Residence to go this way. "There's an awful lot of work involved, sir. I think—"

"Okay. Here's what I need. I'm giving you another week off. I need to see a completed draft by next Friday, July 6. Does that work?"

Martin considered the week he just had, the amount of journal he still had to type, the editing ... "I think so."

"How about this? Draft manuscript on my desk, July 6, at noon. Can you do it?"

Martin was afraid to commit. It was going to be a horrendous amount of work.

"The President's counting on you," Kellner added.

"I'll do my best, sir."

.   .   .

At 11:50 A.M. on July 6th, Martin walked into the White House. He didn't even stop in his office but walked straight to Kellner's. He was carrying the draft manuscript in a manila envelope under his arm. It wasn't complete.

The White House was quiet. The Chief of Staff's door was shut, so Martin knocked.

"In," Kellner called.

Martin opened the door. Kellner looked up from his computer, pulled his reading glasses from his face, and smiled. "Jermanski, come in. Sit down. Is that the manuscript?"

"It's only a draft, sir. It's rough."

The smile disappeared from Kellner's face. "Oh."

"At this point, it's my journal typed. And edited. But it's not ready for ... It's not ready."

"I see. Well, there are two paths forward. One. You can leave it with me; I'll read it over the weekend and give you feedback on Monday. Or two. You take a few more days to work on it, and then you leave it with me for feedback."

'Leave it with the Chief of Staff?!'

"Martin. You'll need someone to read it before you put it in front of the President. His time is too valuable to give him a draft without outside review."

Martin hadn't considered that. But the thought of having the Chief of Staff read it terrified him. He felt the color draining from his face.

"I can tell you don't think it's ready," Kellner said. "I'll walk you out, and you can take a few more days."

Before he knew what was happening, the Chief of Staff had walked Martin to the West Wing exit. Kellner had spoken the whole time, offering reassuring words and motivating Martin 'to do great things for the President'.

"What about Ms. Chung, sir?"

"I'll let Amanda know you're not going to be in next week. She did just fine this past week. Remember, she's been in the job a lot longer than you have."

"Thank you, sir."

·   ·   ·

At noon on July 13th, Martin reported to the White House feeling much better about the manuscript. He had spent the entire week finishing, editing, and organizing it. He had been so busy that he turned down social engagements with fellow staffers to work into the evenings. It wasn't a masterpiece, but he felt okay about putting it in front of Kellner.

As he'd done the week before, Martin went directly to the Chief of Staff's office. He knocked. There was no answer. Undeterred, he walked back to his office.

"Holy shit! He returns! Three weeks, now, bitch? If you're going to be gone, just make it official. Quit. If this place is too much, do us all a favor and quit!"

"Do you know if the Chief of Staff is around?" He decided to skip the pleasantries; they never went anywhere with Amanda anyway.

"What?"

"Kellner? Is he around?"

"Unavailable. And the President's in Europe. London, NATO, heading to Helsinki."

'Oh, shit'.

"I see you don't pay any attention when you're not actually here," Amanda said dismissively. "You won't make it in this town unless you keep track, even during your off time."

"What's in Helsinki?"

"What the shit, bitch? 'What's in Helsinki?' He's meeting with his idol! He's sitting down with his buddy Vlad! He's chatting with President Putin!"

Martin had entirely forgotten the Helsinki Conference. "When do they return?"

"You can check the schedule. Don't ask me."

HELSINKI BLUES

Martin spent most of the weekend polishing the draft. Although willing to give it to Kellner on Friday, he felt that every extra bit of time spent editing made it better.

He even decided to take the next Monday off. Amanda would be upset, but that was nothing new. The President was going to still be in Europe, so Martin felt no great pull to be in the White House.

That afternoon, his phone rang.

"Hello?"

"Marty, Scott. A bunch of us are meeting up to drink and watch the President's press conference with Putin this evening. Want to join us?"

Martin had no plans and needed to get away from the manuscript anyway. "Are we drinking or are we watching the press conference?"

"Yes," Scott said.

"Yeah. I'm in. Where?"

•   •   •

"You gotta be fucking shitting me!" Rick shouted at the television. Rick, who Martin hadn't seen since Easter Sunday, the day before he was fired for calling the President an idiot, apparently still lived in DC and hung with some of the staffers.

Martin, Rick, and several others were sitting around a television in Scott's apartment, watching the Helsinki press conference live.

"What's going on?" Jason asked.

"What's going on? I'll tell you what's going on," Brandon said. Brandon, formerly known only as Wrestler Ear to Martin, chugged a quick mouthful of beer. "The President is fucking up. All he has to do is voice some support for the intelligence community. That's all he has to do. And he can't seem to muster the courage to do it!"

"What do you think that's about?" Martin asked. "Do you believe the collusion thing?"

"Collusion? Who knows?" Brandon asked. "But if he did collude with the Russians, telling the press that he fully supports his own intelligence community would go a long way toward dispelling the idea."

"And it wouldn't cost him anything to say he supports his own personnel," Rick added. "It costs him absolutely nothing."

"What if he didn't collude, but Putin has something on him?" Scott asked.

"Shit," Brandon said. "He should just come out and admit whatever it is that Putin has on him. How bad could it be? The guy was a playboy; everyone knows it. He's been married three times; he cheated on the first two—probably cheated on Melanya, too. He partied with strippers and hookers. All the rich fuckers in New York City probably did so. Just own it. Own it, and then stop acting like you're guilty of something worse."

"What if Putin has something worse on him?" Martin asked.

"Worse than peeing on prostitutes or having them pee on you?" Brandon asked. "What could be worse?"

"I don't get what the big deal is with a golden shower," Rick said. "Urine is mostly salty water that stinks a little bit."

"What the fuck?" Jason asked, and then mockingly, "'Mostly just salty water that stinks a little bit.' Dude. That's some nasty shit."

"It ain't that bad," Rick insisted.

"No one wants to hear about your sick habits," Brandon said. "Can we just get back to the President and Putin?"

"I don't think I could keep working for him if it came out that he colluded," Jason said.

"Are you serious?" Martin asked.

"Yeah," Jason answered. "My great grandfather fought in World War Two, and then stayed in the Army for several years. He swore up and down that the Soviets, the Russians, were almost as evil as the Germans."

"But leave the Administration?" Scott asked.

"Yeah," Jason said. "Absolutely."

"Fuck that shit," Brandon said. "So what if he colluded? The country is way better off than if Hillary had won. If it took a little Russian help to get there, then so be it."

"Uh, no," Jason said.

"Naw, dude," Rick said. "I'd jump."

"Dude," Brandon said. "You were already fired. You don't work for the administration anymore."

"Well, shit," Rick said. "If I was. What about you?"

"I don't know; that's tough," Martin said.

"You're wishy-washy on most things, Marty," Scott said and then turned to Jason and Rick. "But you two'd leave?"

"You guys are fucking retarded," Brandon said.

"Hey, man," Rick said. "There's gotta be a line somewhere."

Martin hadn't really considered what he would do if it turned out that Drumpf had colluded. What did it even mean, really? Was talking to them really that bad? Probably not, he supposed. The worse crime was swearing up and down for months that he hadn't, if in fact he had. But even then, Martin wasn't sure what he'd do.

·   ·   ·

The next day at the White House, the conversation that was had the night before at Scott's apartment was repeated almost every time different staffers got together. In offices in the White House and the

Eisenhower Building, in hallways, outside in the short distance between the two buildings, at eateries across the city, staffers discussed the President's performance in Helsinki.

Martin participated in a number of them and heard from people who had participated in others. Most conversations followed the same themes, and most staffers felt as those the night before had. About half had serious reservations about Drumpf's performance during the press conference and questioned their own continued employment. About a quarter were on the fence, as Martin had been. The final quarter felt as Brandon had, that the President's performance in office far outweighed the particulars of the election or Helsinki.

But amongst all the staffers, those who continued to fully support the President and those who were less sure, the mood after Helsinki was low. Almost universally, the staffers lamented the President's performance.

"He could have at least lied and said that he believed our people over Putin," Brandon said shaking his head. "Who does that? Who throws his own people under the bus and supports Vladimir Putin?"

The Helsinki press conference was all the staffers in the PPO could talk about the next day.

"Why is it that he can tell some lies, so easily, and not others—ones that would really benefit him?" Baggy Khakis asked.

"The President doesn't lie," Hawk Nose said. "No more so than any other President."

The comment drew incredulous stares from every person in the small office.

"What?" Hawk Nose asked.

"Let me break this to you softly," Tall and Creepy said. "President Drumpf lies all the time. Through his teeth. Repeatedly. Incessantly. Continuously. Always. Through his teeth. Through his teeth."

"What the shit?" Hawk Nose asked.

"Who uses the phrase, 'Lying through his teeth?' Are you my grandmother?" another staffer asked.

"Oh, don't get me wrong," Tall and Creepy said. "I still support him. I love him. He's doing what needs to be done."

"Drumpf doesn't lie," Hawk Nose insisted. "He's maybe the most honest President we've ever had. That's why the libtards don't like him. He tells the truth."

"Yeeeeaaah," said a guy wearing a hideous paisley shirt, drawing out the word for effect. "No."

"I'm with them," said a short and pale staffer, cocking his head in Hideous Paisley and Tall and Creepy's direction. "The man lies. But that's cool. I'm okay with it."

Hawk Nose looked around. Everyone nodded.

"I can't believe what I'm hearing," Hawk Nose said. "You people have all lost your shit."

"Seriously?" Martin asked.

"Yeah, seriously," Hawk Nose replied. "Drumpf is easily the greatest President we've had in a hundred years, and you people are talking shit about him."

"Whoa, there, big boy," Hideous Paisley said. "It's gonna be okay."

Martin left the PPO and made his way back to his office. Amanda had already unloaded on him that morning for his failure to come to work the day prior. He expected a quiet time.

What he didn't expect was Amanda's first words to him when he walked in: "Hey, bitch. Whaddya think? Does our friend Vlad have the President over a barrel?"

"Don't really know. What d'you think?"

"It's not looking good for the home team. That's what I think."

"What're you going to do?" he asked.

"I don't know," Amanda said quietly. "The question to ask yourself is this: If all this is real, if the President colluded or is trapped, how far downhill will the shit roll?"

"What d'you mean?"

"This job, this White House gig, it's a ticket to bigger and better things, okay? Do this well and other opportunities will come. That's what I've told myself all along."

She paused; he waited.

"What if that's not true?" she asked. "What if we're somehow tainted by having worked here? What if all this gig is, is a one-way ticket to shitsville?"

Martin had no answer for her.

FARM AID

Martin was moving almost as fast as possible without actually jogging down the White House hallway. The phone call had said that the President was upset.

Martin knocked on the door of his immediate destination and waited. "Come on," he muttered to himself. He knocked a second time, more insistently.

The door clicked, a loud metallic click from the magnetic lock. Martin pushed it open and stepped through.

The young man in civilian clothes looked up at him. "Jermanski?"

Martin had to bite his tongue. The kid knew who he was, but he, and the others who worked in that office, asked every time.

"Yes. Martin Jermanski." He held up the security badge.

"Sign here, please."

A clipboard was slid across the counter at Martin. He took it, signed his name, printed his name, wrote down the date, and then waited.

The young man slid the box across the counter; it came to rest right next to the clipboard.

"Serial number is on the side," the young man droned. "The yellow sticky has the serial number for the current. Please verify it before you bring it back. Last month ..."

Martin stopped listening. He had already heard the story. Last month, someone failed to follow proper security protocols. A lot of people got upset. Actually, the people in *this* office got upset. To Martin's knowledge, no one else did. In fact, most of the staffers laughed about it. 'Seriously,' Martin thought. 'What's the big deal?'

"Got it," Martin said. "Anything else?"

"Have a nice day." Perfectly monotone.

Martin left the office and took off at a full jog.

Lex saw him coming. "You have the package?"

"Wouldn't be worth much if I didn't," Martin breathed through his gasps.

"Couple of others in there already," said Lex.

"Shit," Martin said. "Really? His calendar was empty." He walked the last few steps to the Oval's entrance.

Lex knocked and opened the door. Martin stepped through without even glancing ahead of him.

A group of Cabinet officials stood around the President's desk. Most ignored his entrance, but the Chief of Staff, as always, saw him enter. In addition to Kellner, the Secretaries of the Treasury, Commerce, and Agriculture were present, with Conville and a few hangers-on for good measure.

Martin had been gone for the better part of the last month, working on *The Art of the Presidency*; he wasn't sure what he was walking into.

"I don't understand it," the President was saying. "The tariffs are a good idea. Hell, they're a great idea! This trade war – which is a stupid name, by the way. We're only attempting to level the playing field. But this trade war is going to be good for America. Good for the American worker. Good for the American farmer."

"Mr. President," Secretary Purdy said. "Tariffs leave a bad taste in the mouths of a lot of people. Farmers, in particular, believe that they do more harm than good."

"Farmers?" the President asked sarcastically. "Since when do I listen to a bunch of hick, hillbilly farmers? But they must be … slow, if they don't see the benefit of tariffs."

"Mr. President," Purdy said. "I know quite a few farmers. Good people, all of them. They work hard."

"Sonny, don't get me wrong," Drumpf interrupted. "I love the farmers, love 'em all. And I love you. But I'm not going to take business advice from a farmer. Could you believe that? Me?! Taking business advice from a farmer?"

"Mr. President," Secretary Rose said. "While I fully support the use of tariffs to level the playing field for America, and you know that I do, we have to be careful with how we structure and establish them."

"Wilbur, duh! Obviously," Drumpf said. "And that's why I have you and your people working on it. But I can come up with the tariffs as well as the next guy. You don't need any expertise to figure out what to tariff. Wilbur – what do we import from China the most?"

"Electronic equipment, sir," Rose said.

"How much?" Drumpf asked.

"About $150 billion a year."

"Okay. So we tariff them. What's next?"

"Machinery," Rose said.

"How much?"

"About $115 billion a year."

"Okay. Tariff that. What else?"

"Furniture, home goods and things. About $35 billion."

"Great," Drump said. "Let's tariff all of it." He paused and shook his head. "That wasn't so hard, was it?" He looked around at the men gathered around him.

That's when the President spotted Martin, standing just inside the entrance to the Oval, holding the box in his hand. "Marty! How've you been?"

The group all turned. Of the Secretaries, one frowned, the other shook his head, and the third muttered "Christ" under his breath. Kellner immediately moved to control the situation.

"Mr. President," Kellner said. "I believe Mr. Jermanski is here with your replacement phone, although his timing is less than perfect."

"Nonsense!" the President insisted. "Marty's timing is perfect. He's one of my best staffers, one of the best!"

Martin cautiously approached the desk. He was getting a bad vibe from Kellner and downright hostility from the Secretaries.

At least the President seemed happy to see him. He sat with a broad grin on his face.

"Mr. President," Kellner said quietly, leaning toward Drumpf. "Your phone."

"What? Oh, of course." He reached into his jacket and pulled out his phone.

Martin stepped up to the desk to take the phone. The President reached out with it and then pulled it away as Martin's fingers were about to close on it. Martin knew the game, so he leaned a little closer and tried again. The President pulled the phone away a second time.

"Too slow, Marty! You're too slow. God, you fall for it every time!"

Martin lunged for the phone and managed to snag it, but the President fought back and pulled hard on it. "Not so fast, Marty! You'll have to do better than that!"

"Jermanski!" The word cut through the air. It was Kellner.

Both Martin and the President froze. Martin was leaning over the President, supporting himself with one hand on the desk; his other hand was wrapped around the President's phone, intertwined with both of the President's hands. The President was leaning back in his chair, one foot braced against the desk to push away from Martin.

Martin let go of the phone and stood up at the same instant that the President did. It fell to the carpet between them. Martin looked down at the phone, then at the President, and then at the others in the Oval. Kellner was shaking his head with a severe frown on his face. Secretary Rose was aghast. The other two stood with neutral expressions on their faces.

Drumpf's laughter broke the silence. "Ah, Marty. You do take your job seriously. That's what makes you a good one." The President bent down, retrieved his phone, and handed it to Martin.

Martin stepped back, embarrassed, but with the bizarre urge to laugh.

"Mr. President," Rose said. "Mr. President."

Drumpf didn't seem to hear the Commerce Secretary. He sat looking at Martin.

Martin had decided that he needed to leave the Oval as quickly as possible. He quickly verified the serial number on the old phone and then placed the new one on the desk in front of the President. Without looking, he could sense Kellner's eyes boring into him.

"Mr. President," Rose said again.

"Yeah, Wilbur?" the President asked, finally pulling his eyes from Martin.

"Instituting these tariffs will require careful thought and planning," Rose said. "I'll bring a proposal back to you early next week."

"And don't forget, sir," Kellner said. "Your meeting with President Juncker is scheduled for next week."

"President who?" Drumpf asked.

"President Juncker, sir. Of the European Union."

"Christ," Drumpf said. "The Europeans? Why do I have to talk to him? And why do they call him President? *I'm* the President!" He turned to Kellner and then looked down at his desk. A single folder sat there. He opened it. "Didn't you bring me a proposal today, Wilbur?"

"Yes, sir," Rose said. "But I think it needs to be revised. I'll have you an updated version first thing on Monday."

The President shrugged. Then he picked up the short stack of papers from the folder. "So this is garbage?" he asked Rose, and then looked around at the others.

It seemed to Martin that they had forgotten him. He began to slowly move toward the entrance.

"Garbage?" Drumpf said. When no one answered, he picked up the papers and ripped them in half. And then in half again.

"Does everyone know what operational security is, OpSec?" Again, no one answered.

"Marty, you know OpSec, right?"

'Shit.' Martin stopped and took a step back toward the desk. "Yes, sir," he said. "We received mandatory training on OpSec."

"Of course, you did," the President said. He ripped the papers into even smaller pieces. "It's important that we keep a close hold on sensitive information, on my secrets, on our nation's secrets."

'Oh, Mike and Luke! If I could stop him, I would!' Martin thought, watching the President create smaller and smaller bits of paper. "Yes, sir. It's vital to the functioning of our democracy."

"Absolutely!" As soon as he finished the word, Drumpf picked up several small pieces of paper and plopped them in his mouth. He chewed a bit. "We can never be too careful about protecting the nation's secrets."

He picked up a whole pile of small pieces and dropped them into his mouth.

Martin struggled to keep his face calm. He wasn't sure whether he should laugh, cry, or gag. He dared not look at any of the others in the room; he wasn't sure if he could control his face looking at anyone else.

The President chewed some more and then turned back to Secretary Rose. Through a mouthful of Presidential paper bits, he asked, "New tariffs proposal on Monday?"

"Yes, sir," Rose said. "You'll have it in time to digest it before your meeting with President Juncker."

"Mr. President," Secretary Purdy said. "I need to strongly advise against these tariffs."

"What are you talking about?" Drumpf asked.

"There is widespread skepticism from the agricultural lobby—"

"Agricultural? Are you talking about farmers again, Sonny? I don't want to hear about the farmers."

"Some of your strongest supporters are farmers," Purdy insisted. "It's important that you maintain your support with them."

That seemed to get the President's attention.

And Martin began moving toward the exit again. He glanced at Kellner to find him still looking at him. Martin began to move a little quicker.

"I'm going forward with the tariffs," the President said.

Martin realized that he missed some of the conversation, but he was more interested in making his escape.

"I promised the American people," Drumpf continued.

"But they are susceptible to retaliation. And the retaliation will hurt them. Badly," Purdy said.

"What do you want me to do?" the President asked pointedly.

Secretary Purdy didn't answer.

"The tariffs are on," Drumpf said. "It's already decided. So what else should I do?"

No one answered. The President looked around, obviously frustrated.

Martin was almost to the door. He was worried that if he moved too quickly, he would call attention to himself. Just a few more steps.

"Marty!"

'Shit. Shit. Shit.' "Yes, sir?" Martin had just reached the exit. 'So close!'

"Sonny is worried about the farmers. He thinks the tariffs are going to hurt them. What should I do?"

From Martin's spot near the exit, Kellner was standing just behind the seated President. Kellner was shaking his head 'No.'

"Sir," Martin said. Classic stalling tactic. He was trying to remember what he knew about tariffs. He wasn't even completely sure he knew what they were.

The President stared at him. Eventually, his eyebrows raised. He was getting impatient.

Martin didn't say anything. Kellner continued to shake his head back and forth.

"Marty. Come on," Drumpf said. "What should I do?"

The three Secretaries stared at him. None were pleased with the President asking him. Kellner's head shaking only sped up.

Agriculture, Treasury, Commerce. Farmers. Money. 'Give the farmers some money.' "Sir," Martin said tentatively.

The President leaned forward. The Secretaries stared harder. Kellner's eyes grew wide.

"Can't we just give the farmers money?" Martin asked.

For a moment, no one responded.

Martin cleared his throat. He was afraid to move, or to say anything else.

Kellner palmed his forehead. Secretary Rose smiled. Secretary Purdy actually laughed. Secretary Munchkin, who hadn't said a word since Martin entered the Oval Office, seemed to sigh in relief.

"Sure!" the President said. "Let's give 'em money!"

Kellner started shaking his head, still being firmly palmed in his hand. Rose seemed shocked. Purdy's laughter turned into coughing. Munchkin looked afraid.

"It's a great idea! We'll just give 'em cash. How much?"

Martin was surprised to realize that Drumpf was asking him. He looked down at his watch. It was almost noon. "Twelve m—?"

"Billion?" the President asked.

"Billion!" Marty said, almost in unison.

Kellner and the three Secretaries were all shaking their heads 'No.'

"Mr. President—" two of them said.

"It's a great idea. One of my best—today! Wilbur, Sonny, the farmers will love this. I mean, who doesn't love free money? It's almost the best kind—of money, that is. It's almost as good as free pu—" The President abruptly shut his mouth.

The three Secretaries all started talking at once.

Martin couldn't understand who was saying what, but he could tell that none of them liked the idea. One thing that Martin did understand was the look on Kellner's face. And he could read Kellner's lips: "Out!"

Martin was only too happy to oblige.

SMALL COUNCIL

Martin stood waiting patiently outside of the Oval Office. The President was receiving his security briefing for the day, and while Martin did possess a clearance, he felt it better to wait until the meeting was complete.

Phil had the duty that day and was standing impassively close by. Then he cocked his head slightly, listened for a moment, and nodded at Martin. "They're done; you can go in."

Phil knocked on the door twice, then opened it for Martin.

"Thanks," Martin said, and then stepped into the Oval. And immediately thought better of it. Andrew Breiburg and Kelly Conville were standing close to the President's desk. And, surprisingly, there was no sign of Watterhoot or Kellner.

Although Breiburg didn't see Martin, the look on his face signaled to Martin that he should be somewhere else. He paused and considered backing out when the President spotted him.

"Marty," Drumpf called out.

"Yes, Mr. President," Martin said.

"Come here," Drumpf said. "I want to run something past you."

Martin approached the desk.

"Do you remember the conversation we had several weeks ago about the Vice President?" Drumpf asked.

Martin didn't. "Yes, sir."

"Him being a risk to me, a bigger risk than Hillary," Drumpf said.

"Yes, sir," Martin said. "I do." The additional information helped.

"Have you seen the article at CNN?" Drumpf asked.

Martin didn't and admitted it this time. "No, sir."

"Here. Read this." The President handed him a sheet of paper. It was a two sided printout of an article from CNN.com.

Martin read it as fast as he could. He wasn't a fast reader, but he was able to get the gist of the article quickly enough. It outlined views the Vice President had expressed many years earlier when Bill Clinton was President. Then-Congressman Spence argued that a President must maintain the highest morals and that an immoral President is a danger to the nation and to the world.

"Well?" Drumpf asked.

Martin felt caught. Conville and Breiburg were both staring at him intently. He didn't know how to answer the question. He suddenly wished that he'd been privy to the conversation before entering—he would then at least know what the others had said about the article.

'What is the President even asking?' Martin wondered. His mind swam with a maelstrom of potential questions, none of which he could fully articulate. Regardless of his inability to understand the question, he believed he was in danger

"Well, Mr. President," Martin began. Stalling always seemed to work in the Oval Office. Especially with others in the room.

Apparently, Breiburg lost his patience before Martin did. "It proves the point that I made to you several weeks ago, sir, that the Vice President is a threat. This is just further proof. He questioned everything about a former President's legitimacy; he's questioning your legitimacy now."

"I think Andrew is reading too much into this, sir," Conville countered. "Mike Spence has proven that he is nothing other than completely loyal. Even if he isn't, as long as the Republican Party is firmly in power, he's not a threat."

Martin was trying to read the President. The very tone of the discussion assumed that the President was everything that the article accused Clinton of being twenty years ago. Had the President made that connection? Did he even care about it? Unfortunately, Drumpf's face belied no emotion other than keen interest in his advisors' argument.

"Kelly is being too nonchalant about this, sir," Breiburg countered. "If Spence thought this way twenty years ago, he thinks the same now. Remember, you brought him onboard to assist with the 'values-voters' vote, and he did that. But those same values may cause people to question your leadership."

"Mr. President, this—" Conville began before being cut off by Breiburg.

"If enough Republicans start to question your leadership, it won't matter if they keep control of Congress," Breiburg argued in a louder voice. "If even a few of them begin to consider the opposition arguments, they are as dangerous to you as a flipped Congress."

"What can I do?" the President asked Breiburg directly. "We spoke to the lawyers. I can't remove Spence in the middle of a term."

"You can't remove him, but you can start a conversation that may lead to his im— ... his removal," Breiburg insisted. "You've gotten rid of a lot of others who didn't fully support you."

"I understand where you're coming from. I really do. But listen," Drumpf said. "My support among the base is rock solid. My support among the evangelicals is rock solid—maybe even more solid. As long as Jeff Sessoms' Religious Liberty Task Force is doing its work, whatever it's supposed to do, the evangelicals will support me. Let's face it; I have them firmly in my hip pocket. They're not gonna do anything to endanger my Presidency, and they'll fight tooth and nail to protect me." The President shifted in his seat. He glanced at Martin but then continued, "I think it's risky to move against Spence before the midterms. Too risky."

"Sir," Breiburg said. "It might be even riskier to wait until after the midterms."

The President took in a deep breath and exhaled it loudly. He looked down at his tie and adjusted it slightly. Finally, he looked up. "Marty, what do you think?"

Martin was relieved. By stalling, he learned the others' view before having to voice his own. Of course, he really didn't have a view on the subject. It was time to come up with one.

"Sir. I think it's one thing to fire staffers, fire administration officials, even fire cabinet officials. You've done all of those things, and it's worked. It's worked fully to your advantage." Martin learned from his earliest days in the White House that it was always wise to start an answer to Drumpf with some kind of compliment. And then to ease into an answer without being too definitive. "But I think that, in this case, in a situation where you could be perceived as attacking your own Vice President, I think it's best to be cautious." And then, to stick the answer, end with another compliment. "Even for someone as bold and decisive as you, someone with a keen instinct on these issues, I think caution is the best approach."

Drumpf bobbed his head from side to side with a distinct 'Meh' look on his face. He was obviously deep in thought.

"And besides," Martin continued. "It's probably fake news. How do we know the Vice President even wrote this?"

"Marty. You haven't let me down yet. I think you're right. You know that my every instinct is to not be cautious, but I think it's the best option in this case."

Conville nodded and smiled. "I think it's the right decision, Mr. President."

"Sir, I think you're putting yourself at risk by not taking action," Breiburg said. "I think you're putting yourself at risk by listening to this, this kid. He's only worked in the White House for six months. He doesn't understand politics. He doesn't understand this city."

Martin realized that the personal attacks were normal in Drumpf's White House. They had become more regular as his apparent influence on the President had grown.

"Fighting is good," Drumpf responded. "Conflict is good. The more you people fight, the better advice I get from you. As far as Marty is concerned, I like him, I trust him; he's given me good advice. He's young, sure. But age isn't all it's cracked up to be."

"Mr. President—" Breiburg began.

"Discussion's over," the President said.

"Mr. President, there's the 25th Amendment to consider."

"Fuck the Constitution!" The President's snarl surprised everyone in the Oval. His face calmed almost immediately and his next words were unusually quiet. "I'll only discuss that with Dan, Rudy, and the others. Do not mention it again."

"Yes, sir," Breiburg said, also quietly.

The President looked down at the folder on his desk. "What's next on the schedule?"

It was Breiburg's and Conville's notice that the meeting was over. They moved toward the exit without another word. Reaching the door, they turned to look at Martin.

Martin merely shrugged and approached the President's desk. It was helpful to know his schedule. "Sir, you have one hour of Executive Time. That's followed by a short Cabinet session later this afternoon."

"Thanks, Marty."

"Sir, do you have any papers for me to dispose of?" Martin asked. The others had left, and only he and the President remained in the Oval Office.

"I probably do." Drumpf seemed to be pondering something. He absently opened the folder sitting on his desk. He pulled a sheet of paper from it, shrugged to himself, and ripped it in half. He ripped it in half a few more times and then crumpled up a few of the resultant pieces of paper into a small ball.

Martin glanced in the Presidential garbage can. There was a small pile of hand-shredded papers at its bottom. He bent to retrieve them and then stood up.

The President tossed the paper ball into the air and caught it in his mouth.

'Nice catch,' Martin thought. 'Ew.'

The President chewed on it for a moment, lost in thought.

"Sir?"

Drumpf looked at Martin, as if noticing him for the first time. "Marty. Hey. How's the manuscript coming?"

"I should have something for you shortly, sir," Martin said. "I'm putting the finishing touches on it."

"That's good, Marty. I'll be tweeting whenever I endorse Republican candidates. I can sway elections with my tweets, you know." He chewed a few more times on the paper in his mouth. "But I'll also be tweeting about the book," Drumpf said. "That should drive sales, and I think it'll definitely help our midterm prospects."

"I think anything that showcases your Presidency will be good for the party and for your popularity," Martin said.

"It's important." Drumpf paused and threw a second paper ball into the air and caught it in his mouth. "Important that the book hits the shelves as soon as possible," Drumpf said. "I want people to have plenty of time to read it before November."

"Completely agree, Mr. President." Martin cleared his throat. "Are you done with that, sir?" He indicated the pile of unballed paper that sat on the desk in front of him.

Drumpf looked down, swirled the papers from individual piles into a large mound, and pushed them toward the edge of his desk. "Yeah, Marty. Thanks."

Martin pulled the pile into the garbage can that he was holding in his hand. "Anything else, sir?"

"No. Thanks, Marty."

Martin turned and walked to the exit. His time in Scotch-Tape Purgatory still haunted him. He shuddered thinking about it.

He reached the door and turned to bid the President a farewell, but the Oval Office behind him was empty. Drumpf could be sneaky and quick when he wanted to.

THE FINAL MANUSCRIPT

Martin stood outside the Oval Office waiting for his meeting with the President. He was actually nervous. He had stood there dozens of times, waiting with other visitors before they were admitted to the Oval. Of course, today the topic of the discussion was his completed manuscript for *The Art of the Presidency*. Martin had no idea how it was going to go.

Chad stood impassively at the door. "Nervous?"

"How could you tell?" A bit of friendly banter was always good to get the shakes out.

"I'm paid to tell."

Martin chuckled; it was typical Chad.

The door opened. Madeleine Watterhoot stuck her head out and nodded to him.

Martin stepped in.

The President stood up from the desk. "Marty! Come in, come in. Here. Take a seat." The President walked over to a plush armchair and directed Martin to the sofa. Sitting on the coffee table between the chair and sofa was the manuscript, almost two inches high. The President's copy was clean and bright, much different than Martin's own working copy.

Martin stood at the sofa and waited for Drumpf to sit.

"This might be the most important conversation we've ever had, don't you think? And probably the first time that we've spoken sitting here. This is it. How do you feel?"

Actually, they *had* sat and talked at the coffee table once or twice before, but Martin wasn't going to tell the President that. "Nervous, sir."

"Of course, I get it," Drumpf said. "It only makes sense you're nervous. But, listen, let's get down to it. I read the manuscript. It's fabulous."

Martin was relieved, and a bit surprised. There were certainly some portions of the book that he thought might upset the President.

Drumpf was smiling at him and enthusiastically continued. "Fabulous! It's definitely worthy of the Drumpf name. And I love the title, *The Art of the Presidency*. It was a brilliant idea of mine to name it that. One of my best ideas. Follows perfectly from *The Art of the Deal*. That's the book that started it all, you know."

"Yes, sir."

"And I really like how the final chapter is called 'The Art of the Presidency' and summarizes, in one short section, all of the wisdom that you've learned from your time here."

"I was able to add some more after you read it the first time," Martin said.

The President nodded absently. He didn't like being interrupted. "Listen, Marty. I had my lawyers write up a contract. They actually wrote up three or four different contracts."

Martin tensed a little. 'Here it comes,' he thought.

"We went round and round. And then some additional lawyers looked at it. Not my personal lawyers, but some government lawyers. There was a big argument. You would have loved it. My lawyers and, and my other lawyers, my personal ones, they just went at it. When it was all said and done, I decided to sign all the rights over to you."

'Wait, what?' "Mr. President?"

"I know you're shocked, Marty. I can see it. What we eventually discovered is that it would be unethical, officially unethical—unethical by some stupid ethics rules, that frankly I don't believe apply to me. But unethical for me to sign a contract where you and I split the proceeds from the sale of the book. What they explained to me, which I still believe is wrong, dead wrong, is that, because you are a Federal employee who works for me in your day job, there are restrictions that say you cannot work for me in other capacities."

Martin could only shake his head, and only slightly so.

"I know—it doesn't make sense to me, either. If you had been an author who came to me and offered to write a book and who didn't already work on my staff, it would have been different. But because you are a White House staffer, different rules apply to you. So I guess it's your lucky day. You know, this'll set you up for life. You'll be rich. Well, not quite, but you'll be extremely well-off. You know, anything with my name on it sells and sells huge. Huge!"

"I don't know what to say, Mr. President. Thank you."

"Marty. Don't thank me, yet. You're not much of a negotiator, are you? Well, not compared to me, at least. We're still going to sign a contract." The President pulled a single sheet of paper from a folder. "It'll give you the rights to the book for as long as I am President, or ten years, whichever comes sooner. At that time, the rights, and all future royalties, revert to me." He handed the contract to Martin.

Martin looked it over; it was short. Not even a full page. He wasn't sure if he should sign it or not. He started to panic and then looked up at the Chief of Staff, standing close to the President's desk.

Kellner nodded to him, *it's safe.*

Martin pulled a pen from his pocket, set the contract down to sign it, and then realized he hadn't read it. It didn't take long, and Martin didn't understand the vast majority of it anyway. He took a deep breath and signed it before his hand could start shaking.

The President reached across the table and pulled the contract toward him. He signed it and slid it back into the folder. "Done!" He smiled his trademarked self-satisfied grin. "How's it feel?"

"Good, I think," Martin said.

"I bet it does! So what're you going to do now?"

Martin didn't understand the question. "Sir?"

"Come on, Marty," the President chided. "You can't write a book about the inner workings of the White House and then remain on staff. It doesn't work that way. They'd eat you alive. It's a wonder you've survived this long. Now, if the book had been purely about me and the tremendous job I'm doing as President, that would have been one thing. But you've also written about other aspects of life here. You can't work with people after you've written about them."

"I hadn't considered that," Martin said. The Chief of Staff had said something along those lines, but Martin really hadn't seriously considered it.

"That's what makes you a good aide, but not much of a strategic thinker," Drumpf said. "But that's okay. So what's next?"

Martin was having trouble coming to grips with the idea of leaving the White House. He certainly hadn't intended to. His mind raced, and he said the first thing that came to mind, "I might try to run for office."

"Tremendous! Marty—brilliant idea!" Drumpf crunched his face up in thought. "I don't think you'd be able to get on any ballot for this fall. Do you think—?" The question was directed at the Chief of Staff.

"No, Mr. President," Kellner responded. "I'm almost certain it's too late for that."

"Too bad. Too bad! I need more allies in office. I need allies that I can trust." Drumpf turned from the Chief of Staff back to Martin. "And I've always been able to trust you, Marty. And your dad. Good man, your dad. But you should. Just think about it: You've worked for almost a year in my White House. You've had the opportunity to learn from the best President in modern times. You've written a book about that experience. You are an expert. And if I endorsed you, you'd be a shoe-in."

"I hadn't considered that, Mr. President."

"It's perfect! Remember, that whole last chapter is my advice to politicians wanting to follow in my footsteps. If you follow that advice, you'd win in a landslide!"

The President paused; Martin waited for more. And then the smile slowly melted from Drumpf's face; his excitement seemed to run out of steam.

Drumpf stood up, abruptly, and then looked down on Martin. "I've things to do, Marty. Let's talk again in a few days; I might have some more advice you can put in that last chapter."

"Yes, sir, Mr. President. Thank you."

And just as Martin had himself done to numerous guests, the Chief of Staff escorted Martin from the Oval Office.

.   .   .

"He didn't read it."

"But, sir," Martin said. "He said he did."

"Martin, he didn't." The Chief of Staff shook his head. "But I did. Cover to cover. There were some surprises in there, for sure. One or two things caught me off guard." The former General looked at him with calm and serious eyes. "You sure you want to do this?"

The eyes were what did it. Martin stopped and took a breath. He had worked hard on the manuscript. It had occupied all of his waking hours for the last six weeks. If he wasn't doing White House business, he was writing about White House business. And he had written about the Chief of Staff. "What did you think of it?"

Kellner thought for a moment before answering. "Ultimately, it doesn't matter what I think. I served in the military for over forty years; you don't do that without growing a thick skin. How thick is *your* skin?"

"Sir?"

"A lot of what the President says is bullshit," the Chief of Staff told him. "Hell, almost all of it, but he's certainly right about one thing. No one in the White House is going to treat you the same after the book hits."

"Well, the contract is already signed," Martin said. "I can't back out now."

"I can arrange it, if you want the book eliminated. No one has to read it. Regardless of the contract. It can all go away."

Martin stood in silence. He wasn't sure what to think, or say.

"You think about it. Take a day or two. Maybe talk to your parents. Then tell me what you want to do. Okay?"

"Thanks, sir."

They had been speaking at the door to the Chief of Staff's office. Both were standing, Kellner just inside his office and Martin just outside. Martin turned to leave.

"Martin," Kellner said. "One last thing."

"Sir?"

"Your last day in the White House is going to be August 17th. The President and I already agreed on the date. You need to seriously start thinking about your plan."

Kellner's words were a body blow. "Yes, sir." Martin felt his innards clench; he was shocked by his own physical reaction to the news.

"I have to admit. I underestimated you," Kellner said. "I didn't think you'd be able to write a book. Didn't think you had a chance in hell. If I had, I would've been more… forceful in my opposition to it."

It seemed to Martin that Kellner was trying to offer him a little pick-me-up after informing him of his last day. Martin was grateful.

"I guess I am full of surprises, sir."

Kellner smirked, nodded once, and then turned and walked to his desk. At his desk, he noticed that Martin was still standing in the doorway. "Good luck, Jermanski."

"Thanks, sir." Martin took the hint and walked back to his own office.

THE ART OF THE PRESIDENCY

Note from Martin Jermanski: This final chapter of the book, unlike all previous chapters, is based directly upon Ronald G. Drumpf's wisdom as the greatest modern President of the United States. It is a distillation of everything that he learned while campaigning for and serving to this point as the 45th President.

This chapter is, in his own words, "the single greatest collection of political advice ever gathered in one place, condensed into a short reading so that anyone, even those who don't like to read, can read it quickly and understand it."

Speaking of this chapter, President Drumpf continued, "Anyone, and I mean anyone, even the libtards and the Democrats, who follow the advice here will succeed in his campaign, succeed more impressively than he thought possible, succeed in ways that other politicians can only hope to. He will, and I guarantee this, win whatever race he enters and win with historic margins of victory, just as my Presidential win was by the widest margin in modern history." The paragraphs that follow encompass Drumpf's philosophy and outline his "keys to victory."

·　　　　·　　　　·

The Art of the Presidency is a style of leadership, a style of governing, that has proven to be very successful over the last two years. It can also be viewed as a collection of advice for aspiring politicians. Political success is all but guaranteed when a candidate closely adheres to this advice. There are three related pillars that define the Art of the Presidency. In order, they are: Media Supremacy, Satisfaction of the Base, and Institutional Supremacy.

Typically, the first (Media Supremacy) should be achieved long before a political campaign but, at the latest, must be achieved early in a campaign. The candidate will lay the groundwork for the second (Satisfaction of the Base) during the campaign and then, once in office, must continually work to maintain it. The third (Institutional Supremacy) begins during the campaign but will bear its greatest fruits once the individual is in office. This final condition is the most important, because it will maintain the politician's popularity for the long term.

Media Supremacy. A politician who desires to succeed in the 21st century must achieve *Media Supremacy*. This is accomplished through four separate but related activities. These activities can be done in any order, but all four are vital to achieving supremacy. These activities are:

1. *Achieve fame and notoriety.* The politician must become well-known to as many people as possible. This is the most important activity within **Media Supremacy**, because everything that follows throughout the Art of the Presidency builds from this fame. The most successful candidates become known to a large audience before ever indicating political aspirations. Name recognition is more important than ideology, political bent, or knowledge of the issues. Note that the fame doesn't have to be positive; notoriety (fame for negative reasons) is just as effective. The only 'bad' fame is a small amount of fame. The more famous, or infamous, a person can become, the better they are laying the groundwork for a successful candidacy.

2. *Control the story through all forms of media.* This is actually a two-parter! The candidate must control the story (Part 1) and must do so through all media (Part 2).

- *Controlling the story* is first and foremost about transmitting more than anyone else. Inundate the media (whichever) with a constant stream of content. A candidate controls the story through the sheer volume of content he creates. Generate more "story" than your competitors and those friendly to you. Ensure that you remain the most talked-about individual.

  - Control also involves having the courage and forethought to choose the story that you want to tell and telling that story. You must have a personal story that is compelling, interesting, and either relatable or aspirational for the audience. The best personal story is one that is both relatable and aspirational. It's why Americans love rags-to-riches stories, stories about underdogs, and comeback stories. If you don't have a personal story that is any of these things, make up a new story. Recreate yourself to fit a story that meets these requirements. Recreation itself is one form of the underdog tale.

  - In additional to your own story, you must shape existing stories to support your fame, your goals, your agenda. EVERY story can be made about you, if you are willing to find the right angle. If you are unsure of the angle, do not hesitate. Inaction is the enemy here. You may choose an angle and then learn, through trial and error or feedback, that you've chosen poorly. Change angles loudly, vociferously, and strongly. And never admit that you've changed angles! Instead, explain to the media and the masses that they misunderstood your angle, and they are only now beginning to understand it. Remember: Every story is about you.

- *Employing all media* is the second part of controlling the story. The more forms of media the better!

    - There are numerous forms available today that enable a brave and determined candidate to control his story. The big four are, of course, print, video, radio, and the internet, and each of those has various subsets. Print includes newspapers, books, magazine, pamphlets, etc. Video refers to television, movies, and anything that involves moving pictures. Radio is just that—radio. In our 21st century world, the internet is quickly becoming the elephant in the room, specifically because it can encompass all of the previous forms. Ebooks are print, typically delivered via the internet. Youtube are videos likewise delivered by the internet. Any audio files, whether in the form of music, podcasts, or otherwise, delivered by the internet subsume radio.

    - The internet has also created its own forms: blogging, vlogging, Facebook, Twitter (of course), Instagram, and the list goes on. The canny candidate will employ all of these and more. He will develop a web presence on as many of these platforms as possible. Even Tinder, the dating app, could be used by a savvy candidate to help control his story. For candidates who are even more shrewd, there are other options: Creating your own app, to be downloaded by your followers, or even just people interested in your story, is now almost required to be seen as a serious contender among a large percentage of the populace. An app that "gamifies" the political process for a given candidate might be the next step in this evolution.

3. *Ensure your story is spun.* The modern candidate must maintain an active propaganda machine. It is impossible today to be the sole proprietor of your story. Therefore, it is a requirement that all candidates foster relationships

with people, groups, media outlets, and "influencers" who are not directly related to him but who can tell the story when he isn't able or in addition to his own telling. These "outside" voices, even when not technically outside of your camp, lend credence and legitimacy to your story. There is one thing better than telling your own story, and that is having others tell your story for you. In some cases, this may be a single voice, another celebrity who supports you; in other cases, it may be an entire television network, or website. Foster these relationships, offer quid pro quo support, build loyalty and, if possible, friendship. However, if at all possible, try to keep the true nature of these relationships secret. There are those who view these relationships with disdain.

4. *Degrade media that does not spin for you.* Spinning your story is not enough; you must shut down the voices who spin against you.

  • In addition to building and maintaining a supportive propaganda machine and lending those who advance your interests support in return, viciously attack all media outlets who are against you. Denigrate them, attack their legitimacy, their honesty, their credentials. Those who would speak against you must be silenced.

  • Attack even those outlets that claim neutrality. There is no neutrality in the modern media landscape. All forms of media are for or against you, and you must, so much as you are able, attack those who are against you. There is no objective truth, that crutch that so-called neutral media lean on to support their lies. There is only *your* truth; you must own it and attack those who don't share it. In so doing, you must keep people ignorant of the "truth" and educate them on *your* truth.

Satisfaction of the Base. *Media Supremacy* will give you the prize and allow you to win any election. To ensure your continued popularity once in office, you must feed the masses. If you feed them well, they will be satisfied, and you will have achieved *Satisfaction of the Masses*. This is both a literal and emotional feeding and is comprised of several related activities; they are:

1. *Find "your" people.* You must choose a group of constituents to be "your" people. Just as achieving fame and notoriety is the most important action in **Media Supremacy**, finding "your" people is the most important action in **Satisfaction of the Base**. It is these people who will support you through thick and thin, who will go to the mat for you, who will bleed for you. Once you are able to find these people, speak directly to them. Coddle them, love them, attempt to satisfy them, through your story and your message. They will become your base, your most ardent supporters.

2. *Select potent issues.* Find issues that your base cares about.

    • There are many ways to do this, but the most straightforward is to speak directly to them. Listen to them. Meet them and shake their hands. Communicate with them on a personal level. If you determine that personal contact with them is too unsavory for you, never fear. You can appear to meet them where they are without "getting your hands dirty." This fact-finding is not to actually make a connection with people, but merely to learn their desires and their fears, in order to exploit that information for your gain.

    • Commandeer those issues as your own. Regardless of your personal feelings for a given issue, claim it as your own and fight for it against all outsiders. The loyalty of your people is wholly dependent on you fighting for those things they believe in. Your personal beliefs do not matter, all that matters is your action to support the beliefs of your people. Frankly, it is possible, and sometimes necessary, to champion issues that you personally disagree with. This is the price you pay to earn the loyalty of your people; it is a small price to pay.

- "Potent" issues are better than impotent issues. For an issue to be potent, it must meet the following conditions:

    - Your people must care strongly about it. If they don't care enough to get angry when discussing it, is not worth your time. A potent issue draws an emotional reaction from your people—the stronger the reaction, the better. You must be prepared to harness that emotion to maintain and build upon the support of your people.

    - Your people must feel that there are forces at work in society, government, or the media that are actively trying to defeat, marginalize, or otherwise act against your issue. An issue is potent if it is being attacked by outside forces. You must position yourself to appear as the defender of that issue against all outside influences. Here, appearance is most important; it doesn't necessarily matter if you are actively defending the issue. What is most important is that your people believe that you are.

    - An issue is potent if you are able to spin the objective truth of the issue to replace it with *your* truth. The first two conditions that define potency above are important; once they are met, this third condition will ensure your ability to exploit it for maximum benefit. The issue in question must be such that you can take ownership for it and convince your people that you alone are able to solve it. The objective truth of this is irrelevant; all that matters is that your people believe that you personally are the key to their issue being successful (if it is attempting to promote change) or well-defended (if it is attempting to resist change).

3. *Build a base of angry, unhappy people.* Once you have found your people and selected those issues in order to maximize the appearance of your support, stoke their anger and resentment. Convince them that they are the targeted minority

battling for their particular issues. Couch the struggle in life-or-death terms. Exaggerate the threat to them and their issue and minimize the influence of anything that may seem to alleviate the danger they face—except for you. The aim of this is to convince them that you are the singular individual who understands their issue, sympathizes with it, and is able to support them in their struggle.

4. *Feed the base.* To this point, the activities that support *Satisfaction of the Base* have mainly been communications issues. This final activity is where the rubber meets the road. You must pass laws, sign orders, and make concrete progress on rectifying your peoples' issues. You must meet your campaign promises. This is the literal feeding of the masses, and it is absolutely essential that you are able to accomplish this. Failure to do so will risk your time in office and almost guarantee that you will not be reelected.

Institutional Supremacy. Once in office, you must assume control of the major institutions in society. Only by assuming this control can you hope to remain in office for the long term.

1. *Attack the "So-Called" Elites.* Anyone who has a vested interest in the status quo can and should be labelled an "Elite," regardless of whether or not they are actually elite in any way; the modifier "So-Called" is important in this context. As long as that group can be denigrated and labelled "other," they should be attacked. Do not be concerned if you actually meet some definition of "elite" or are even a member of the group you are attacking; distance yourself from them in all ways. Use your story to show the vast differences between the enemy elite and you. You can and should attack in every way imaginable; you should insult, brow-beat, marginalize, objectify, dehumanize, and embarrass your opponents at every opportunity. You should never let up. If they attack you, attack them tenfold in return.

2. *Attack education and the sciences.* Attack the institutions that claim to support objective truth. Remove funding from schools, ensure that quality education is hard to come by, if not downright nonexistent, and viciously attack those who support said institutions. Denigrate the importance of education and the sciences. Convince your people that (all) science is merely a ploy by the educated elite to control the masses. In place of education and the sciences, promote your truth as the only objective fact worth believing. While the educated elite use the smoke-screen of science to keep your people in shackles, you will present them with truth that will free them and lead them to live brighter, healthier, more-fulfilling, and freer lives.

3. *Obtain control of the police and justice systems.* Once your truth is widely accepted as the only truth, you can bend the norms of justice within your town, city, municipality, county, state, or country to ensure your hold on power. Vigorously support the police force to gain their approval. Profess that you are "protecting" the population. Further, claim that you are the only one capable of protecting them. Appoint judges that are loyal to you, over the rule of law. Control of the police and justice systems is the final victory.

Media Supremacy, Satisfaction of the Base, and Institutional Supremacy: These are the pillars that make up the Art of the Presidency. Master these pillars! Political and personal success are within your reach when you apply the wisdom found herein to all of your endeavors.

EPILOGUE

Martin didn't know that the process of leaving the Federal Government would be as complicated as it was. There were checklists to follow, forms to complete, IT accounts to scrub and then close down.

It was his very last morning in the White House, and he still wasn't complete with wiping his email account. But he had purposefully come in early to beat Amanda and get the computer. So many unread emails to delete.

After Amanda had come in and after deleting over a hundred emails, he came across one that caught his eye. He opened it and read it. 'What?!' He couldn't believe it. He jumped up from his desk and ran from his office.

"Bitch! Where are you going?"

He didn't bother to answer her. He quickly made his way into the Eisenhower Building. He came to the office and knocked on the door.

Not waiting for a response, he burst into the room. Two guys looked up from the desk. They were bent over torn-up pieces of paper, trying to reconstruct them.

"Who're you guys?" he asked.

"Maybe you don't know," the first said to him. He wore a mullet and had traces of long-ago acne around his forehead. "This is the Document Reconstruction Team, the DRT. I'm Theo." He stood up and offered Martin his hand.

The second one also stood up. He was short, shorter than Martin, and wore a too-wide tie. "Fred."

Martin shook both of their hands. They both had decent grips. 'Not too bad.' "I'm Martin. Nice to meet you guys. Hey, uh, question for you. Where're Mike and Luke?"

"Those guys?" Fred asked. "Mike left the DRT about a week and a half ago. He got a position in International Negotiations. He deserved it; did he ever show you his resume? It was a crime he was here for so long."

"And Luke's last day was actually yesterday," said Theo. "He moved to National Security Affairs. Just where he belonged."

"No shit," Martin said as a massive smile engulfed his face. 'They made it!' he thought to himself. 'They actually made it out! And they did it early!'

"Okay, well, thanks," Martin said. "Good luck." 'You're gonna need it.'

He whistled a happy tune for the entire walk back to his office. When he got there, a cardboard box had appeared on his desk. Amanda told him it was for him to carry his 'personal effects' out. He looked around. He didn't have any.

"Oh," she said, sitting at the computer, now under her login. "I deleted the rest of your emails. Nothing looked important."

"Thank you? But that was the last thing on my checklist," he said. "I guess it's time for me to go."

"You ain't leaving that box here, bitch," Amanda had said. "Get that shit outta here."

So Martin carried the empty box out of the White House. For some reason, Amanda accompanied him. They stood on the sidewalk between the White House and the Eisenhower Building. He didn't know what to say and was curious to hear what Amanda was going to say.

"Now give me the fucking phone," she said.

"Wait. What?"

"You don't get to keep your official phone, bitch," she spat. "I know you ignored that item on all of your checkout sheets, but I'd be the one to get in trouble if you don't turn it in. Hand it over."

Martin laughed. He put the empty cardboard box on the ground at his feet and pulled the phone from his pocket. "You're right. I just need to scan my contacts."

"Fucking shit. Seriously?"

'This girl knows how to get angry,' Martin thought, as he started scrolling through the phone's contacts.

"Just delete them all; none of those people are going to talk to you after you leave," she insisted. "You can forget all of them."

'She's probably right,' Martin thought. So he started deleting contact after contact.

"Tick tock, bitch. You do know you can mass-delete them, right? Are you that much of an idiot?"

"Come on, Amanda," Martin said. "I'm trying to prolong this goodbye for your sake. I know you're going to be heartbroken when you walk back into that lonely office."

"Fuck that. I've been waiting for you to leave since the day you got here." She clapped her hands. "Get my old office back. Can't wait!"

Martin was deleting as fast as he could. And then he came across one contact that he wanted. He pulled his personal phone from his other pocket and transferred the information. He handed the phone to Amanda.

"You know, you're right, Amanda," he said. "I *am* an idiot. You can mass-delete the rest."

Martin paused and looked at her. He had thought they might have a profound goodbye; it wasn't going to happen. He bent down to retrieve his empty cardboard box.

"Goodbye," he said. And turned and walked away.

·   ·   ·

"Yeah, mom. I'm going to stay through the weekend, at least. But I was able to get out of the lease on my apartment early, so that's good."

"That sounds great, Martin. We're excited to have you coming home."

"You know I don't know what I'm going to do, right, mom? Maybe I'll come back to DC."

"But you're leaving the administration, after all the good work you did for them. Why would you go back? What would you do?"

"I don't know, mom. Just keeping my options open."

"Okay, Martin. That's fine. We're excited to see you."

"I know, mom. I love you. But I have to run, okay? Got some things to take care of."

"I love you, Martin. Bye."

He ended the call and looked at his ancient iPhone. "Like maybe get a new phone," he said aloud to no one.

He opened his contacts and found the one contact that he copied over from his official phone. He looked at it for a moment and then hit dial.

"Hello?" A pleasant voice answered.

"Hey, Gabby. This is Marty. I'm calling, because I no longer work for the administration."